I0435146

United States
Department
of Agriculture

Forest Service

**Rocky Mountain
Research Station**

Resource Bulletin
RMRS-RB-14

July 2012

Idaho's Forest Resources, 2004–2009

Chris Witt, John D. Shaw, Michael T. Thompson,
Sara A. Goeking, Jim Menlove, Michael C. Amacher,
Todd A. Morgan, Charles Werstak

Abstract

This report presents a summary of the most recent inventory information for Idaho's forest lands. The report includes descriptive highlights and tables of area, number of trees, biomass, volume, growth, mortality, and removals. Most of the tables are organized by forest type, species, diameter class, or owner group. The report also describes inventory design, inventory terminology, and data reliability. Results show that Idaho's forest land totals 21.4 million acres. Nearly 76 percent (16.2 million acres) of this forest land is administered by the USDA Forest Service. Douglas-fir forests cover almost 6.3 million acres or roughly 29 percent of Idaho's forested lands, making it the most abundant forest type in the State. The lodgepole pine type is the second-most common type comprising 11.5 percent of Idaho's forest land. In terms of number of individual trees, subalpine fir is the single most abundant tree species in Idaho. Net annual growth of all live trees 5.0 inches diameter and greater on Idaho forest land totaled 376.2 million cubic feet. Average annual mortality totaled nearly 814.6 million cubic feet.

The Authors

Chris Witt is an Ecologist and a member of the Analysis Team with the Interior West Inventory and Analysis Program at the USFS Rocky Mountain Research Station in Ogden, Utah. He holds B.S. and M.S. degrees in ecology from Idaho State University (contact: chriswitt@fs.fed.us, 208-373-4370).

John D. Shaw is a Forester and Analysis Team Leader with the Interior West Inventory and Analysis Program at the USFS Rocky Mountain Research Station in Ogden, Utah. He holds B.S. and M.S. degrees in natural resources management from the University of Alaska, Fairbanks and a Ph.D. in forest ecology from Utah State University.

Michael T. Thompson is a Forester and a member of the Analysis Team with the Interior West Inventory and Analysis Program at the USFS Rocky Mountain Research Station in Ogden, Utah. He holds a B.S. degree in forestry from North Carolina State University.

Sara A. Goeking is a Biological Scientist and a member of the Analysis Team with the Interior West Forest Inventory and Analysis Program at the Rocky Mountain Research Station in Ogden, Utah. She holds a B.S. degree in environmental studies and an M.S. degree in forest ecology, both from Utah State University.

Jim Menlove is an Ecologist and a member of the Analysis Team with the Interior West Inventory and Analysis Program at the Rocky Mountain Research Station in Ogden, Utah. He holds a B.S. degree in biology from the University of Utah and an M.S. degree in zoology and physiology from the University of Wyoming, both with an emphasis in ecology.

Michael C. Amacher is a Research Soil Scientist in the Forest and Woodland Ecosystems Research Program at the USFS Rocky Mountain Research Station in Logan, Utah. He also serves as the western soils Indicator Advisor in the Indicators of Forest Health program. He has B.S. and M.S. degrees in chemistry and a Ph.D. in soil chemistry, all from Pennsylvania State University.

Todd A. Morgan is the director of the Forest Industry Research Program at The University of Montana's Bureau of Business and Economic Research in Missoula, Montana. He received a B.A. degree in philosophy and a B.S. degree in forest science from Pennsylvania State University and an M.S. degree in forestry from The University of Montana.

Charles Werstak is a Biological Scientist and a member of the Analysis Team with the Interior West Inventory and Analysis Program at the USFS Rocky Mountain Research Station in Ogden, Utah. He holds a B.S. degree in geography from Western Illinois University and an M.S. degree in geography from Utah State University.

Acknowledgments

The Rocky Mountain Research Station gratefully acknowledges the cooperation and assistance of the Rocky Mountain Region, Forest Service, U.S. Department of Agriculture; the Bureau of Land Management and Indian Affairs; and the National Park Service, U.S. Department of Interior. The authors extend a special note of thanks to the private landowners who provided information and access to field sample plots.

Report Highlights

Forest Area

- Idaho's forest land area totals 21.4 million acres.
- Unreserved forest land accounts for most (83 percent) of the forest land in Idaho and totals 17.8 million acres.
- Ninety-three percent of Idaho's unreserved forest land is classified as timberland and 7 percent is classified as unproductive forest land.
- Nearly 76 percent of Idaho's total forest land area, about 16.2 million acres, is administered by the USDA Forest Service.
- Douglas-fir forests cover almost 6.3 million acres and account for 29 percent of forest land in Idaho.
- Lodgepole pine forests cover about 2.5 million acres and are the second most abundant forest type.
- After the Douglas-fir forest type group, the fir / spruce / mountain hemlock group is the second most abundant with 6.0 million acres in Idaho.

Numbers of Trees, Volume, and Biomass

- There are an estimated 7.8 billion live trees in Idaho.
- Softwood species total 7.1 billion trees or 92 percent of all live trees.
- Numbers of subalpine fir trees total nearly 1.5 billion, making this species the single most abundant tree in Idaho.
- The net volume of live trees in Idaho on forest land totals 46.6 billion cubic feet.
- Growing-stock volume on timberland in Idaho totals 39.7 billion cubic feet, or 84 percent of the total live volume on forest land.
- The Douglas-fir species group accounted for the greatest growing-stock volume with over 11.5 billion cubic feet present in Idaho timberlands.
- The total weight of oven-dry biomass on Idaho forest land is 835 million tons.
- Net volume of sawtimber trees on timberland totals 200 billion board feet.

Forest Growth and Mortality

- Net annual growth of all live trees 5.0 inches diameter and greater on Idaho forest land totaled 219.6 million cubic feet.
- Average annual mortality totaled nearly 376.2 million cubic feet
- Mortality exceeded net growth for four major tree species groups.
- Timber harvest for 2010 was 830 MMBF (Scribner), up about 10 percent from 2009 and approximately equal to 2008; the annual harvest each year for 2008-2010 were the three lowest harvest totals in Idaho since the second World War.

- The annual level of mortality of whitebark pine trees is greatly outpacing the combined annual basal area growth of survivor trees and ingrowth trees.

- Damage agents related to merchantability accounted for the majority of primary damage agents in Idaho's forests, with diseases being the second most frequently recorded damage.

- A pronounced upward trend in mortality has occurred in lodgepole pine due to mountain pine beetle infestation outbreaks during the 6 years of annual inventories in Idaho.

- Current inventory data show that there are nearly 708,000 acres of the aspen forest type in Idaho, as compared to nearly 532,000 acres found during the previous inventory.

- Sixteen different invasive species were documented on 9 percent of the forested plots in Idaho. Canada thistle, spotted knapweed, and meadow hawkweed were the most common species detected.

Contents

Introduction

Idaho's Forest Inventory

This report contains highlights of the status of Idaho's forest resources, with discussions of pertinent issues based on the first 6 years of inventory under the new Forest Inventory and Analysis (FIA) annual system (Gillespie 1999). Resource issues covered in this report were derived from scoping meetings with Idaho data users conducted in 2009-2010. In 1998, the Agricultural Research Extension and Education Reform Act (also known as the Farm Bill) mandated that inventories would be conducted throughout United States' forests on an annual basis. This annual system integrates FIA and Forest Health Monitoring (FHM) sampling designs resulting in the mapped-plot design, which includes a nationally consistent plot configuration with four fixed-radius subplots; a systematic national sampling design consisting of one plot in each approximately 6,000-acre hexagon; annual measurement of a proportion of permanent plots; data or data summaries within 6 months after yearly sampling is completed; and a State summary report after 5 years.

Interior West Forest Inventory and Analysis (IWFIA) implemented the new annual inventory strategy starting in Idaho in 2004. The strategy for the Western United States involves measurement of 10 systematic samples (or subpanels) each of which represents approximately 10 percent of all plots in the State. The six inventory years covered in this report are 2004 through 2009, with a few sections using additional periodic inventory data from earlier years and the "Idaho Timber Harvest and Forest Products" section using ancillary data from 2010. Although the Farm Bill requires reports after 5 years, the Idaho report was delayed to give the IWFIA program time to work through national inconsistencies with past and current forest land definitions.

Comparison With Previous Inventories

Past inventories of Idaho were referred to as periodic inventories where estimates were derived from measurements of all plots in the State over a period of two to three years. Numerous previous inventories of Idaho's forest resources have been completed, most recently in 1981 (Benson and others 1987) and 1991 (Brown and Chojnacky 1996). Data from new inventories are often compared with data from earlier inventories to determine trends in forest resources. However, for the comparisons to be valid, the procedures used in the inventories must be compatible. Idaho's procedures for past inventories are different enough from present procedures that comparisons between them are not recommended. For example, past Idaho inventories often did not sample National Forest Systems lands or woodlands. Some data on these lands were provided by the Forest Service National Forest System staffs, but these data were not collected using IWFIA protocols so any temporal comparisons are difficult to make. In addition, many definitions of forest resource attributes have changed since 1981. The impact of these changes varies by inventory estimate. Forest land definitions, plot configuration, and procedures used to estimate forest type and stand size are some of the significant changes that have occurred since the previous inventory. Some of the factors affecting definitional differences, such as stocking or crown cover, have been reconciled with the past through a process called "plot-filtering," which re-classified forest land with 5 to 9 percent cover as a potentially new land class called "other wooded land." A more complete description of this process can be found in "Utah's Forest Reources, 2000-2005" (DeBlander and others 2010) and a detailed discussion on comparing periodic to annual data can be found as a "Special Topic" in the "Issues in Idaho's Forests" section of this report.

Annual inventory summaries are updated each spring to include the most recent subpanels of data available to the public. Data may be downloaded in table form or queried using a variety of online tools (http://fia.fs.fed.us/tools-data/default. asp). After 2013, a full assessment of ten subpanels of data will be included in the upcoming 10-year (full cycle) report. In 2014, the re-measurement phase of the inventory will begin by re-measuring the first subpanel of plot data collected in 2004.

Inventory Methods

Plot Configuration

The national FIA plot design consists of four 24-foot radius subplots configured as a central subplot and three peripheral subplots. Centers of the peripheral subplots are located at distances of 120 feet and at azimuths of 360 degrees, 120 degrees, and 240 degrees from the center of the central subplot. Each standing tree with a diameter 5 inches or larger at breast height (d.b.h.) for timber trees, or at root collar (d.r.c.) for woodland trees, is measured on these subplots. Each subplot contains a 6.8-foot radius microplot with its center located 12 feet east of the subplot center on which each tree with a d.b.h./ d.r.c. from 1 inch to 4.9 inches is measured.

In addition to the trees measured on FIA plots, data are also gathered about the stand or area in which the trees are located. Area classifications are useful for partitioning the forest into meaningful categories for analysis. Some of these area attributes are measured (e.g., percent slope), some are assigned by definition (e.g., ownership group), and some are computed from tree data (e.g., percent stocking).

To enable division of the forest into various domains of interest for analysis, it is important that the tree data recorded on these plots are properly associated with the area classifications. To accomplish this, plots are mapped by condition class. A condition class (or condition) is the combination of discrete attributes that describe the area associated with a plot. These attributes include land use, forest type, stand origin, stand size, owner group, reserve status, and stand density as well as other ancillary and computed attributes (Bechtold and Patterson 2005). In some cases, the plot footprint spans two or more conditions. Field crews assign a number to the first condition class encountered on a plot. This condition is then defined by a series of discrete variables attached to it (i.e., land use, stand size, regeneration status, tree density, stand origin, ownership group, and disturbance history). Additional conditions are identified if there is a distinct change in any of the condition-class variables on the plot.

2

USDA Forest Service Resour. Bull. RMRS-RB-14. 2012

Sample Design

Based on historic national standards, a sampling intensity of approximately one plot per 6,000 acres is necessary to satisfy national FIA precision guidelines for area and volume. Therefore, FIA divided the area of the United States into non-overlapping, 5,937-acre hexagons and established a plot in each hexagon using procedures designed to preserve existing plot locations from previous inventories. This base sample, designated as the Federal base sample, was systematically divided into a number of non-overlapping panels, each of which provides systematic coverage of the State. Each year the plots in a single subpanel are measured, and subpanels are selected on either a 5-year (eastern regions) or 10-year (western regions) rotating basis (Gillespie 1999). For estimation purposes, the measurement of each subpanel of plots can be considered an independent, equal probability sample of all lands in a State, or all plots can be combined to represent the State.

Three-Phase Inventory

FIA conducts inventories in three phases. Phase 1 uses remotely sensed data to obtain initial plot land cover observations and to stratify land area in the population of interest, such as counties, to increase the precision of estimates. In phase 2, field crews visit the physical locations of permanent field plots to measure traditional inventory variables such as tree species, diameter, and height. In phase 3, field crews visit a subset of phase 2 plots to obtain measurements for an additional suite of variables associated with forest and ecosystem health. The three phases of the enhanced FIA program are discussed in the following sections.

Phase 1—Remotely sensed data in the form of aerial photographs, digital orthoquads, and satellite imagery are used for initial plot establishment. Each plot is assigned a digitized geographic location, and a human interpreter determines whether a plot has the potential to sample forest or other wooded land based on remotely sensed data. Plot locations that are accessible to field crews and have the potential to sample forest or other wooded land are selected for further measurement via field crew visits in phase 2.

The only remote sensing medium used for stratification in Idaho was 2004 MODIS satellite imagery. The spatial resolution of the MODIS imagery used was 250 meters. Three strata were recognized: forest/other wooded land, nonforest land, and census water. Depending on geography and sampling intensity, geographic divisions are identified within a State for area computation and are referred to as estimation units. In Idaho, individual counties served as the estimation units. The area of each estimation unit is divided into strata of known size using the satellite imagery and computer-aided classification. The classified imagery divides the total area of the estimation unit into pixels of equal size and assigns each pixel to one of H strata. Each stratum, h, then contains n_h ground plots where the phase 2 attributes of interest are observed.

To illustrate, the area estimator for forest land for an estimation unit in Idaho is defined as:

$$\hat{A}_g = A_{Tg} \sum_{h=1}^{H} \frac{n'_{hg}}{n'_g} \frac{\sum_{i=1}^{n_{hg}} y_{ihg}}{n_{hg}}$$

where:

USDA Forest Service Resour. Bull. RMRS-RB-14. 2012

3

$\hat{A}_g$ = total forest area (acres) for estimation unit g

A_{Tg} = total land area (acres) in estimation unit g

H = number of strata (3)

n'_{hg} = number of phase 1 points in stratum h in estimation unit g

n'_g = total number of phase 1 points in estimation unit g

y_{ihg} = forest land condition proportion on phase 2 plot i in stratum h in estimation unit g

n_{hg} = number of phase 2 plots in stratum h in estimation unit g

Phase 2—Field crews record a variety of data for plot locations determined in phase 1 to sample accessible forest land. Before visiting privately owned plot locations, field crews consult county land records to determine the ownership of plots and then seek permission from private landowners to measure plots on their lands. The field crews determine the location of the geographic center of the center subplot using geographic positioning system (GPS) receivers. They record condition-level variables that include land use, forest type, stand origin, stand-size class, site productivity class, forest disturbance history, slope, aspect, and physiographic class. For each tree, field crews record a variety of variables including species, live/dead status, diameter, height, crown ratio, crown class, damage, and decay status. Office staff apply statistical models using field crew measurements to calculate values for additional variables such as individual tree volume and per unit area estimates of number of trees, volume, biomass, growth, and mortality.

The standard suite of phase 2 attributes is collected by all FIA regions in a consistent manner. In addition to these national "core" variables, IWFIA collects data on forest attributes that regional stakeholders find informative and useful. These include understory vegetation cover and species dominance, noxious weeds, and down woody material. These data are collected through documented protocols on all accessible phase 2 forested plots in the Interior West (USFS 2011). These regional attributes are used in the "Noxious Weeds" and "Down Woody Material" analyses of this report.

Phase 3—The third phase of the enhanced FIA program focuses on forest health. Phase 3 is administered cooperatively by the FIA program, other Forest Service programs, other Federal agencies, State natural resource agencies, universities, and the Forest Health Monitoring (FHM) program. Phase 3 is the ground survey portion of the Forest Health Monitoring (FHM) program and was integrated into the FIA program in 1999. The phase 3 sample consists of a 1/16 subset of the phase 2 plots, which equates to one phase 3 plot for approximately every 95,000 acres. Phase 3 measurements are obtained by field crews during the growing season and include an extended suite of ecological data. Because each phase 3 plot is also a phase 2 plot, the entire suite of phase 2 measurements is collected on each phase 3 plot at the same time as the phase 3 measurements. Soil structure and chemistry, and crown condition are two attributes collected at the phase 3 subsample. Phase 3 soil data is used in the "Soil Resources" section of this report.

Sources of Error

Sampling error—The process of sampling (selecting a random subset of a population and calculating estimates from this subset) causes estimates to contain error they would not have if every member of the population had been observed and included in the estimate. The 2004-2009 FIA inventory of Idaho is based on a sample of 5,295 plots systematically located across the State (a total area of 53.5 million acres); a sampling rate of approximately one plot for every 10,101 acres.

The statistical estimation procedures used to provide the estimates of the population totals presented in this report are described in detail in Bechtold and Patterson (2005). Along with every estimate is an associated sampling error that is typically expressed as a percentage of the estimated value but that can also be expressed in the same units as the estimate or as a confidence interval (the estimated value plus or minus the sampling error). This sampling error is the primary measure of the reliability of an estimate. An approximate 67 percent confidence interval constructed from the sampling error can be interpreted to mean that under hypothetical repeated sampling approximately 67 percent of the confidence intervals calculated from the individual repeat samples would include the true population parameter if it were computed from a 100-percent inventory. The sampling errors for State-level estimates are presented in Appendix D (table 37).

Users may compute statistical confidence for subdivisions of the reported data using the formula below. Because sampling error increases as the area or volume considered decreases, users should aggregate data categories as much as possible. Sampling errors obtained from this method are only approximations of reliability because homogeneity of variances is assumed. The formula is:

$$SE_s = SE_t \frac{\sqrt{X_t}}{\sqrt{X_s}}$$

SE_s = sampling error for subdivision of State total.

SE_t = sampling error for State total.

X_s = sum of values for the variable of interest (area, volume, biomass, etc.) for subdivision of State total.

X_t = sum of values (area, volume, biomass, etc.) for State total.

Measurement Error—Errors associated with the methods and instruments used to observe and record the sample attributes are called measurement errors. On FIA plots, attributes such as the diameter and height of a tree are measured with different instruments, and other attributes such as species and crown class are observed without the aid of an instrument. On a typical FIA plot, 30 to 70 trees are observed with 15 to 20 attributes recorded on each tree. In addition, many attributes that describe the plot and conditions on the plot are observed. Errors in any of these observations affect the quality of the estimates. If a measurement is biased—such as tree diameter consistently taken at an incorrect place on the tree—then the estimates that use this observation (e.g., calculated volume) will reflect this bias. Even if measurements are unbiased, high levels of random error in the measurements will add to the total random error of the estimation process. To ensure that all FIA observations are made to the highest standards possible, a Quality Assurance Program is an integral part of all FIA data collection efforts (see the "Quality Assurance Analysis" section of this report for more details).

Prediction error—Errors associated with using mathematical models (such as volume models) to provide information about attributes of interest based on sample attributes are referred to as prediction errors. Area, number of trees, volume, biomass, growth, removals, and mortality are the primary attributes of interest presented in this report. Area and number of trees estimates are based on direct observation and do not involve the use of prediction models; however, FIA estimates of volume, biomass, growth, and mortality used model-based predictions in the estimation process.

Overview of Tables

Forest Inventory and Analysis is currently working on a revised national core table set that will expand the suite of tabular information to incorporate more of the core FIA Program, using both phase 2 and 3 data. Appendix D contains an interim set of tables supporting this report, using Idaho annual data for the years 2004 through 2009. There are a total of 37 tables with statistics for land area, number of trees, wood volume, biomass (weight), growth, mortality, and sampling errors. Table 1 is the only table that includes all land types or land status; the rest include only accessible forest land or timberland. Table 37 shows sampling errors for area, volume, net growth, and mortality at the 67 percent confidence level. Appendix E includes tables derived from soil data collected from the phase 3 subsample. Additional tables that supplement specific sections are included in the body of this report and are numbered consecutively, using Roman numerals, as they appear in the document.

Overview of Idaho's Forest Resources

Ecoregion Provinces of Idaho

Issues and events that influence forest conditions often occur across forest types, ownerships, and political boundaries. As a result, scientists, researchers, and land managers must also find a way to assess and treat these issues in a boundaryless way. Ecoregions are often used as a non-political land division to help researchers study forest conditions. An ecoregion is a large landscape area that has relatively consistent patterns of topography, geology, soils, vegetation, climate, and natural processes (Shinneman and others 2000). Many smaller ecosystems may reside within an ecoregion.

Idaho is at the confluence of five ecoprovinces: (1) the Intermountain Semi-Desert Province dominates the southern part of the State, (2) the Great Plains-Palouse Dry Steppe Province encompasses a small portion of the northwestern part of the State, (3) the Northern Rocky Mountain Forest—Steppe-Coniferous Forest Alpine Meadow Province encompasses the northern part, (4) the Middle Rocky Mountain Forest—Steppe-Coniferous Forest Alpine Meadow Province in the central portion of the State, and (5) the Southern Rocky Mountain Forest—Steppe-Coniferous Forest Alpine Meadow Province in the southeast (Bailey 1995).

The Northern, Middle, and Southern Rocky Mountain Steppe ecoprovinces contain the majority of Idaho's forest resources. These provinces also contain the most forested area and greatest variety of forest types. Bailey (1995) describes these areas as follows:

Northern Rocky Mountain Forest—Steppe-Coniferous Forest Alpine Meadow Province:

Well-marked life belts are a striking feature of the Northern Rocky Mountain Steppe Province. In the uppermost (alpine) belt, trees are absent. The subalpine belt is dominated in most places by Engelmann spruce and subalpine fir. Western redcedar and western hemlock are characteristic of the montane belt. Associated trees include Douglas-fir (found throughout the region), along with western white pine, western larch, grand fir, and western ponderosa pine (found in the south). In these forests, areas that have been burned or cut are invaded first by larch, a deciduous conifer. White pine may crowd out the larch, then be replaced by hemlock, redcedar, and lowland white fir. Depending on latitude, the lower part of the montane belt may be interspersed with grass and sagebrush.

Middle Rocky Mountain Forest—Steppe-Coniferous Forest Alpine Meadow Province:

Altitudinal zones are also evident in the Middle Rocky Mountain Steppe Province. Below the subalpine zone, Douglas-fir is the climax dominant, with grand fir as an associate west of the continental divide, chiefly on west-facing slopes. Lodgepole pines and grasses grow principally in the basins and ranges in the eastern and southeastern part of the province. Below the Douglas-fir belt, ponderosa pine is dominant to the west of the continental divide, constituting a xerophytic forest. The lower slopes of the mountains and the basal plain are dominated by sagebrush semidesert or steppe.

Southern Rocky Mountain Forest—Steppe-Coniferous Forest Alpine Meadow Province:

The Southern Rocky Mountain Steppe province is noted for its pronounced vegetational zonation, controlled by a combination of altitude, latitude, direction of prevailing winds, and slope exposure. Generally, the various zones are at higher altitudes in the southern part of the province than in the northern, and they extend downward on east-facing and north-facing slopes and in narrow ravines and valleys subject to cold air drainage. The uppermost (alpine) zone is characterized by alpine tundra and the absence of trees. Directly below it is the subalpine zone, dominated in most places by Engelmann spruce and subalpine fir. Below this area lies the montane zone, characterized by ponderosa pine and Douglas-fir, which frequently alternate--ponderosa pine dominates on lower, drier, more exposed slopes, and Douglas-fir is predominant in higher, moister, more sheltered areas. After fire in the subalpine zone and in the upper part of the montane zone, the original forest trees are usually replaced by aspen or lodgepole pine.

The remaining two provinces are characterized by dry rocky foothills, mesas, and plateaus, north and south running basins and ranges, and lava fields. The predominant community types in the areas are sagebrush steppe and shortgrass prairie. Forest types in these regions include western juniper, with some Douglas-fir, aspen, and other hardwood species found along riparian zones and where soils and moisture permit.

Forest Land Classification

Historically, FIA has used a nationally consistent standard for defining different categories of forest land. These categories were originally developed for the purpose of separating forest land deemed suitable for timber production from forest land that was either not suitable or unavailable for timber harvesting activity. The first division of forest land is unreserved forest land and reserved forest land. Unreserved forest land is considered available for harvesting activity where wood volume can be removed for timber products. Reserved forest land is considered unavailable for any type of wood utilization management practice through administrative legislation.

Unreserved forest land is further divided into timberland and unproductive forests. In the past, forest types have often been separated into timber and woodland types. Timber types are characterized by stands where the plurality of stocking is from species where diameter is measured at breast height, as opposed to root collar (woodland types). Timberland is further defined as forest land capable of producing 20 cubic feet of wood per acre per year of trees designated as a timber species and not withdrawn from timber production. Unproductive forests are, because of species characteristics and site conditions, not capable of producing 20 cubic feet of wood per acre per year of trees designated as a timber species and not withdrawn from timber production (see the "Standard Forest Inventory and Analysis Terminology" section of this document).

Reserved forest land is further divided into productive and unproductive forests. Productive forest land is capable of producing 20 cubic feet of wood per acre per year of trees designated as a timber species but is withdrawn from timber production. Unproductive reserved land is, because of a combination of species characteristics and site conditions, not capable of producing 20 cubic feet of wood per acre per year of trees designated as a timber species and withdrawn from timber production.

The State of Idaho encompasses 53.5 million acres of land area, of which 21.4 million acres were estimated by FIA as forest land (fig. 1). Unreserved forest land accounts for most (83 percent) of the forest land in Idaho and totals 17.8 million acres (table 2). Ninety-three percent of Idaho's unreserved forest land is classified as timberland and 7 percent is classified as unproductive forest land. Reserved forests account for 17 percent, or 3.6 million acres of total forest land.

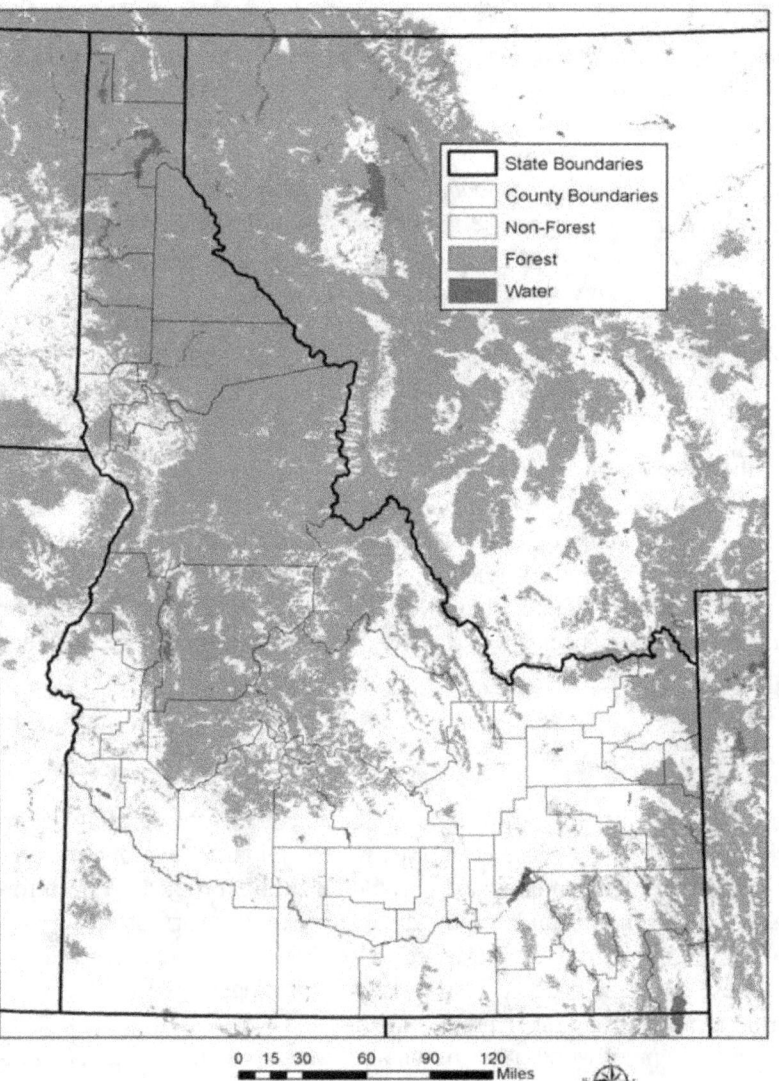

Figure 1: Land class map depicting lands with 10 percent or more forest cover in Idaho.

8

USDA Forest Service Resour. Bull. RMRS-RB-14. 2012

Forest Land Ownership

Nearly 76 percent of Idaho's total forest land area, about 16.2 million acres, is administered by the USDA Forest Service (fig. 2). The National Forest Service System's land in Idaho consists of 11 different National Forests. Almost 79 percent of National Forest System's forest land is classified as unreserved forest land. About 12.2 million acres, or 96 percent, of National Forest System's forest land is classified as unreserved timberland (table 2). The State government manages 1.3 million acres of forest land in Idaho. Most of this forest land—about 98 percent—is classified as unreserved. Over 91 percent of Idaho's State controlled forest land meets the conditions to qualify as unreserved timberland. Privately owned forest land totals 2.8 million acres. Private landowners are a diverse group in Idaho consisting of private individuals and corporations. All private forest land is in the unreserved owner class and 91 percent is classified as timberland. The remaining amount of forest land in Idaho is controlled by the National Park Service (NPS), the Bureau of Land Management (BLM), and the Department of Defense. Over 944 thousand acres are controlled by the BLM, another 80 thousand acres are controlled by the NPS, and 32 thousand acres are controlled by the Department of Defense.

Forest Type

Forest type is a classification of forest land based on the species forming a plurality of living trees growing in a particular forest. The distribution of forest types across the landscape is determined by factors such as climate, soil, elevation, aspect, and disturbance history. Forest type names may be based on a single species or groups of species. Forest types are an important measure of diversity, structure, and successional stage. Loss or gain of a particular forest type over time can be used to assess the impact of major disturbances such as fire, weather, insects, disease, and man-caused disturbances such as timber harvesting activity.

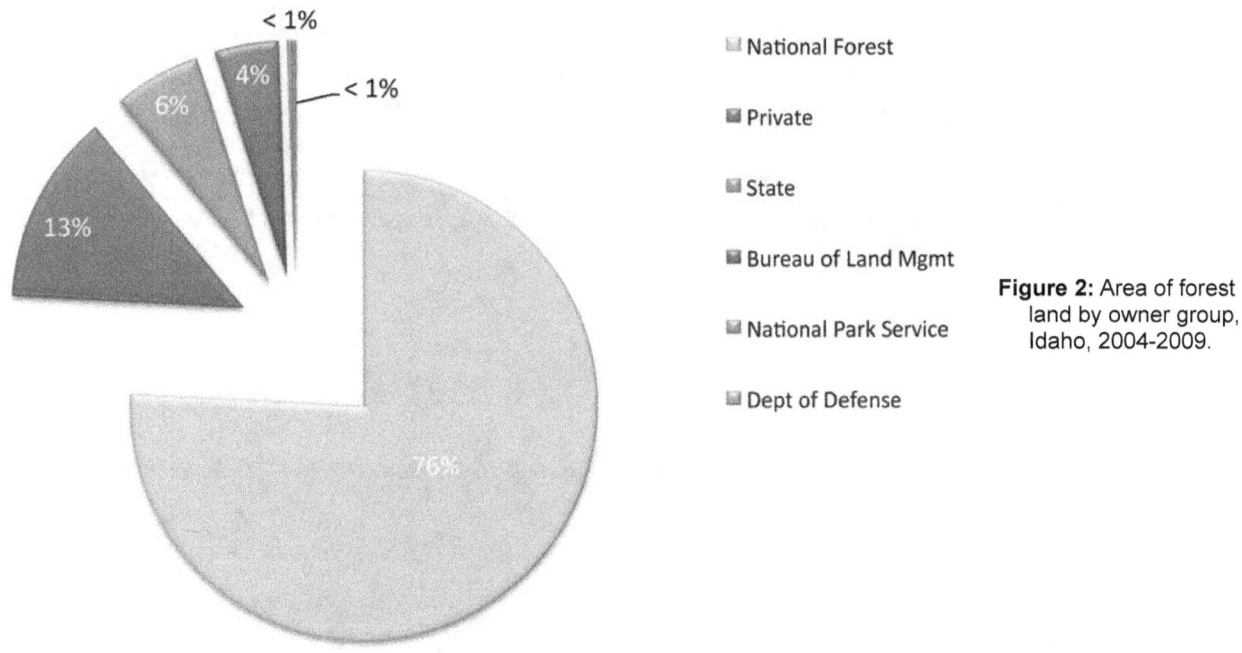

National Forest

Private

State

Bureau of Land Mgmt

National Park Service

Dept of Defense

Figure 2: Area of forest land by owner group, Idaho, 2004-2009.

USDA Forest Service Resour. Bull. RMRS-RB-14. 2012

9

The most abundant forest type group in Idaho is the Douglas-fir group (fig. 3). Douglas-fir forests cover nearly 6.3 million acres and account for 29 percent of forest land in the State (fig. 4a, table 3). Second in abundance, the fir/ spruce/ mountain hemlock forest type group totals just over 6 million acres (fig. 4b). Subalpine fir accounts for the largest portion (2.3 million acres) of the forest area classified in the fir/spruce/mountain hemlock type group. Lodgepole pine forest types cover 2.5 million acres and are the third most abundant forest type group (fig. 4c). Next in order of abundance are non-stocked forests (1.7 million acres), the ponderosa pine group (1.6 million acres), the hemlock/ sitka spruce group (887 thousand acres), and the aspen/ birch group (795 thousand acres).

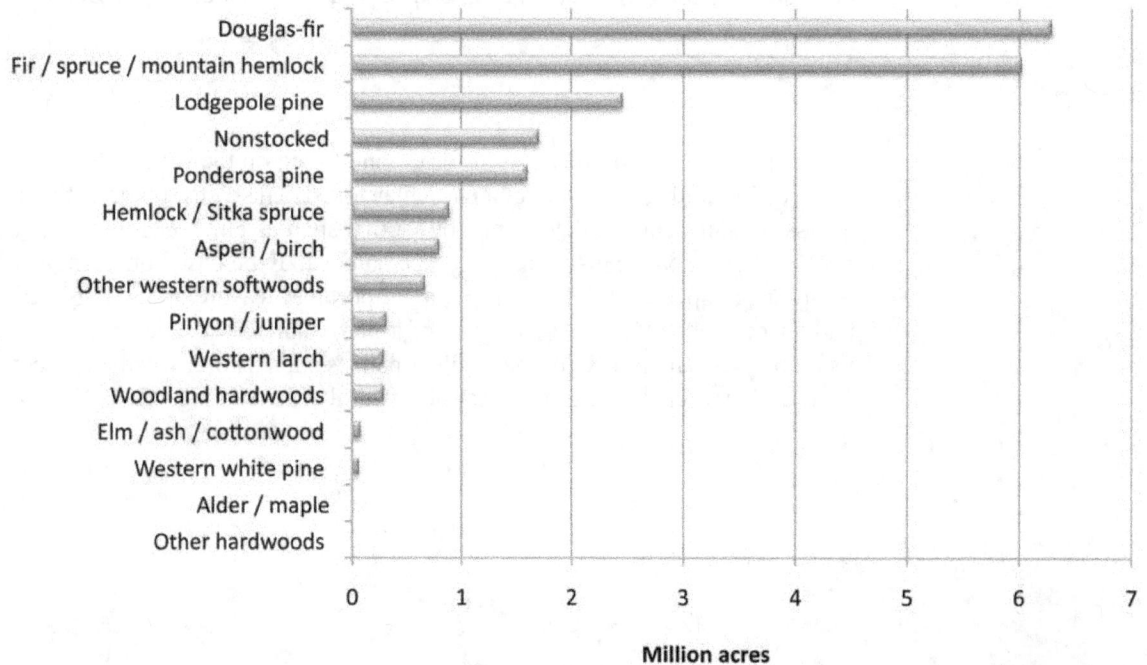

Figure 3: Area of forest land by forest type group, Idaho, 2004-2009. See appendix A and B for species and forest types included in each group.

USDA Forest Service Resour. Bull. RMRS-RB-14. 2012

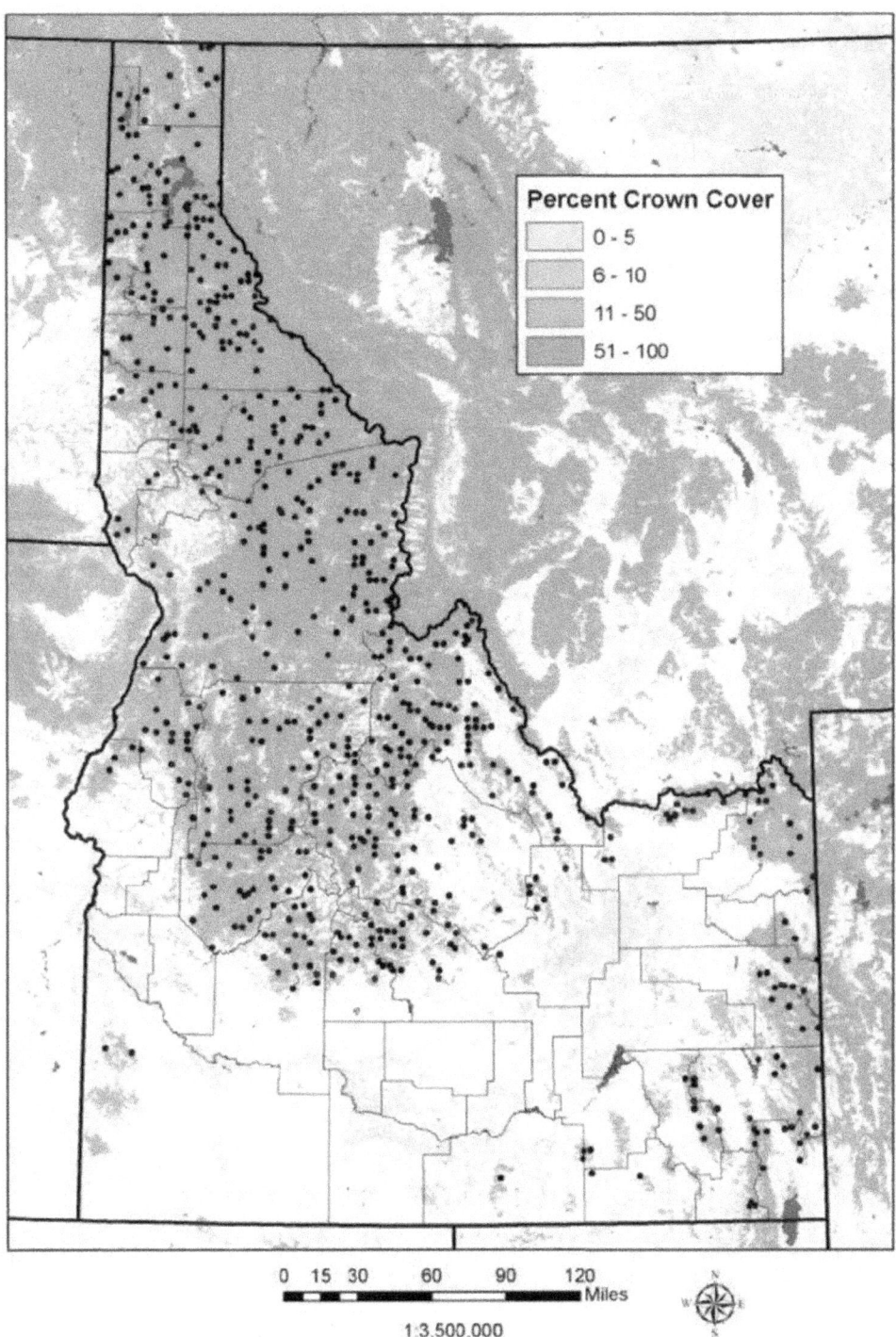

Percent Crown Cover

	0 - 5
	6 - 10
	11 - 50
	51 - 100

0 15 30   60   90   120
                                    Miles
1:3,500,000

Figure 4a: Land class map depicting crown forest cover in Idaho with the general locations of plots containing the Douglas-fir forest type group, Idaho, 2004-2009.

USDA Forest Service Resour. Bull. RMRS-RB-14. 2012

11

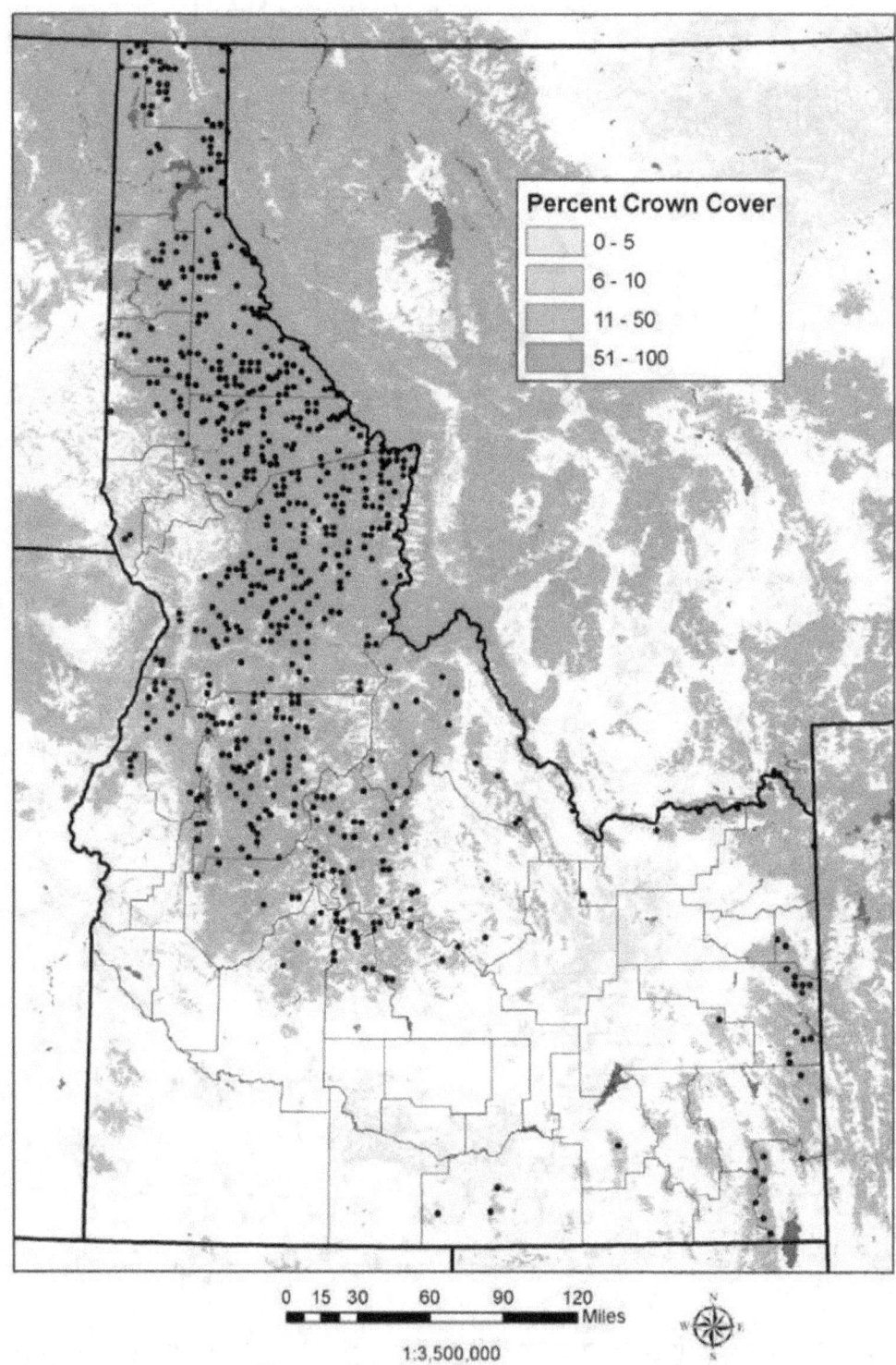

Figure 4b: Land class map depicting percent crown cover in Idaho with the general locations of plots containing fir/spruce/mountain hemlock forest type group, Idaho, 2004-2009.

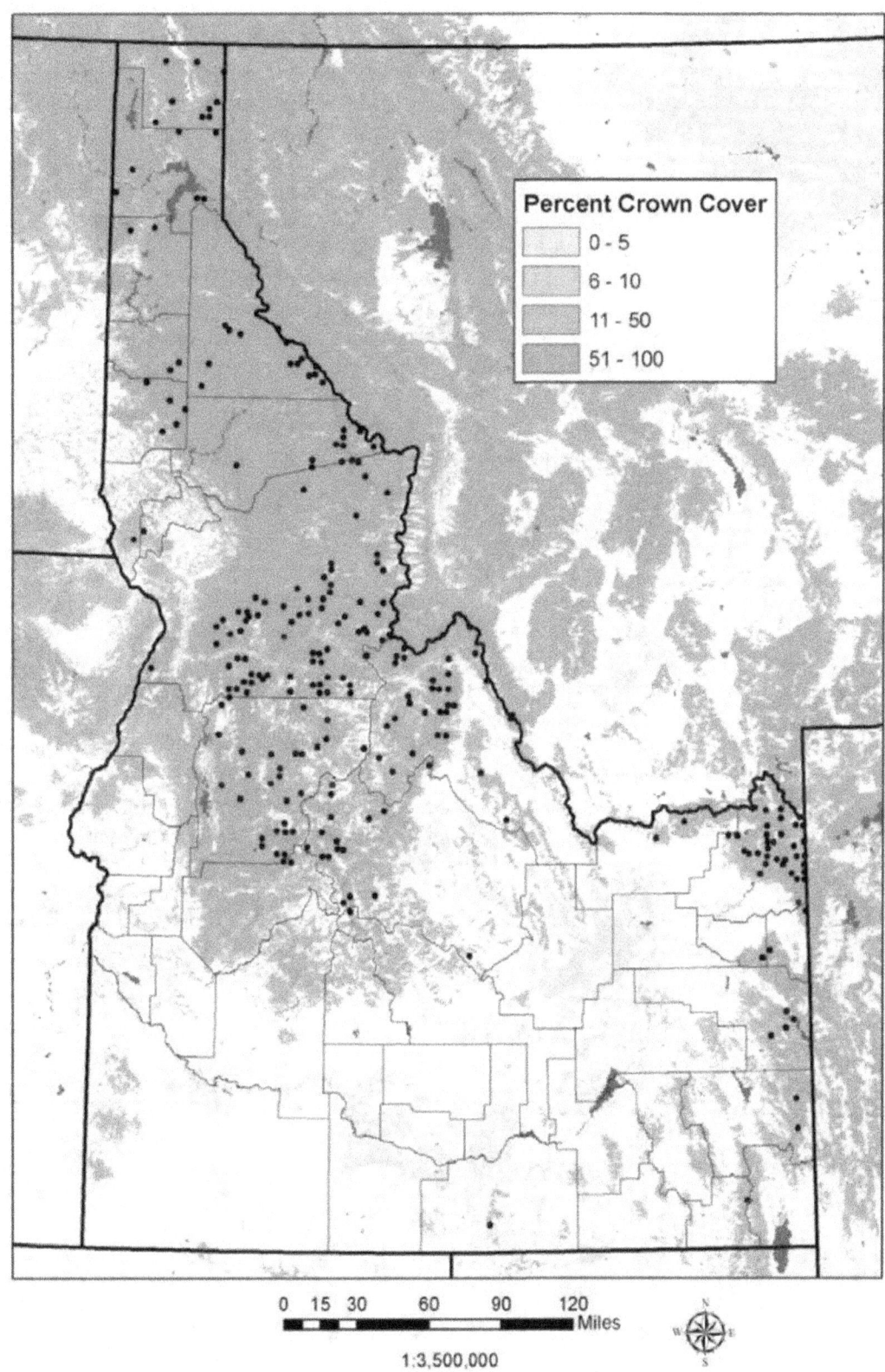

Figure 4c: Land class map depicting percent crown cover in Idaho with the general locations of plots containing lodgepole pine forest type group, Idaho, 2004-2009.

Stand Age

The present age structure of Idaho's forest area, in terms of stand age and forest type group composition, provides insight into prospective shifts in stand composition over time. On every FIA plot that samples forest land, a stand age is calculated. If there are trees available for suitable increment core extraction, a stand age is estimated based upon the average age of only those trees that fall within the calculated stand-size assignment. For example, suppose an FIA plot sampled a softwood forest type where about 30 percent of the live trees were in the large diameter stand-size (trees at least 9.0 inches d.b.h. and larger) and 70 percent were in the medium diameter stand-size class (trees between 5.0 and 9.0 inches d.b.h.). Since the stand would be classified as a medium diameter stand size class, only the medium size trees would be used in determining stand age. There are limitations to collecting data for stand age computation. Certain tree species, especially those that are very old, prohibit repeatable measures of increment cores. Certain stand types, such as Gambel oak, that are dominated by small-diameter trees are very difficult to accurately assign a stand age. All nonstocked forest conditions—i.e., those forested areas that have less than 10 percent stocking of live trees because of disturbance—are assigned a stand age of zero.

The largest proportion of Idaho's forested land is between 60 and 120 years of age (table 6). Over 46 percent, or almost 10 million acres, of the forest land is between 60 and 120 years of age. About 20 percent of the forest land is in stands under 21 years of age and 3 percent are over 200 years of age.

There is a considerable difference in stand age distribution between the major forest type groups in the State (figs. 5a and 5b). The other western hardwoods group is the oldest with half of the forest area in stands over 140 years old. Twenty percent of pinyon-juniper stands are over 140 years old, making it the next oldest group. Aspen, which is generally shorter lived than most Idaho conifer species, is characterized by a larger number of stands in the younger age classes with over 98

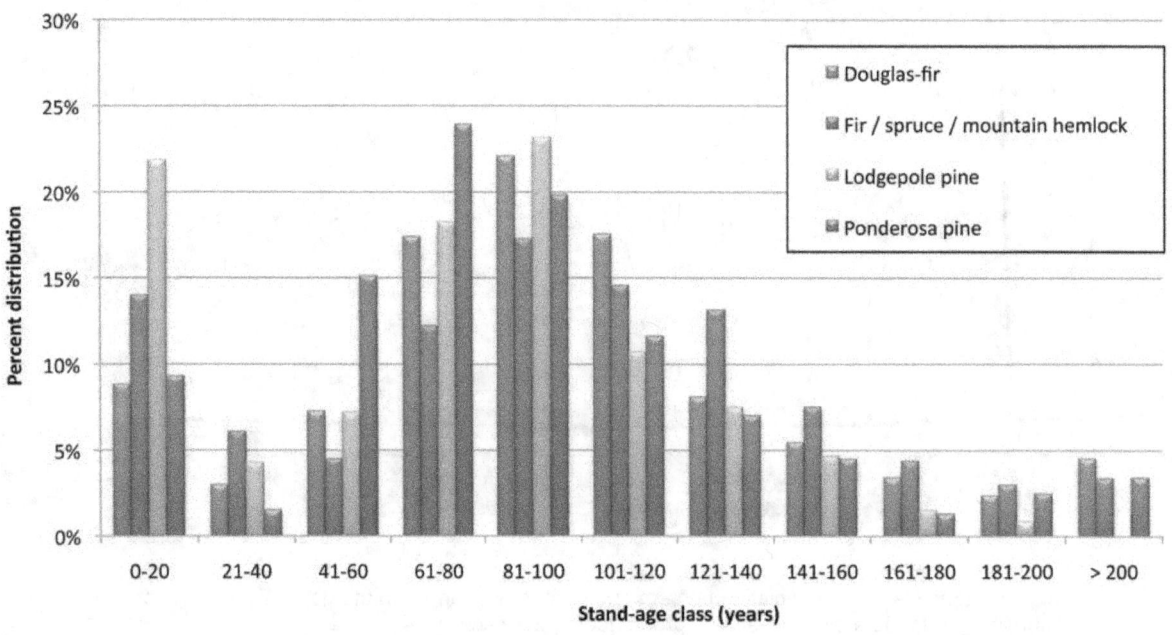

Figure 5a: Distribution of forest land by stand age class and more common forest type groups in Idaho, 2004-2009.

                                    USDA Forest Service Resour. Bull. RMRS-RB-14. 2012

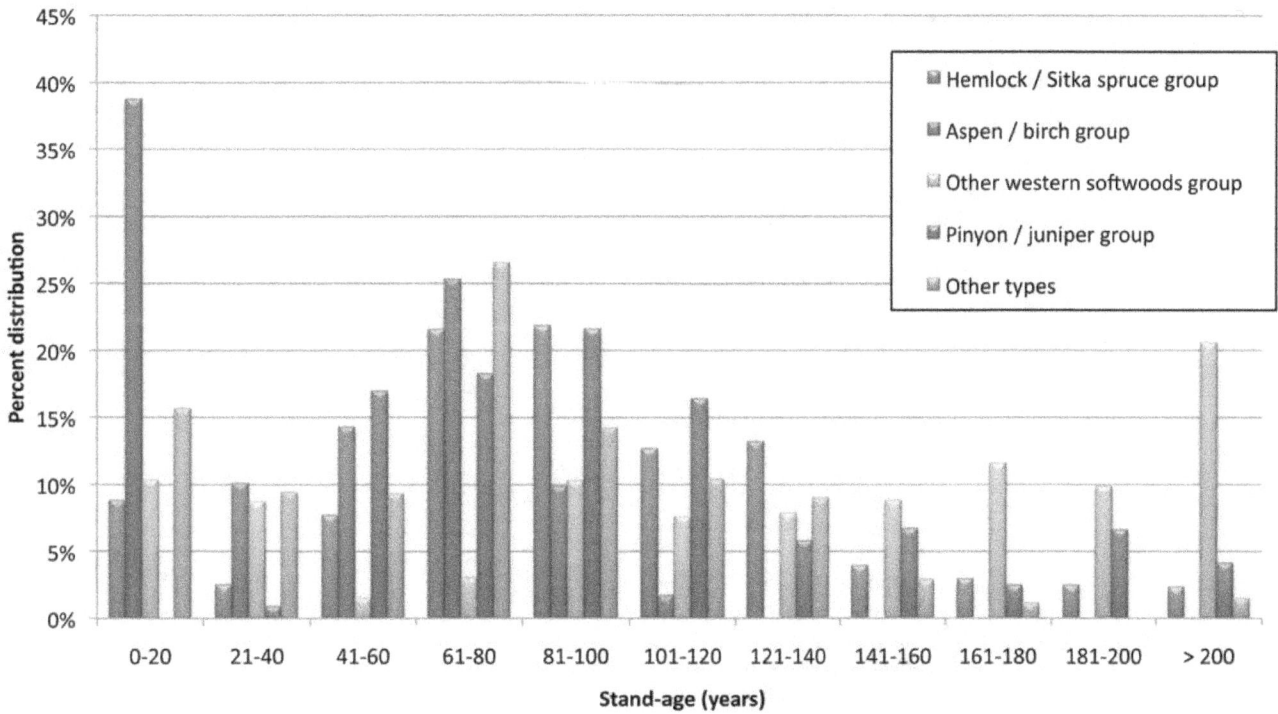

Figure 5b: Distribution of forest land by stand age class and less common forest type groups in Idaho, 2004-2009.

percent of aspen forests in stands less than 100 years old. This makes the aspen/ birch forest type group the youngest of those occupying greater than 100 thousand acres in Idaho. All three of the most abundant groups—the Douglas-fir, the spruce/ fir/ mountain hemlock, and the lodgepole pine groups—have their highest proportion of area in the 81 to 100 year age class at 22 percent, 17 percent, and 23 percent respectively.

Stand Density Index (SDI)

Stand density index (SDI) (Reineke 1933) is a relative measure of stand density, based on quadratic mean diameter of the stand and the number of live trees per acre. In the western States, silviculturists often use SDI as one measure of stand structure to meet diverse objectives such as ecological restoration and wildlife habitat (e.g., Smith and Long 1987; Lilieholm and others 1994; Long and Shaw 2005).

SDI is usually presented as a percentage of a maximum SDI for each forest type. Maximum SDI is rarely, if ever, observed in nature at the stand scale because the onset of competition-induced (self-thinning) mortality begins to occur at about 60 percent of the maximum SDI. Average maximum density, which is used in normal yield tables, and is equivalent to the A-line in Gingrich-type stocking diagrams (Gingrich 1967) is equal to approximately 80 percent of maximum SDI. There are several reasons why stands may have low SDI. Stands typically have low SDI following major disturbances, such as fire, insect attack, or harvesting. These stands remain in a low-density condition until regeneration fills available growing space. Stands that are over-mature can also have low SDI, because growing space may not be re-occupied as fast as it is released by the mortality of large, old trees. Finally, stands that occur on very thin soils or rocky sites may remain

USDA Forest Service Resour. Bull. RMRS-RB-14. 2012

15

Table I: Maximum Stand Density Index (SDI) of forest types found in Idaho.

Forest Type	Maximum SDI
Western juniper	320
Cottonwood	360
Pinyon-juniper woodland	370
Ponderosa pine	375
Juniper woodland	385
Limber pine	410
Cercocarpus woodland	415
Rocky Mountain juniper	425
Western larch	430
Subalpine fir	470
Grand fir	475
Unknown / nonstocked	475
Douglas-fir	485
Engelmann spruce / subalpine fir	485
Aspen	490
Whitebark pine	500
Engelmann spruce	500
Lodgepole pine	530
Intermountain maple woodland	540
Mountain hemlock	56
Western hemlock	600
Other hardwoods	645

at low density indefinitely, because limitations on physical growing space do not permit full site occupancy. A site is considered to be fully occupied at 35 percent of maximum SDI. At lower densities, individual tree growth is maximized but stand growth is below potential, while at higher densities, individual tree growth is below potential, but stand growth is maximized (Long 1985).

Originally developed for even-aged stands, SDI can also be applied to uneven-aged stands (Long and Daniel 1990; Shaw 2000). Stand structure can influence the computation of SDI, so the definition of maximum SDI must be compatible with the computation method. Because FIA data include stands covering the full range of structure, the maximum SDIs are currently being revised for FIA forest types (Shaw and Long, in prep.). The provisional revised maximum SDIs, which are compatible with FIA computation methods, are shown in table I. SDI was computed for each condition that sampled forest land using the summation method (Shaw 2000), and the SDI percentage was calculated using the maximum SDI for the forest type found on the condition.

The distribution of SDI values in Idaho is relatively balanced. Figure 6 shows that stands appear to be well-stocked, with over 47 percent of forest acres at least fully occupied (SDI equal to 35 percent or greater). The other 53 percent is relatively evenly distributed over the lower range of stocking. Over 14 percent of Idaho's forests are in the range where competition-induced mortality is expected (SDI equal to 60 percent or greater).

Stands with SDI between 35 and 60 percent of maximum SDI (full stocking zone) are desirable from a forest management perspective because that density range maximizes stand growth and minimizes competition-induced mortality; other objectives, such as fuel reduction or maintenance of wildlife habitat characteristics, may warrant lower relative densities. The proportion of Idaho's forests in the full stocking zone (32.7%) is comparable to the proportions found in other

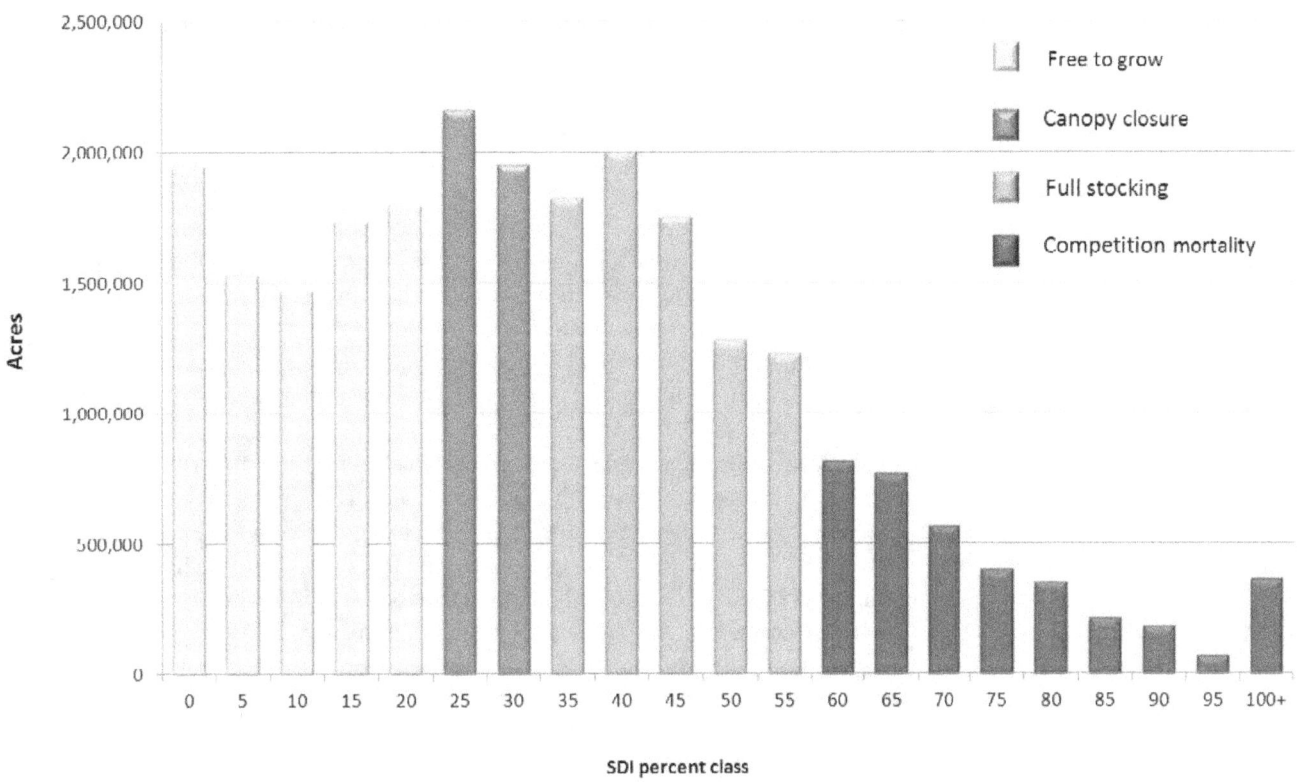

Figure 6: Distribution of stand density on Idaho forest land, Idaho, 2004-2009.

interior western States (Arizona 25.2%, Colorado 34.9%, Montana 32.5%, Utah 32.0%). At 14.4 percent, the proportion of area in the competition mortality zone is somewhat lower than is found in other interior western States (Arizona 15.8%; Colorado 25.3%, Montana 19.6%, Utah 20.0%). The relatively small proportion of acreage in this density range is likely due to a combination of density-reducing natural disturbances, such as fire and insect infestation, and management activities, such as thinning treatments. Because excessive density is considered a risk factor for many damaging agents, Idaho forests may have a lower risk rating for certain agents. Given that several damaging agents are currently active in Idaho (see the "Issues in Idaho's Forests" section of this document), it is expected that the proportion of high-density acreage will decrease further over time. Management activities designed to reduce risks, such as fuel reduction treatments, will have a similar effect. At the same time, many lower-density stands should increase in relative density. This may lead to an eventual increase in the area of well-stocked forest land.

Number of Trees

A measure of the number of live trees is needed in a variety of silvicultural, forest health, and habitat management applications. To be meaningful, numbers of trees are usually combined with information about the size of the trees. Younger

USDA Forest Service Resour. Bull. RMRS-RB-14. 2012

17

forest stands are usually comprised of large numbers of small-diameter trees, whereas older forest stands contain small numbers of large-diameter trees.

There are an estimated 7.8 billion live trees ≥1 inch d.b.h. or d.r.c. in Idaho (table 10). Softwood species total 7.1 billion trees or 92 percent of the trees in Idaho (fig. 7). Over 65 percent of softwood trees are under 5.0 inches in diameter and nearly 5 percent are 15.0-inches and larger in diameter. The true fir species group is the most abundant softwood species group accounting for 38 percent (2.7 billion trees) of the softwood total. This group consists of grand fir and subalpine fir. Next in abundance is the Douglas-fir group at 1.3 billion trees. The Douglas-fir species accounts for all trees in this group. Third in abundance is the lodgepole pine species group at 1.26 billion trees. Lodgepole pine is the only species represented in this group. Tables 10 and 11 in Appendix D show the size-class distribution by species group for these trees.

The cottonwood and aspen species group accounts for the majority (51 percent) of the hardwood species occurring in Idaho. Quaking aspen is a very important tree in Idaho. Stands of aspen are esthetically appealing and provide excellent habitat for a wide variety of wildlife. Numbers of aspen trees total nearly 330 million making this species the single most abundant hardwood tree in Idaho. Most aspen trees in Idaho are concentrated in the smaller diameter classes. Sixty-five percent of all live aspen stems are less than three inches in diameter. The western woodland hardwoods species group is the next most abundant group with an estimated 276 million trees. This group includes bigtooth maple and curlleaf mountain-mahogany.

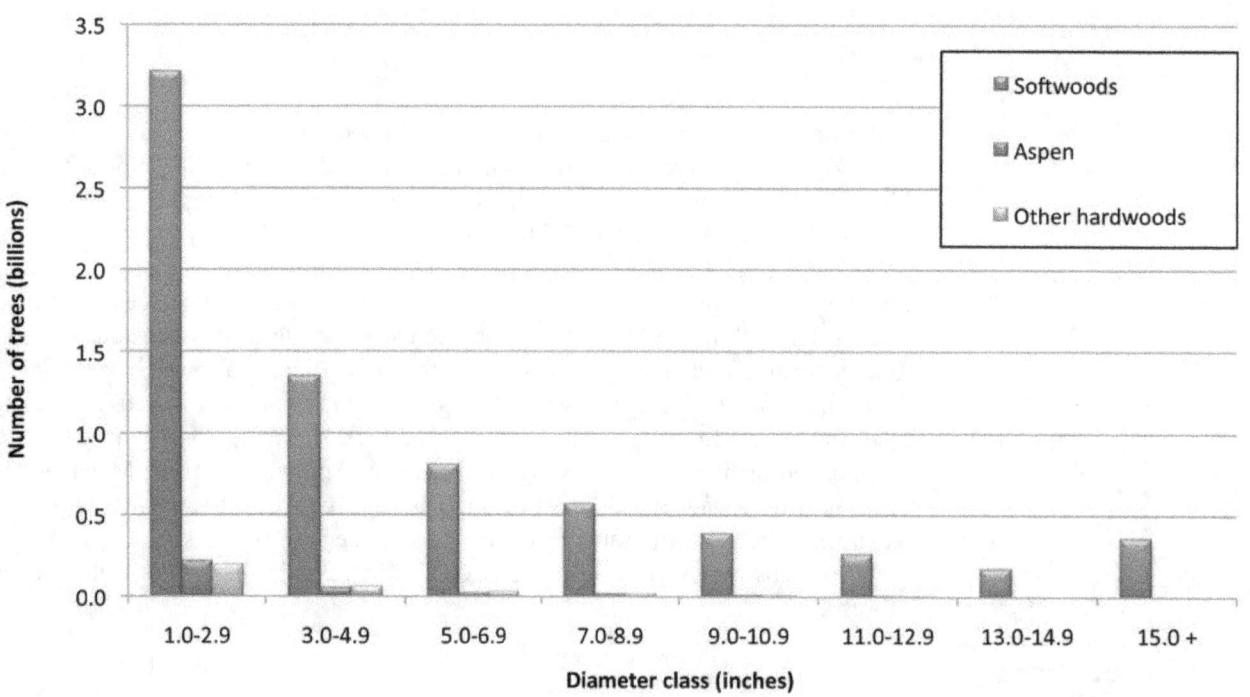

Figure 7: Number of live trees ≥1 inch d.b.h./ d.r.c on forest land by species group and diameter class, Idaho, 2004-2009.

Live Tree Volume, Biomass, and Sawtimber

The amount of cubic-foot volume of wood in a forest is important for determining the sustainability of current and future wood utilization. The forest products industry is interested in knowing where available timber volume is located, who owns it, the species composition, and the size distribution. Biomass estimates are based on gross volumes; they exclude foliage and include all live trees 1.0 inches in diameter and larger.

The net volume of live trees in Idaho on forest land totals 47.2 billion cubic feet (table 12). Eighty percent, or 37.8 billion cubic feet, is located on lands managed by the National Forest System. Ten percent, or 4.8 billion cubic feet, is under private ownership. Three percent, or 1.4 billion cubic feet, is on Federal lands other than national forests. The remainder, about 3.2 billion cubic feet, is on lands administered by the State of Idaho. The total weight of oven-dry aboveground biomass on Idaho forest land (using regional equations, see table 29a) is 853 million tons, of which 734 million tons reside on Federal lands, 56 million tons on State lands, and the remaining 92 million tons on private land.

Various factors affect whether timber is available for harvest. Three significant factors are ownership status, productivity, and merchantability standards. Timber volume on reserved forest land—land permanently reserved from wood products utilization through statute or administrative designation—is considered land that will not be harvested. Timberland is unreserved forest land capable of producing in excess of 20 cubic feet per acre per year of wood. Forest land not capable of meeting this productivity threshold is assumed to have a low probability of being harvested. Historically, FIA has segregated live-tree volume based on growing-stock classification. Growing-stock trees are live trees that possess, or have the potential, to produce an 8-foot sawlog that meets required merchantability standards (see the "Standard Forest Inventory and Analysis Terminology" section of this document). Therefore, the amount of growing-stock volume on timberland can be considered a reasonable benchmark for the amount of timber that is potentially available for harvest. Growing-stock volume on timberland in Idaho totals 40 billion cubic feet, or 84 percent of the total live volume on forest land (fig. 8). Net volume of sawtimber trees on timberland totals 200 billion board feet (table 19).

Douglas-fir and grand fir together account for almost half (49 percent) of all growing-stock volume on timberland (fig. 9). Next in abundance, lodgepole pine totals 4.3 billion cubic feet of growing-stock volume. Growing-stock volume of subalpine fir total 3.4 billion cubic feet and ranks fourth. Douglas-fir and grand fir also account for the majority of sawtimber volume (103 billion board feet).

USDA Forest Service Resour. Bull. RMRS-RB-14. 2012

19

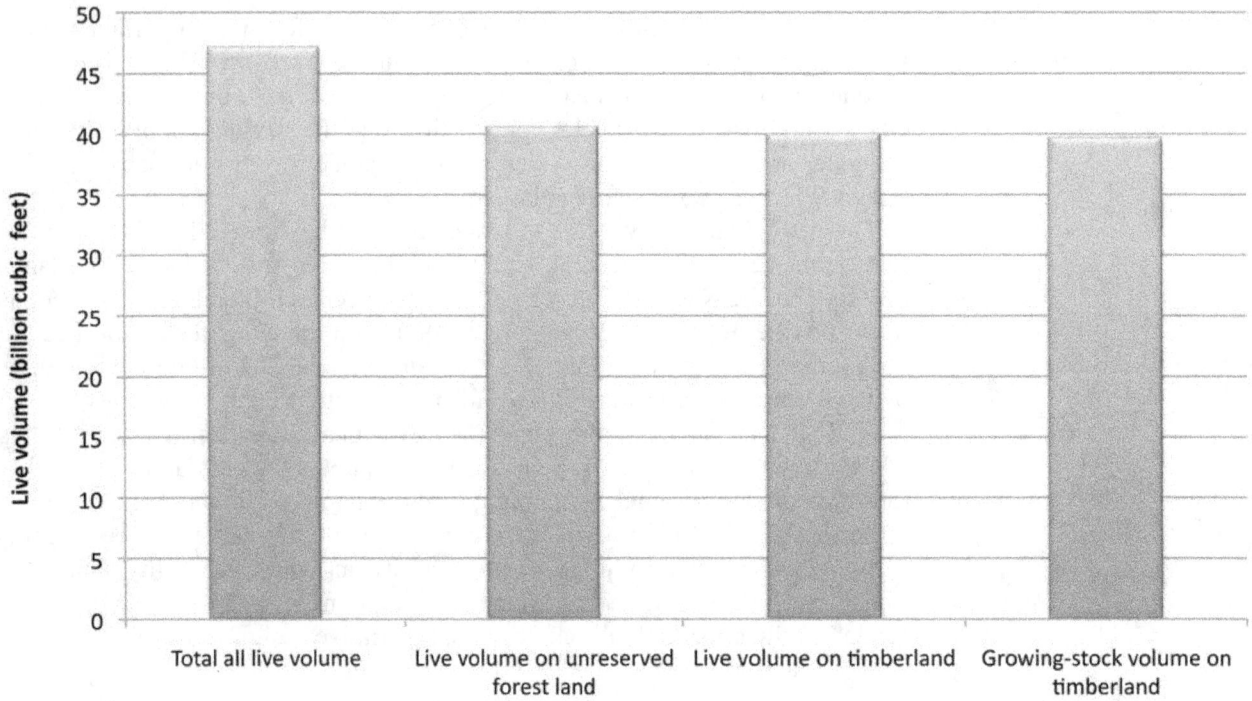

Figure 8: Volume of live trees on forest land by ownership status, productivity, and merchantability status, Idaho, 2004-2009.

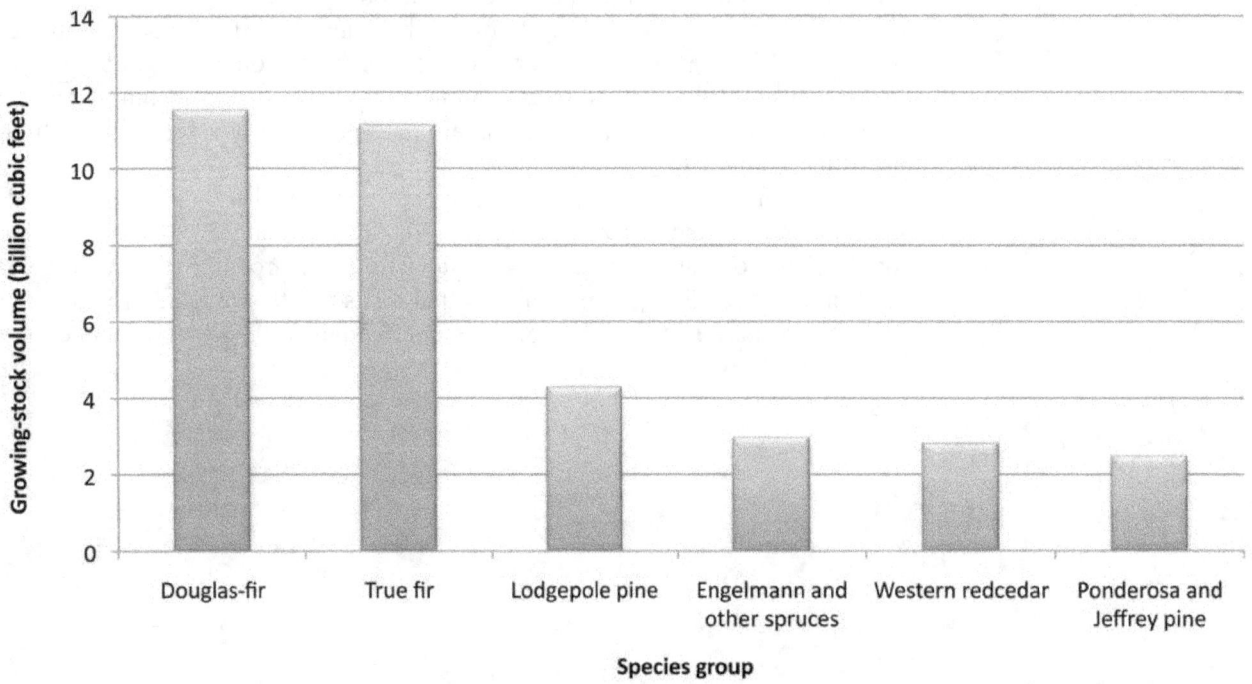

Figure 9: Volume of growing-stock trees on timberland by species group, Idaho, 2004-2009.

USDA Forest Service Resour. Bull. RMRS-RB-14. 2012

Forest Growth and Mortality

Two common measures of forest vigor and sustainability are tree growth and mortality. Growth, as reported here, is the average annual growth volume calculated from a sample of tree increment core measurements based on the previous 10 years of radial growth. Mortality, as reported here, is the average annual net volume of trees that have died in the 5 years prior to the year of measurement. The reason behind this growth and mortality estimation procedure in Idaho is that the inventory data are limited to initial plot measurements. Complete remeasurement data for the State—where the status of the plot and all trees on the plot are known at two points in time—will not be available until all ten panels of data are completed and remeasurement begins in the eleventh year.

The relationship between growth and mortality quantifies the change in inventory volume over time. Gross growth minus mortality approximates the average annual change in inventory volume not including the average annual volume removed through timber harvesting. Net annual growth of all live trees 5.0 inches diameter and greater on Idaho forest land totaled 376.2 million cubic feet while mortality totaled nearly 814.6 million cubic feet (tables 22 and 25). Figure 10 illustrates the relationship between net growth and mortality by ownership group in Idaho. Mortality of all trees on forest land controlled by National Forest Systems lands totaled 757.9 million cubic feet and exceeded net growth on this owner group by more than sevenfold. In contrast, net growth exceeded mortality on privately owned forests: net growth totaled 168.8 million cubic feet compared to 25.9 million cubic feet of mortality.

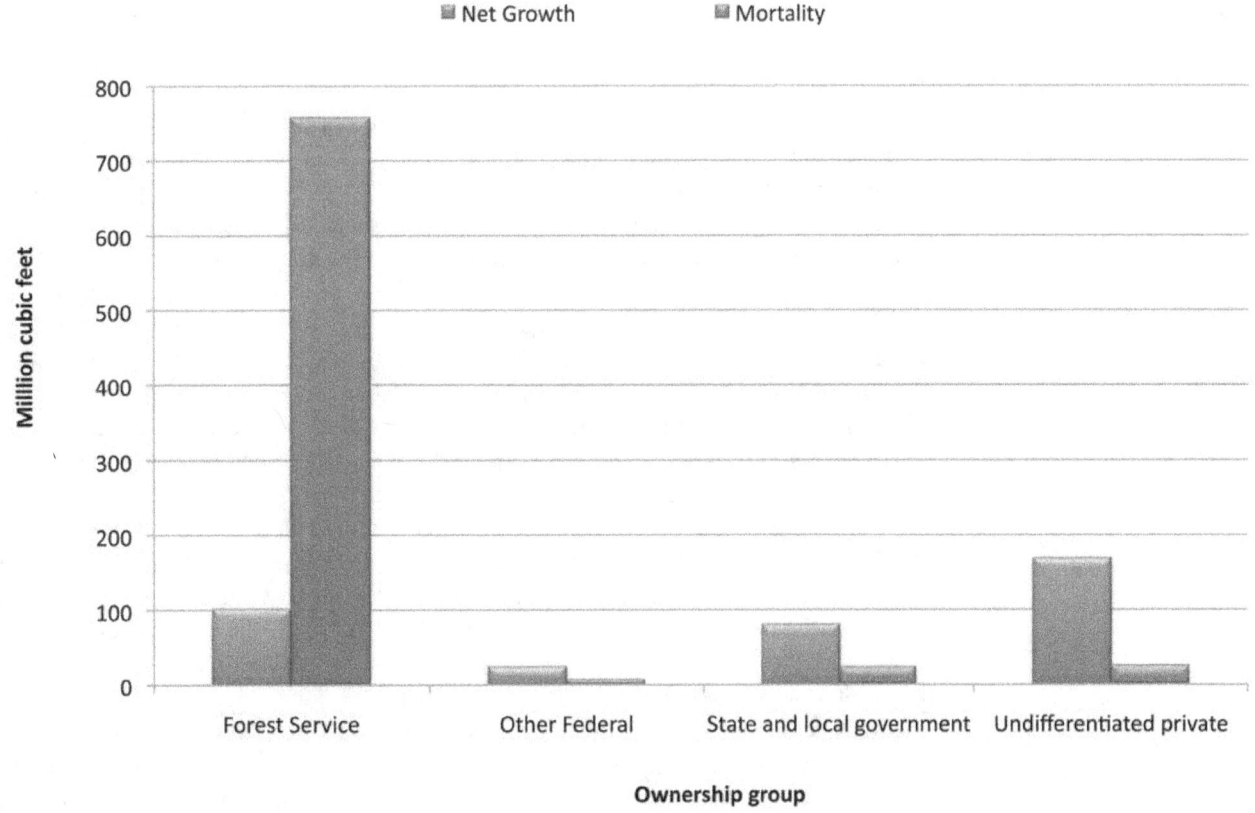

Figure 10: Net annual growth and mortality on forest land by ownership group, Idaho, 2004-2009.

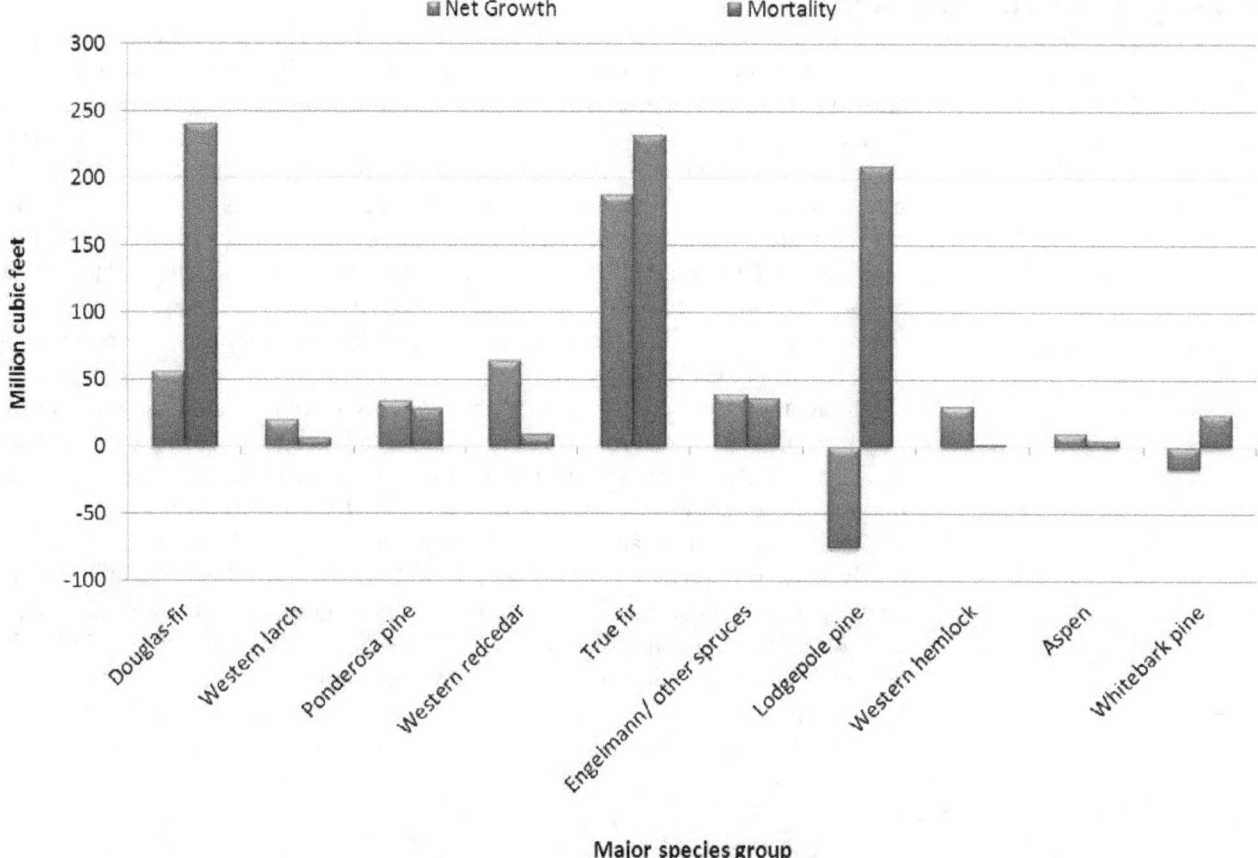

Figure 11: Net annual growth and mortality on forest land by species and species group, Idaho, 2004-2009.

Figure 11 illustrates the relationship between net growth and mortality for the major species and species groups in Idaho. Of the ten species groups listed, mortality exceeded net growth for four species groups. The most striking relationship between net growth and mortality occurred in lodgepole pine. Lodgepole pine recorded –75.3 million cubic feet of net growth compared to 209 million cubic feet of mortality. Whitebark pine—an important producer of food for wildlife in Idaho and other States—also recorded a negative net growth of –16.4 million cubic feet compared to 23.9 million cubic feet of mortality. Mortality of Douglas-fir totaled 240.7 million cubic feet compared to 56.3 million cubic feet of net growth. Mortality of the true fir group also exceeded net growth. Net growth exceeded mortality for the ponderosa pine, western larch, western redcedar, western hemlock, Engelmann and other spruces, and aspen species groups.

Since high mortality is the driving force behind the large reductions in gross growth, further examination of this change component by other resource attributes can help explain the factors behind the high level of tree volume estimated to have died in the previous 5 years. Significant differences were observed in per-acre estimates of mortality between major ownership groups and reserved status. Converting the State-level estimates of mortality into per-acre estimates removes the effect of differences in the amount of forest land controlled by different ownership groups. Across all ownerships, the per-acre estimate of annual mortality volume averages 38.1 cubic feet per year on forest land. Mortality on reserved forest land was substantially higher than unreserved land. Average annual mortality on reserved land

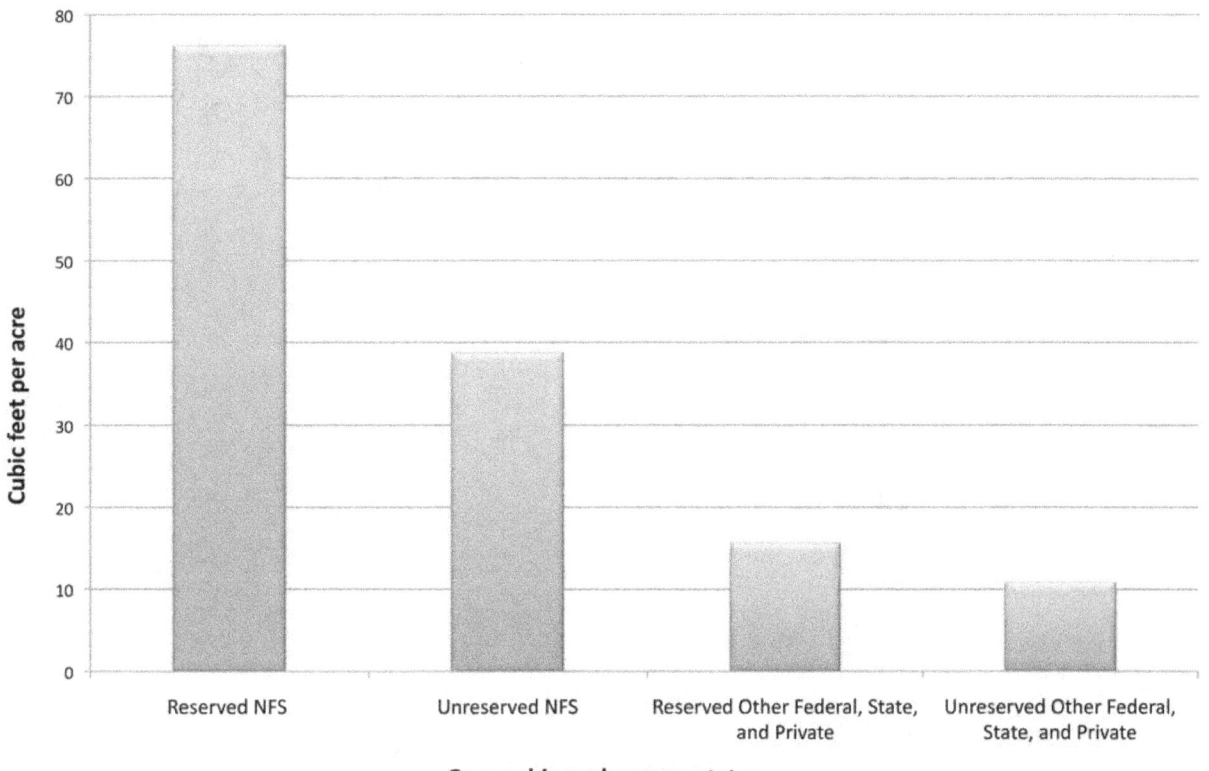

Figure 12: Average annual per-acre mortality on forest land by two major owner categories and reserved status, Idaho, 2004-2009.

averaged 74.3 cubic feet per acre compared to 30.8 cubic feet per acre on unreserved forest land. Figure 12 illustrates per-acre estimates of mortality by two major owner categories and reserved status. National Forest Systems lands classified as reserved recorded the highest average level of per-acre mortality at 76.2 cubic feet, which is over seven times higher than the per-acre estimate recorded on unreserved land controlled by private landowners, other Federal agencies, and State agencies.

Figure 13 illustrates per-acre estimates of mortality by reserved status and cause of death. All trees classified as mortality are assigned a cause of death in the field. Drawing conclusions from mortality estimates by cause of death should be done with caution. The actual agent that caused a tree's death may be difficult, if not impossible, to determine. The cause of death category of "other" includes trees that have died due to reasons the field crews are unable to determine. Interactions between insects and diseases are complex and make identification of damaging agents difficult. Mortality due to fire accounted for the majority (37.9 percent) of total mortality. Insects were the second leading contributor to mortality, accounting for 26 percent of total mortality. Disease accounted for 20 percent. There was a very significant difference in the level of fire-caused per-acre mortality recorded on reserved forest land (fig. 13).

The high mortality resulted in a very significant reduction in gross growth for several species and species groups. By ownership, mortality is highest on National Forest System's forest land especially forest land classified as reserved. Mountain pine beetle infestations are likely contributing to much of the lodgepole pine mortality. Lodgepole pine accounted for 68 percent of the mortality volume determined to be caused by insects. Trends in lodgepole pine mortality believed to have been caused by mountain pine beetle are examined in the "Mountain Pine Beetle" section in the "Issues in Idaho's Forests" chapter.

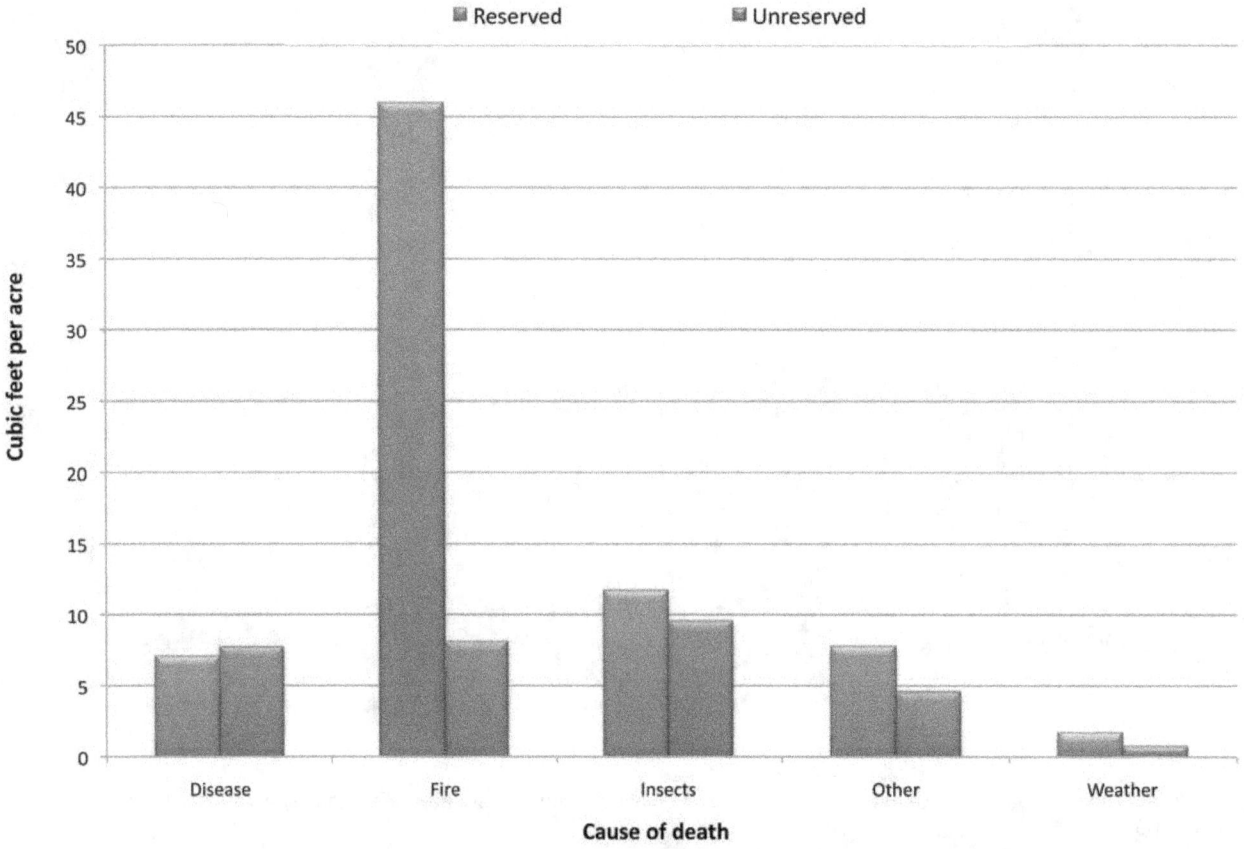

Figure 13: Average annual per-acre mortality on forest land by reserved status and cause of death, Idaho, 2004-2009.

Quality Assurance Analysis

FIA employs a Quality Assurance (QA) Program to ensure the quality of all collected data. The goal of the QA program is to provide a framework to assure the production of complete, accurate, and unbiased forest information of known quality. Specific Measurement Quality Objectives (MQO) for precision are designed to provide a performance objective that FIA strives to achieve for every field measurement. These data quality objectives were developed from knowledge of measurement processes in forestry and forest ecology, as well as the program needs of FIA. The practicality of these MQOs, as well as the measurement uncertainty associated with a given field measurement, can be tested by comparing data from blind check plots. Blind check data are paired observations where, in addition to the field measurements of the standard FIA crew, a second QA measurement of the plot is taken by a crew without knowledge of the first crew's results (Pollard and others 2006). The QA data for this analysis were collected between 2001 and 2005 and then compared for measurement precision between two independent FIA crews' observations. Therefore, for many FIA variables, the data quality is measured by the repeatability of two independent measurements.

The results of the QA analysis for this reporting period are presented in tables II and III. Table II describes tolerances for condition-level variables, and table III describes tree-level variables. Tolerances are the "accepted" range of variability between two independent observations, for checking or comparison purposes.

Table II: QA Results for Condition-Level Variables from 100 Conditions in Idaho, 2004-2009

Variable	Tolerance	Percentage of data within tolerance				Number of times data exceeded tolerance				Records
		@1x	@2x	@3x	@4x	@1x	@2x	@3x	@4x	
Condition Status	No Tolerance	99.00%				1				100
Reserve Status	No Tolerance	99.00%				1				100
Owner Group	No Tolerance	100.00%				0				100
Forest Type (Type)	No Tolerance	85.90%				13				92
Stand Size	No Tolerance	85.90%				13				92
Regeneration Status	No Tolerance	95.70%				4				92
Tree Density	No Tolerance	97.80%				2				92
Owner Class	No Tolerance	99.00%				1				100
Owner Status	No Tolerance	100.00%				0				12
Stand Age	±10 %	95.60%	95.60%	96.70%	96.70%	4	4	3	3	90
Disturbance 1	No Tolerance	79.30%				19				92
Disturbance Year 1	±1 yr	66.70%	66.70%	66.70%	66.70%	1	1	1	1	3
Disturbance 2	No Tolerance	100.00%				0				92
Disturbance 3	No Tolerance	100.00%				0				92
Treatment 1	No Tolerance	96.80%				3				92
Treatment 2	No Tolerance	100.00%				0				92
Treatment 3	No Tolerance	100.00%				0				92
Physiographic Class	No Tolerance	55.40%				41				92
Present Nonforest Use	No Tolerance	100.00%				0				5
Regional Variables										
Percent Crown Cover	±10 %	79.30%	91.30%	96.70%	97.80%	19	8	3	2	92
Percent Bare Ground	±10 .	95.70%	95.70%	95.70%	95.70%	4	4	4	4	92
Habitat Type 1	No Tolerance	44.60%				51				92
Habitat Type 2	No Tolerance	44.60%				51				92

USDA Forest Service Resour. Bull. RMRS-RB-14. 2012

25

Table III: QA results for tree-level variables from 2,224 trees in Idaho, 2004-2009.

Variable	Tolerance	Percentage of data within tolerance				Number of times data exceeded tolerance				Records
		@1x	@2x	@3x	@4x	@1x	@2x	@3x	@4x	
DBH	±0.1 /20 in.	88.6%	93.3%	95.0%	96.0%	242	141	105	84	2119
DRC	±0.1 /20 in.	45.7%	60.0%	70.5%	72.4%	57	42	31	29	105
Azimuth	±10 °	96.3%	98.6%	98.9%	99.0%	82	32	24	23	2224
Horizontal Distance	±0.2 /1.0 ft	93.5%	96.4%	98.0%	98.5%	145	81	45	33	2224
Species	No Tolerance	96.4%				79				2224
Tree Status	No Tolerance	95.9%				92				2224
Rotten/Missing Cull	±10 %	94.0%	97.1%	98.3%	98.8%	116	55	32	23	1928
Total Length	±10 %	80.4%	93.3%	97.6%	99.0%	436	149	54	22	2224
Actual Length	±10 %	80.7%	93.3%	97.3%	98.5%	429	148	61	34	2224
Compacted Crown Ratio	±10 %	69.6%	91.0%	96.4%	98.7%	521	155	61	22	1716
Uncompacted Crown Ratio (P3)	±10 %	83.7%	94.4%	98.0%	99.4%	256	88	31	9	1567
Crown Class	No Tolerance	78.4%				371				1716
Decay Class	±1 class	100.0%				0				413
Cause of Death	No Tolerance	69.7%				27				89
Mortality Year	No Tolerance	29.2%				63				89
Condition Class	No Tolerance	94.3%				126				2224
Regional Variables										
Lean Angle	No Tolerance									–
Mistletoe	±1 class	97.7%	98.4%	99.2%	99.8%	40	27	14	3	1716
Number of Stems	No Tolerance	61.0%				41				105
Percent Missing Top	±10 %	94.6%	96.9%	97.8%	98.4%	105	59	43	31	1928
Sound Dead	±10 %	85.5%	91.9%	93.9%	95.3%	279	156	117	91	1928
Form Defect	±10 %	95.4%	97.9%	98.6%	98.9%	66	30	20	16	1426
Current Tree Class	No Tolerance	96.3%				80				2140
Tree Age	±5 %	12.3%	22.8%	29.8%	42.1%	50	44	40	33	57
DRC using IW MQO	±0.2 in/stem	88.6%	96.2%	98.1%	98.1%	12	4	2	2	105
Horiz Dist-timberland	±0.2 /1.0 ft	95.8%	98.0%	98.8%	98.9%	89	42	25	23	105
Horiz Dist-woodland	±0.2 /1.0 ft	46.7%	62.9%	81.0%	89.5%	56	39	20	11	105

26

USDA Forest Service Resour. Bull. RMRS-RB-14. 2012

Each variable and its associated tolerance are followed by the percentage of total paired records that fall within one, two, three, and four times the tolerance. The last four columns show the number of times out of the total records the data fell outside the tolerance. For example, table III shows that there were 2,119 paired records for the variable "d.b.h." (diameter at breast height). At the 1X tolerance level, almost 89 percent of those records fell within plus or minus one-tenth inch of each other, for each 20.0 inches of d.b.h. observed. This percentage is referred to as the observed compliance rate. MQOs for each variable consist of two parts, a compliance standard and a measurement tolerance, and can be compared to the observed compliance rate to determine that variable's performance.

The information in tables II and III shows variables with varying degrees of repeatability. For example, one condition-level regional variable that appears fairly repeatable is "percent bare ground." At the 1X tolerance level, its observed compliance rate was 96 percent for 92 paired observations that were within plus or minus 10 percent of each other. In contrast, the compliance rate for "habitat type 1," which has no tolerance variability, was only 45 percent for the same observations. Habitat types are an important variable for forest management. Accurate determination could provide an insight to successional status when combined with existing vegetation (such as tree numbers, size class, and species by habitat types or series) thus warranting further investigations into the potential repeatability issues associated with evaluating habitat type.

The tree-level variable "d.b.h.," as mentioned above, is more repeatable when compared to the regional variable "tree age," which has a 1X tolerance compliance rate of only 12 percent. This is probably due to the difficulty of obtaining accurate tree ages. Several factors that might affect inconsistent tree ages are (1) tree too large to reach the center, (2) rings too close or faded to read accurately, and (3) variation in age estimation when not hitting tree center (pith). Although not much can be done about the first two situations, QA data can be used to develop better field procedures for the last, especially for critical variables such as tree age.

As more blind check information becomes available, it might become apparent that a variable's MQO needs to be adjusted accordingly to better reflect the realistic expectation of quality for that variable. As a result, MQO's should be used not only to assess the reliability of FIA measurements and whether current standards are being met, but also to provide data collection experts with the information necessary to improve the current data collection system. This process can improve repeatability, or lead to elimination of variables that prove to be unrepeatable.

Other Resources in Idaho's Forests

Down Woody Material

Down woody material (DWM) is an important component of forests that greatly impacts fire behavior, wildlife habitat, soil stabilization, and carbon sources. Some examples of DWM are fallen trees, branches, and leaf litter commonly found within forests in various stages of decay. The main components of DWM include fine woody debris (FWD), coarse woody debris (CWD), litter, and duff. FWD comprises the small diameter (1- to 3-inch) fire-related fuel classes (1-hr, 10-hr, 100-hr), and CWD comprises the large diameter (3-inch +) 1000-hr fuels.

USDA Forest Service Resour. Bull. RMRS-RB-14. 2012

27

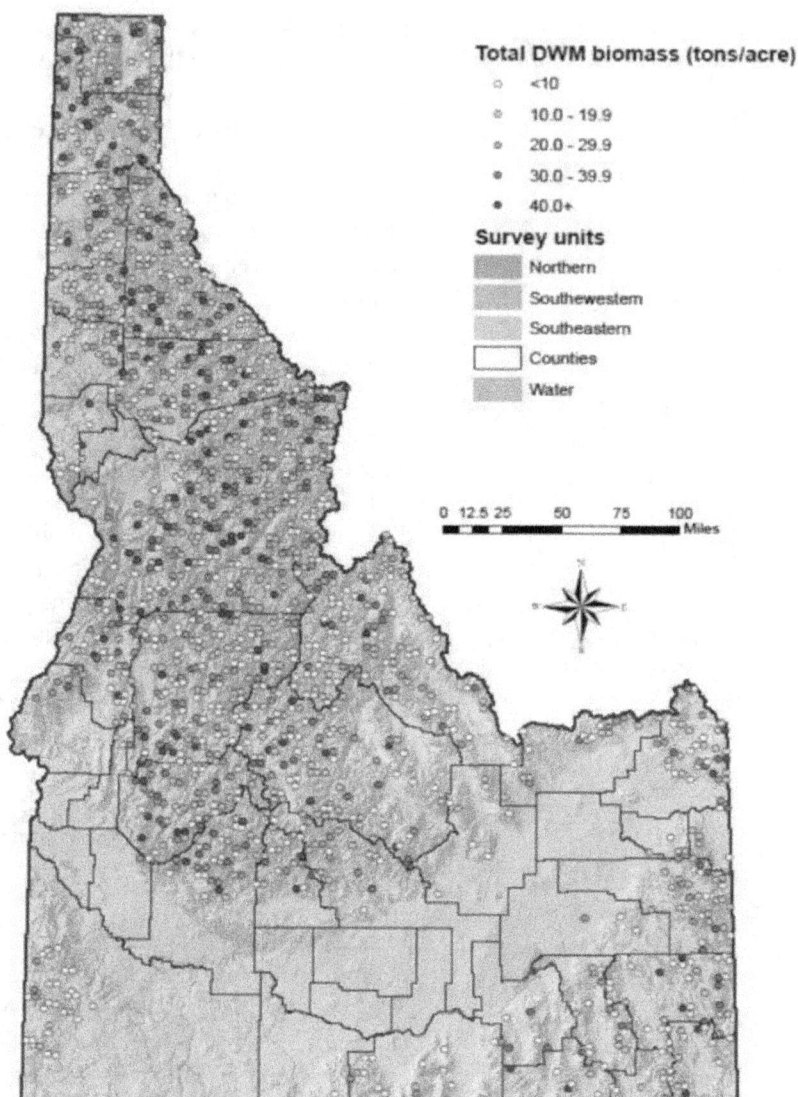

Figure 14: Plot distribution of total DWM biomass (tons per acre) by FIA survey unit, Idaho, cycle 2, subcycles 3-6, 2006-2009.

Total DWM biomass (tons/acre)
- ○ <10
- ◎ 10.0 - 19.9
- ◉ 20.0 - 29.9
- ● 30.0 - 39.9
- ● 40.0+

Survey units
- Northern
- Southewestern
- Southeastern
- Counties
- Water

Nationally, DWM are measured on phase 3 (P3) plots. In 2006, due to the increasing need for more intensive DWM information, IWFIA initiated a phase 2 (P2) DWM inventory in all its annual States. This DWM analysis used regional P2 protocols (USFS 2006-2009) for data collected from 2006 to 2009. Due to the presence of snow or other hazardous conditions, not all DWM components were able to be sampled on all plots. Only plots that sampled all six DWM components were included.

The random distribution of four annual subcycles of P2 DWM plots is displayed in figure 14. This shows the total DWM biomass (tons per acre) by FIA survey unit for 1,553 plot/conditions in Idaho. In general, DWM biomass is highest in the northern and central parts of the State; this distribution reflects the distribution of forest types. The northern forest types western larch, western hemlock, and western redcedar have the highest DWM biomass estimates; while the southern forest types western juniper, Rocky Mountain juniper, and juniper woodlands have the lowest.

Table IV shows the mean biomass (tons per acre) by DWM component, number of sampled plot/conditions, and average elevation for FIA survey units. The

Table IV—Average elevation and DWM loadings by FIA survey unit with number of plots, Idaho 2006-2009.

FIA Survey Unit	Number of plots	Elevation	CWD	FWD large	FWD medium	FWD small	Duff	Litter	Total DWM
Northern	741	4,458	7.4	2.4	0.5	0.2	8.7	3.1	22.4
Southwestern	327	6,110	5.4	1.7	0.4	0.1	6.2	3.8	17.7
Southeastern	485	7,164	5.4	1.6	0.3	0.1	5.5	2.5	15.5
Totals	1,553	5,651	6.4	2.0	0.4	0.2	7.2	3.1	19.2

northern survey unit has the highest mean DWM, at 22.4 tons/acre, and the southeastern survey unit has the lowest, at 15.49 tons/acre. The mean DWM for the entire State is 19.2 tons/acre. Specific DWM components mostly show a similar pattern, with the southeastern and southwestern units sometimes showing values similar to one another. The exception is the litter component, where the southwestern survey unit has the highest mean tons/acre. Table V shows the mean biomass (tons per acre) by DWM component, number of plot/conditions sampled, and average elevation for forest type groups and forest types. Western larch has the highest mean DWM at 33.6 tons/acre, and the lowest is 3.7 tons/acre for juniper woodland. Some of the forest types in this analysis may not be representative due to small sample sizes.

Table V—Average elevation and DWM loadings by forest type group and forest type. Idaho, 2006-2009.

Forest type group and forest type	Number of plots	Elevation	CWD	FWD large	FWD medium	FWD small	Duff	Litter	Total DWM
Pinyon-juniper group									
Rocky Mountain juniper	4	5,913	1.7	0.9	0.3	0.0	0.9	1.2	5.0
Juniper woodland	15	5,466	0.0	0.1	0.1	0.0	1.5	1.9	3.7
Total	19	5,560	0.4	0.3	0.2	0.0	1.3	1.7	3.9
Douglas-fir group									
Douglas-fir	447	5,548	4.7	1.9	0.5	0.2	5.7	2.4	15.4
Total	447	5,548	4.7	1.9	0.5	0.2	5.7	2.4	15.4
Ponderosa pine group									
Ponderosa pine	117	4,571	4.2	1.6	0.4	0.1	9.2	6.9	22.4
Total	117	4,571	4.2	1.6	0.4	0.1	9.2	6.9	22.4
Western white pine group									
Western white pine	3	4,078	6.0	1.1	0.3	0.1	7.2	3.8	18.6
Total	3	4,078	6.0	1.1	0.3	0.1	7.2	3.8	18.6
Fir-spruce-mountain hemlock group									
Engelmann spruce	52	6,505	12.0	1.1	0.3	0.1	8.2	1.9	23.5
Engelmann spruce-subalpine fir	44	6,347	10.0	1.6	0.4	0.2	10.6	2.4	25.2
Grand fir	141	4,134	9.0	4.9	0.9	0.3	8.9	3.0	26.8
Subalpine fir	152	6,979	8.6	1.3	0.3	0.1	6.0	1.7	18.0
Mountain hemlock	16	5,584	7.8	1.3	0.5	0.2	3.5	1.1	14.3
Total	405	5,804	9.3	2.5	0.5	0.2	7.7	2.2	22.4

USDA Forest Service Resour. Bull. RMRS-RB-14. 2012

29

Table V—*Continued.*

Forest type group and forest type	Number of plots	Elevation	CWD	FWD large	FWD medium	FWD small	Duff	Litter	Total DWM
Lodgepole pine group									
Lodgepole pine	177	6,324	7.3	1.5	0.3	0.1	9.6	3.3	22.0
Total	177	6,324	7.3	1.5	0.3	0.1	9.6	3.3	22.0
Hemlock-Sitka spruce group									
Western hemlock	27	3,435	11.4	3.1	0.6	0.3	14.8	3.2	33.4
Western redcedar	48	3,449	14.0	2.2	0.5	0.2	11.8	3.7	32.4
Total	75	3,444	13.0	2.5	0.5	0.3	12.9	3.5	32.8
Western larch group									
Western larch	25	3,684	7.4	4.0	0.7	0.4	14.8	6.3	33.6
Total	25	3,684	7.4	4.0	0.7	0.4	14.8	6.3	33.6
Other western softwoods group									
Limber pine	8	8,259	5.2	0.6	0.2	0.1	3.1	2.0	11.0
Whitebark pine	19	8,951	6.2	0.7	0.2	0.1	2.7	1.3	11.1
Western juniper	18	5,816	0.8	1.2	0.3	0.1	1.2	2.4	5.9
Total	45	7,574	3.9	0.9	0.2	0.1	2.1	1.9	9.0
Elm-ash-cottonwood group									
Cottonwood	6	3,671	2.8	4.2	0.7	0.1	2.3	1.6	11.8
Total	6	3,671	2.8	4.2	0.7	0.1	2.3	1.6	11.8
Aspen-birch group									
Aspen	65	6,446	4.2	2.1	0.3	0.1	6.5	4.9	18.1
Paper birch	3	2,411	1.9	1.9	0.2	0.2	17.6	10.2	31.9
Total	68	6,268	4.1	2.1	0.3	0.1	7.0	5.2	18.7
Other hardwoods group									
Other hardwoods	1	5,456	3.6	5.3	0.5	0.1	4.2	4.9	18.5
Total	1	5,456	3.6	5.3	0.5	0.1	4.2	4.9	18.5
Woodland hardwoods group									
Cercocarpus (mountain brush) woodland	16	6,882	1.1	0.3	0.2	0.1	2.0	3.6	7.2
Intermountain maple woodland	13	6,382	0.6	3.2	0.3	0.1	5.7	4.6	14.4
Total	29	6,658	0.9	1.6	0.2	0.1	3.6	4.1	10.5
Nonstocked									
Nonstocked	136	6,140	4.2	1.5	0.3	0.1	4.7	3.1	13.9
Total	136	6,140	4.2	1.5	0.3	0.1	4.7	3.1	13.9
Totals	1,553	5,651	6.4	2.0	0.4	0.2	7.2	3.1	19.2

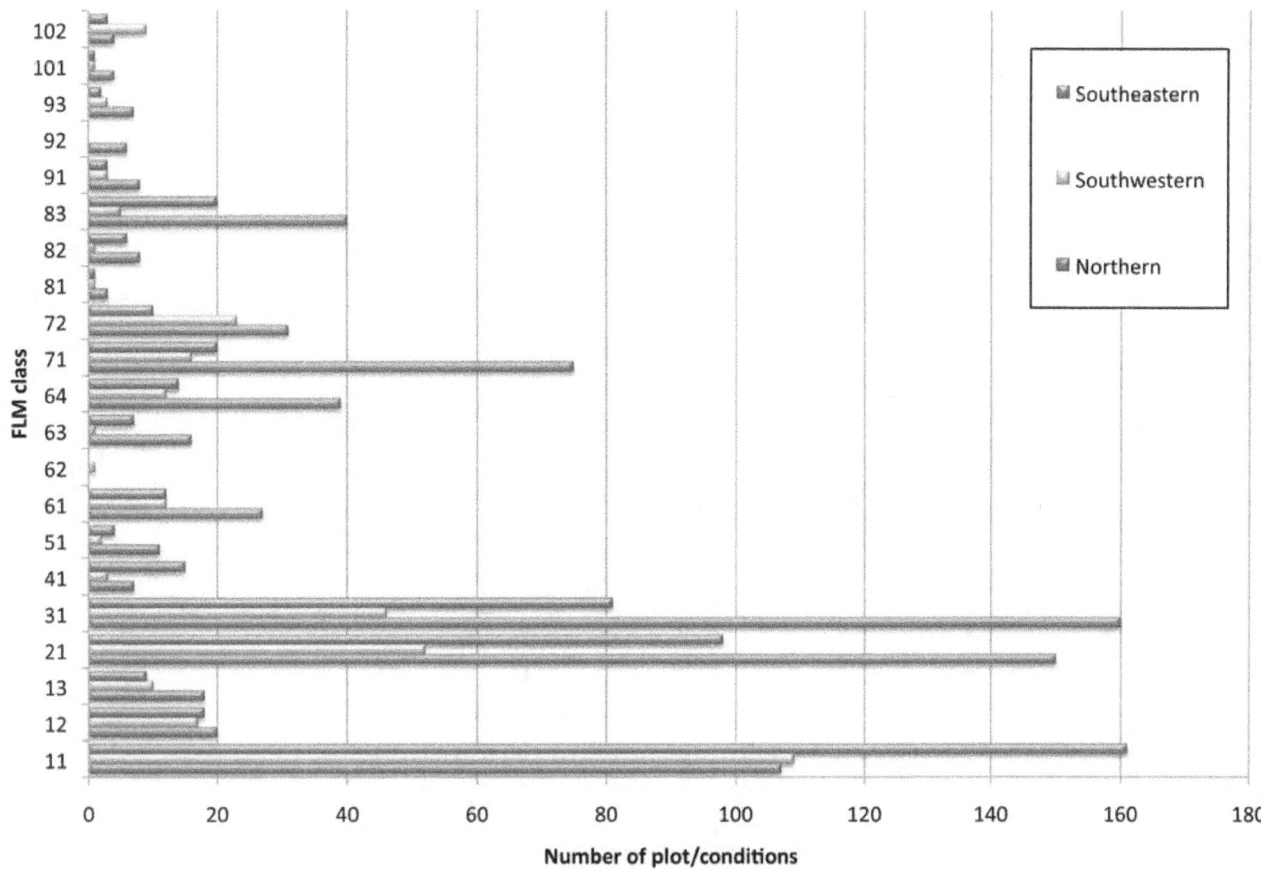

Figure 15: Number of plot/conditions by fuel loading model (FLM) class and FIA survey unit, Idaho, 2006-2009.

Fuel loadings by DWM component are essential for predicting fire behavior. Table V also shows that the duff DWM component has the highest mean fuel loadings over all, followed by the CWD component and then the litter component. Several forest types show some variation from this general trend. Also, fuel loading variation among forest types in the three FWD classes is not as great as in the CWD, duff, and litter classes.

Surface fuel classifications of duff, litter, FWD, and CWD for estimating fire effects were compiled from a wide variety of recent fuel sampling projects conducted across the contiguous United States (Lutes and others 2009). For each FIA plot/condition, fuel loading ranges from these four classes were used to identify one of 21 potential fuel loading models (FLM) described by Lutes and others (2009). Figure 15 displays the number of plot/conditions identified by FLM class for the three survey units in Idaho. This shows that for this DWM dataset all of the 21 possible FLM's were identified, and the largest proportion of all the plot/conditions (377) occurred in the class 11 FLM, followed by classes 21 (300 plot/conditions) and 31 (287 plot/conditions). Class 11 was the most common FLM for the southeastern and southwestern survey units; class 31 was the most common FLM for the northern survey unit. Although these plot classifications are currently under review, once they are objectively classified they can be used as inputs to fire effects models to compute smoke emissions, fuel consumption, and carbon released to the atmosphere.

USDA Forest Service Resour. Bull. RMRS-RB-14. 2012

31

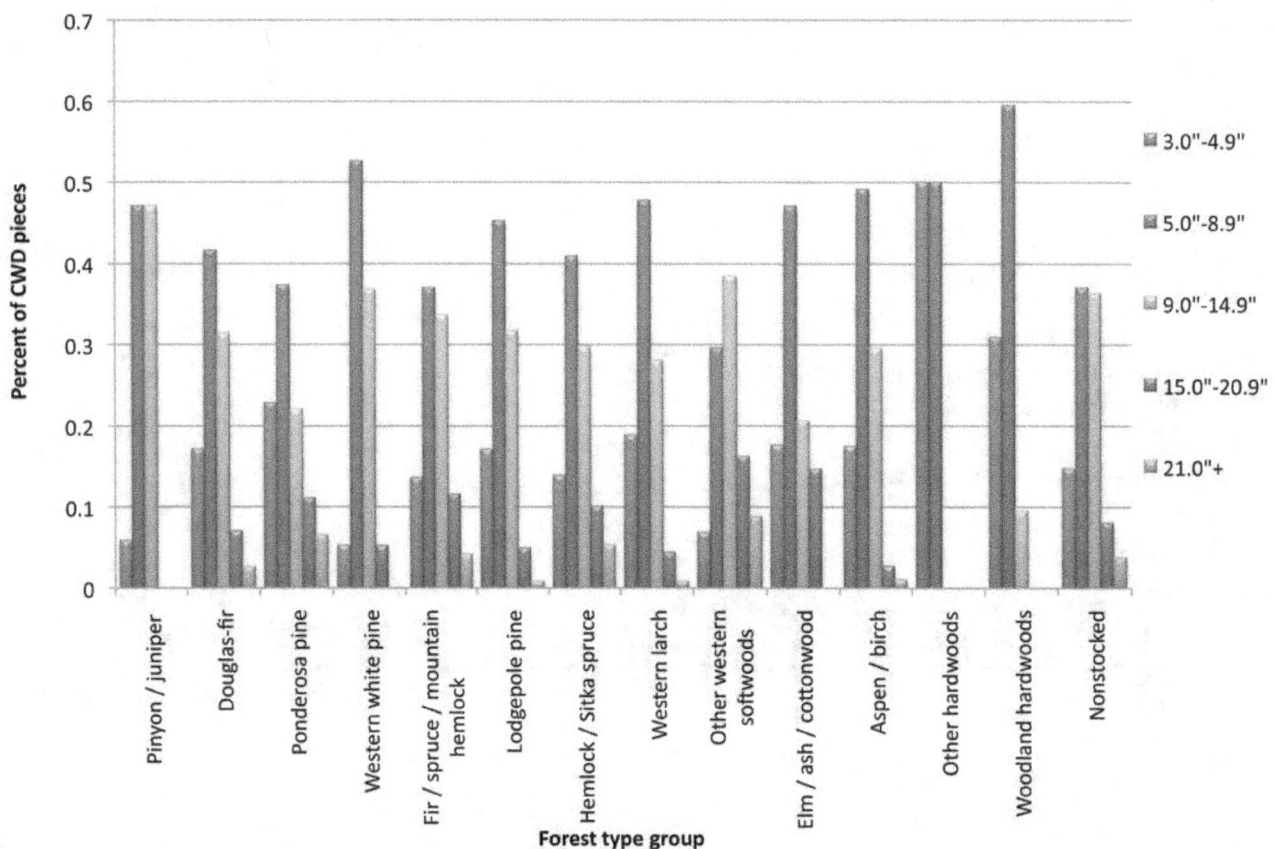

Figure 16: Percentage distribution of course woody debris (CWD) pieces (decay class 1-4) by large-end diameter class and forest type group, Idaho, cycle 2, subcycles 3-6, 2006-2009.

Structural diversity in terms of CWD diameters and decay classes are important criteria for wildlife habitat. IWFIA field crews identify one of five large-end diameter classes for each P2 CWD piece tallied. This information may be critical for wildlife species that use large-diameter logs for habitat. Figure 16 displays the percentage of CWD pieces for decay classes 1 through 4 in each large-end diameter class by forest type. Although they contribute to biomass and carbon pools, large-end diameter class is not recorded for pieces in decay-class 5 due to their degree of decomposition. At 9 percent, the other western softwoods forest type group (consisting of the whitebark pine, limber pine, and western juniper forest types) has the highest percentage of CWD pieces in the 21.0-inch and greater class, followed by the ponderosa pine forest type / group at 7 percent, the hemlock/Sitka spruce forest type group (consisting of the western hemlock and western redcedar forest types) at 5 percent, and the fir / spruce/ mountain hemlock group (consisting of the Engelmann spruce, Engelmann spruce / subalpine fire, subalpine fir, grand fir and mountain hemlock forest types) and nonstocked at 4 percent each. At 15.0 to 20.9 inches large-end diameter, the other western softwoods forest type group again has the most at 16 percent, followed by the elm / ash / cottonwood group (with only the cottonwood forest type) at 15 percent, although this percentage is derived from a relatively small sample (34 CWD pieces on 4 plot/conditions). The fir / spruce/ mountain hemlock group has 12 percent, and the ponderosa pine forest type / group had 11 percent of their CWD pieces in the 15.0 to 20.9 inches large-end diameter class.

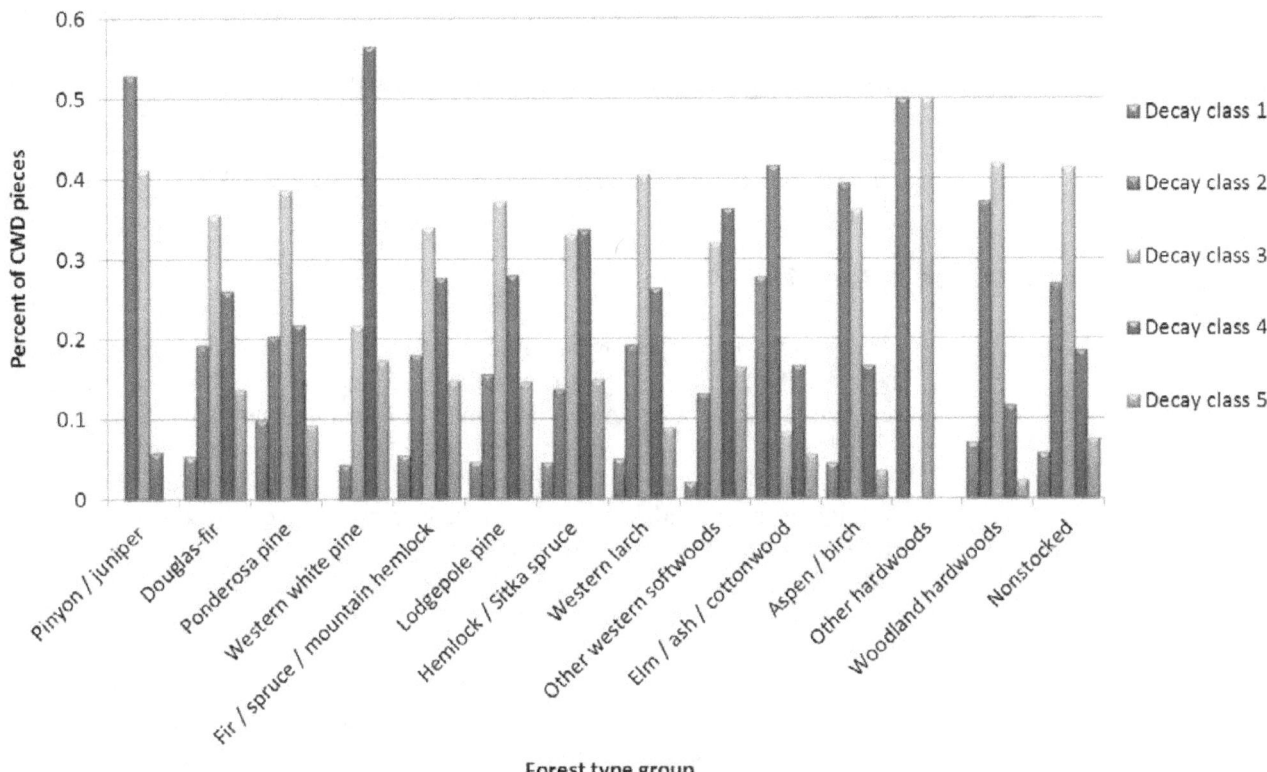

Figure 17: Percentage distribution of course woody debris (CWD) pieces by decay class and forest type group, Idaho, cycle 2, subcycles 3-6, 2006-2009.

Another consideration other than size is the degree of decay of individual logs. Decay classes can range from class 1, which are newly fallen trees with no decay, to class 5, which still resemble a log but often blend into the duff and litter layers. Figure 17 shows the percentage of CWD pieces by forest type and decay class. In general, the wetter types have a higher percentage of CWD pieces in the advanced decomposition classes, while drier types have a lower percentage.

The annual FIA system supports live and standing dead tree inventories but does not include down dead trees as did some past periodic inventories. The current P3 DWM protocols and estimation procedures (Woodall and Monleon 2008) include improvements such as population estimation, and are designed to capture some important aspects that serve as a better surrogate for answering relevant questions about the various components of down woody materials in forests. However, P3 is a 1/16th sample of P2, and although it may be adequate at the regional or national level, it is often inadequate for many DWM applications at the State level.

Although this analysis included only plot-level per acre estimates and analysis, soon IWFIA will have population estimate capabilities for its regional P2 DWM database. This will allow analyses of the impacts and implications of expanding plot level information to the State. For example, table V shows that although the western larch forest type in Idaho has over twice the total per acre DWM biomass as the Douglas-fir type, the area of the Douglas-fir type is over 20 times that of the western larch type (table 3). Once population estimates are factored in, the Douglas-fir type will likely contain more total DWM biomass and carbon than many of the types with high per acre estimates in Idaho.

USDA Forest Service Resour. Bull. RMRS-RB-14. 2012

33

The Pacific Northwest FIA and IWFIA are jointly investigating a national P2 inventory version of DWM to support a more robust dataset for future fire fuel, wildlife structure, and carbon assessments. These protocols should be complementary and compatible with the current regional P2 variations. As estimates of DWM are improved and refined, along with FIA's understory vegetation and standing tree inventory, FIA will be better positioned for addressing estimates of total forest biomass.

Soil Resources in Idaho's Forests

Soils on the landscape are the product of five interacting soil forming factors. These are parent material, climate, landscape position (topography), organisms (vegetation, microbes, other soil organisms), and time (Jenny 1994). Many external forces can have a profound influence on forest soil condition and hence forest health. These include agents of change or disturbances to apparent steady-state conditions such as shifts in climate, fire, insect and disease activities, land use activities, and land management actions.

The Soil Indicator of forest health was developed to assess the status and trend of forest soil resources in the United States across all ecoregions, forest types, and land ownership categories. For this report, data were analyzed and are being reported by forest type groups. This forest type stratification not only reflects the influence of forest vegetation on soil properties, but also the interaction of parent material, climate, landscape position, and time with forest vegetation and soil organisms. A complete listing of mean soil properties in Idaho, organized by forest

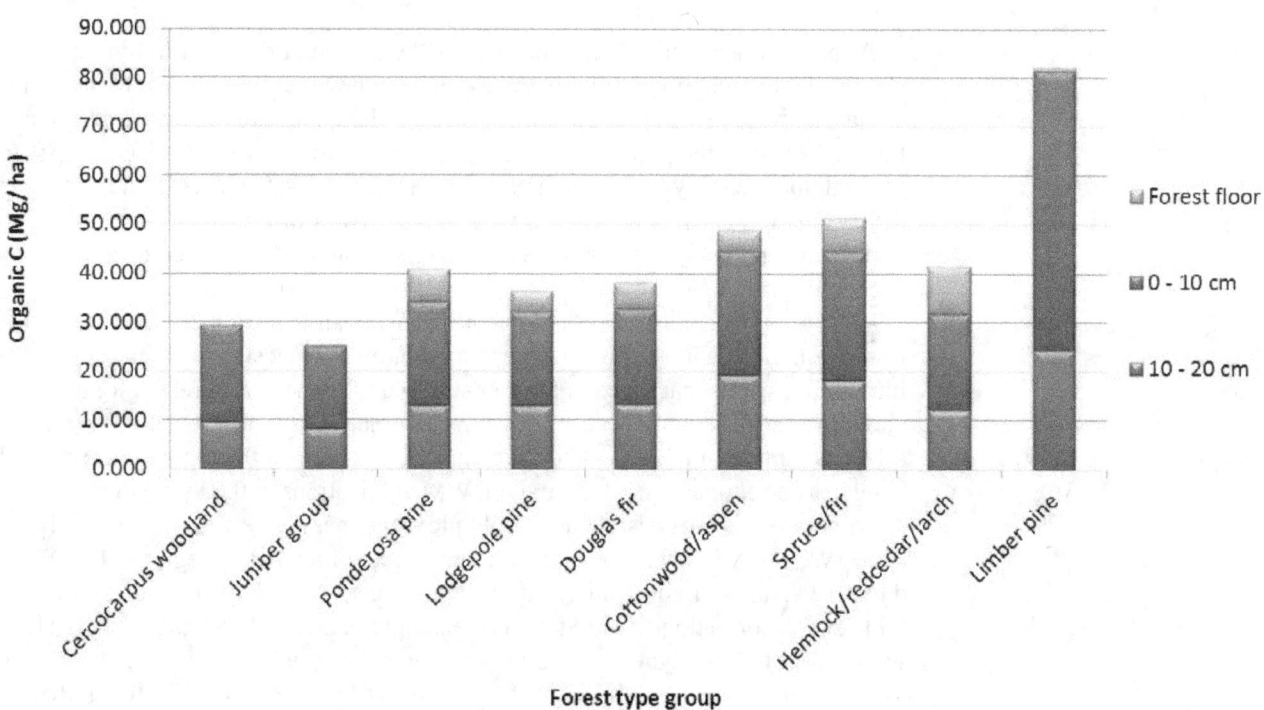

Figure 18: Soil organic carbon stocks (Mg/ha) in the forest floor and 0-10 and 10-20 cm soil layers arranged by forest type groups in Idaho. The forest type groups are arranged left to right in order of increasing latitude, elevation, and precipitation with some overlap among forest types. The juniper group in Idaho includes Rocky Mountain juniper and western juniper. The spruce/fir group in Idaho includes grand fir, Engelmann spruce, subalpine fir, and mixed Engelmann spruce/subalpine fir.

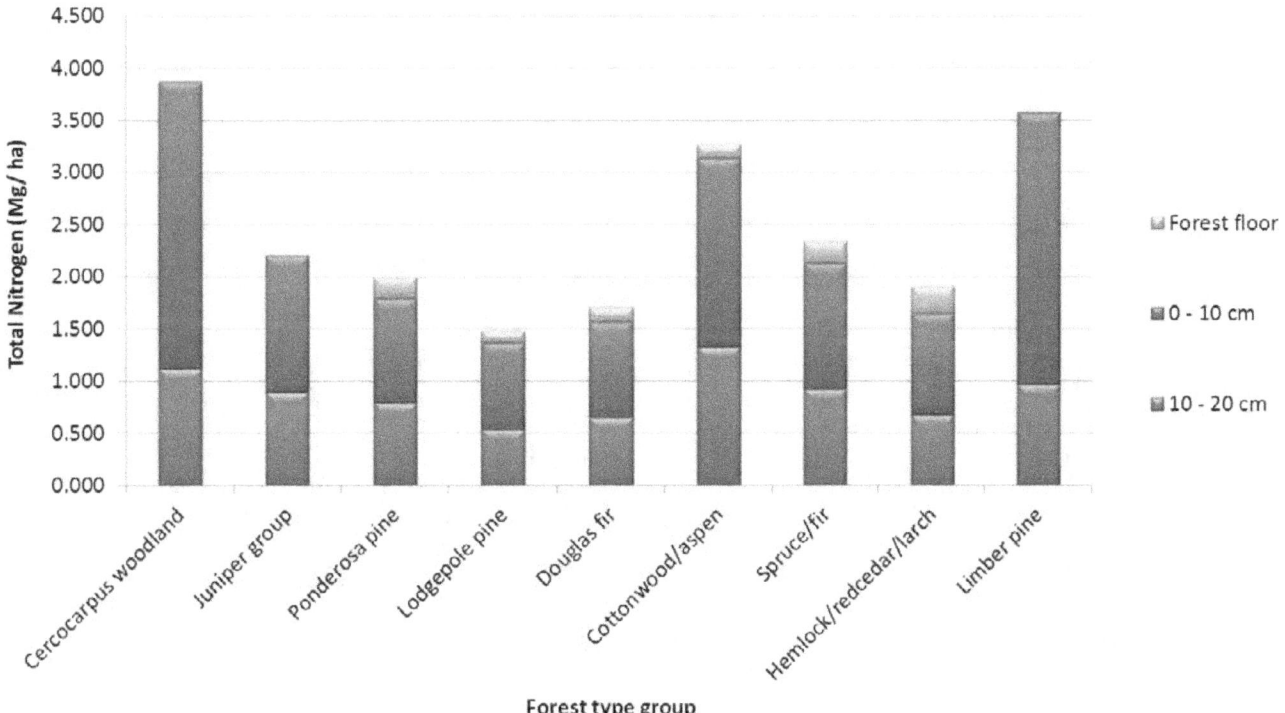

Figure 19: Soil organic nitrogen stocks (Mg/ha) in the forest floor and 0-10 and 10-20 cm soil layers arranged by forest type groups in Idaho. The forest types and type groups are arranged left to right in order of increasing latitude, elevation, and precipitation with some overlap among forest types. The juniper group in Idaho includes Rocky Mountain juniper and western juniper. The spruce/fir group in Idaho includes grand fir, Engelmann spruce, subalpine fir, and mixed Engelmann spruce/subalpine fir.

type, can be found in appendix E. These are least-squares means generated by the SAS GLMMIX data analysis software program. Some plots had a repeat visit so the data are summarized by visit number (1 or 2) and by forest type. Plots visited for the first Soil Indicator measurements were sampled in 2000, 2001, 2002, 2004, 2007, and 2008. Only a small subset of plots have been re-visited thus far in 2006, 2007, and 2009 so there is not yet enough data to run a valid repeated measures analysis. Nevertheless, we report the data for the re-visited plots summarized by forest type in the Soil Indicator core tables. Some of the key soil properties were graphed by forest type group in Idaho and are highlighted in the discussion below.

Generally, soil moisture increases with elevation and latitude (associated with cooler temperatures) and forest types tend to reflect this climatic gradient. When expressed in terms of megagrams of carbon (C) per hectare of forest area, C stocks generally increase with elevation and/or soil moisture storage (fig. 19). Soil nitrogen (N) stocks in cercocarpus woodland, cottonwood/aspen, and limber pine forests in Idaho tend to be higher than those in other forest types (fig. 19). The high soil N under cercocarpus in Idaho is based on only one plot, but these results are similar to those in Utah (DeBlander and others 2010). High soil N stocks under cottonwood/aspen in Idaho mirror data from Utah and Colorado where higher amounts of N are stored in aspen-dominated landscapes (DeBlander and others 2010; Thompson and others 2010). The high C and N stocks in limber pine are from a single plot and may not be representative. This is far too small a sampling to generalize findings for this forest type across the State as a whole.

Soils in drier areas such as soils under cercocarpus and juniper woodland tend to be less weathered and have higher amounts of exchangeable base cations such

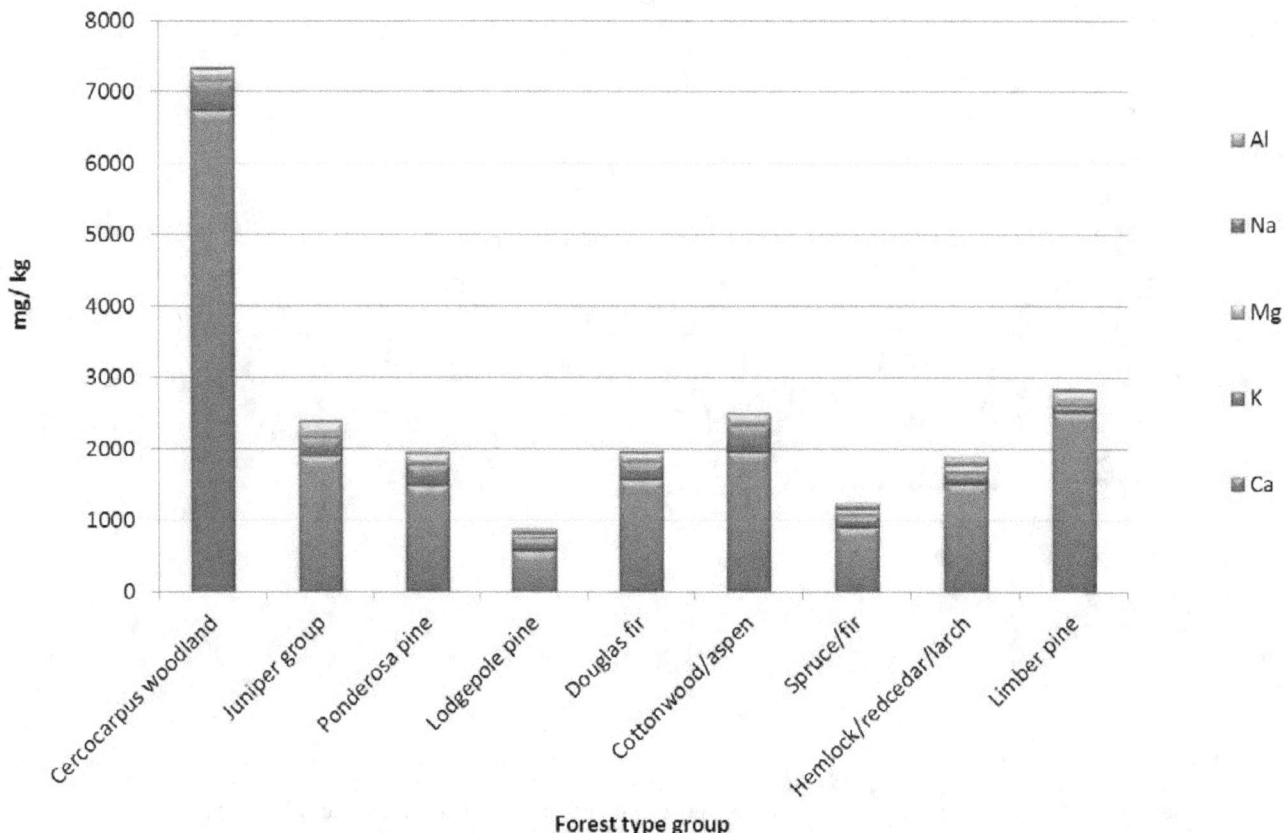

Figure 20a: Exchangeable cations (aluminum, sodium, magnesium, potassium, and calcium) in the 0-10 cm soil layer arranged by forest type groups in Idaho.

as sodium, potassium, magnesium, and calcium (figs. 20a and 20b). Acidic soils, many of which are found in wetter, higher elevation environments (e.g., spruce/fir) tend to have lower levels of exchangeable base cations and have measureable levels of exchangeable aluminum. In none of the plots sampled are soil exchangeable aluminum levels high enough to pose a toxicity risk to tree roots given the ample supply of exchangeable calcium. Exchangeable base cation concentrations are also high under cottonwood/aspen forests.

Soil pH in drier calcareous soils tends to be near-neutral to alkaline (fig. 21 top) and such soils are found under cercocarpus woodland in Idaho. The lowest pH soils are found under lodgepole pine and spruce/fir forests and these tend to be only moderately acid as a whole in Idaho. Moderately acid soils often have elevated levels of extractable manganese (fig. 21 middle). Although elevated levels of manganese present some toxicity risk to sensitive species, potentially toxic levels of extractable manganese have yet to be established for most forest plant species. In general, only about 3.4 percent of the 0-10 cm forest soil layers in the Interior West contain extractable Mn levels greater than 100 mg/kg (Amacher and Perry 2011). In Idaho, most of the forest soils with elevated levels of extractable Mn are found under spruce/fir (mean extractable Mn = 35 mg/kg in 0-10 cm layer). The lowest levels of extractable phosphorus by the Olsen method were found in soils under cercocarpus woodland, whereas the highest levels were found under cottonwood/aspen (fig. 21 bottom). The lower levels of extractable P in the calcareous soils reflect strong attenuation of plant-available P by the abundant calcium minerals in these soils.

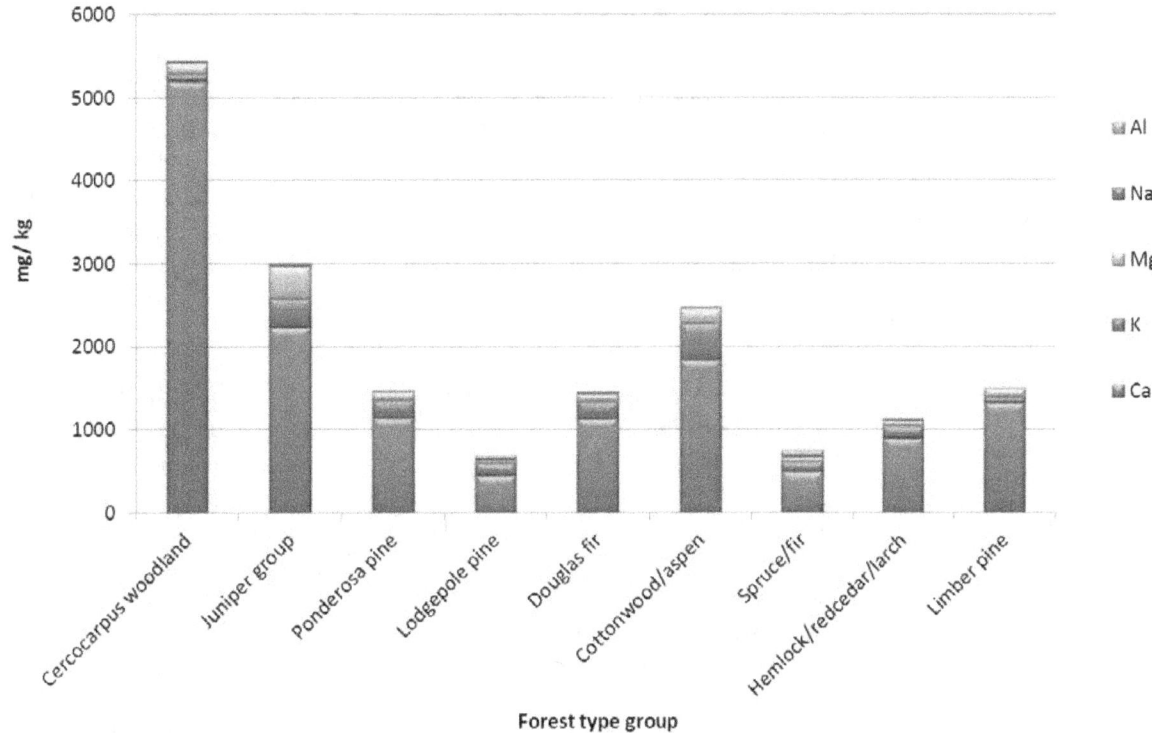

Figure 20b: Exchangeable cations (aluminum, sodium, magnesium, potassium, and calcium) in the 10-20 cm soil layer arranged by forest type groups in Idaho.

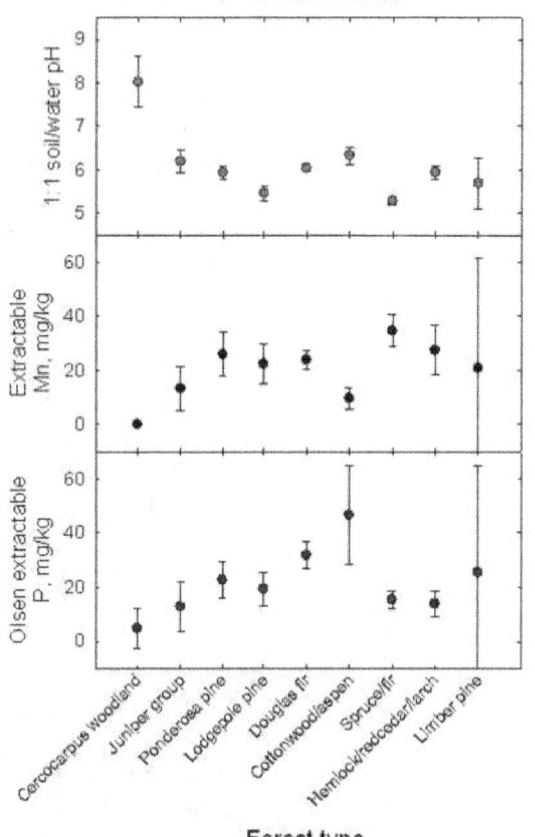

Figure 21: Soil pH (top), 1 M NH₄Cl-extractable manganese (middle), and Olsen (pH 8.5 0.5 M NaHCO₃)-extractable phosphorus (bottom) in the 0-10 cm soil layer arranged by forest type groups in Idaho. Whiskers represent standard error.

Overall, soils under lodgepole pine in Idaho tended to have the least nitrogen stocks, the lowest levels of exchangeable bases, and the lowest pH. This probably reflects the ability of the widely distributed lodgepole species to occupy lower fertility soils, whereas many other species prefer richer deeper soils. Throughout the Interior West as a whole and in Idaho, aspen, for example, tends to occupy deeper, richer, wetter soils and is associated with sites with higher nitrogen and potassium reserves, near-neutral pH levels, and a general absence of exchangeable aluminum (DeBlander and others 2010).

Snags as Wildlife Habitat

Standing dead trees (snags) provide important habitat in the forested ecosystems of Idaho. There are many organisms that utilize snags at some point in their life history. These include, but are not limited to, bacteria, fungi, insects, rodents, cavity-nesting birds, bats, raptors, mustelids, and black bears. The height, diameter, and decay status of a standing dead tree are some of the important attributes for species that use snags as a nesting, roosting, or den site. Individual tree data collected by FIA field crews allow for population-level analysis of the availability of individual snags that meet criteria important to wildlife.

Cavity-nesting birds in Idaho are especially dependent on snags for both nesting and foraging activities. There are a handful of bird species that act as primary excavators of nest sites. These birds create a cavity during one breeding season, but often abandon it and create a new cavity the following year. The old cavities are then occupied by secondary nesting birds. Secondary cavity-nesters do not excavate their own nest sites and are dependent on primary excavators for their cavities. The suitability of an old cavity for a secondary nester often depends on the species of primary excavator that created it. Here we present data reflecting the number of snags in Idaho that are suitable for three important primary excavators. These birds provide the bulk of cavities for secondary nesters in Idaho. The Hairy Woodpecker (*Picoides villosus*), Red-naped Sapsucker (*Sphyrapicus nuchalis*), and Northern Flicker (*Colaptes auratus*) create different sized openings and cavities and are also relatively abundant and wide spread throughout the different forest types of Idaho. Therefore they provide suitable nest sites for a wide variety of secondary nesting species. The distribution of suitable snags by stand-age is also presented. Suitability is based on mean tree diameters found to be used by these birds (Flack 1976; McClelland and others 1979; Dobkin and others 1995; Martin and others 2004).

There are almost 283 million snags in Idaho that meet the size preferences of the Hairy Woodpecker (≥25cm (9.8 in.) d.b.h). The most abundant tree species contributing to these bird's nesting sites are Douglas-fir (80.1 million snags), subalpine fir (59.1 million), and lodgepole pine (53.8 million) (fig. 22). These snags are predominately found in the Douglas-fir, subalpine fir, and non-stocked forest types. Nearly 167 million snags meet the diameter preferences of the Red-naped Sapsucker (≥31cm (12.2 in.) d.b.h.). Douglas-fir, subalpine fir and lodgepole pine again contribute the majority of these snags at 58.6, 31.9, and 20.3 million snags respectively. The forest types where most of these snags can be found are Douglas-fir, non-stocked, and subalpine fir. Potential Northern Flicker snags (≥35cm (13.8 in.) d.b.h.) are found in the same forest types as the two aforementioned bird species. The tree species that comprise most of the suitable snag population for this species are Douglas-fir (46.6 million), subalpine fir (20.7 million), and grand fir (10.4 million). The non-stocked forest type often includes areas disturbed by

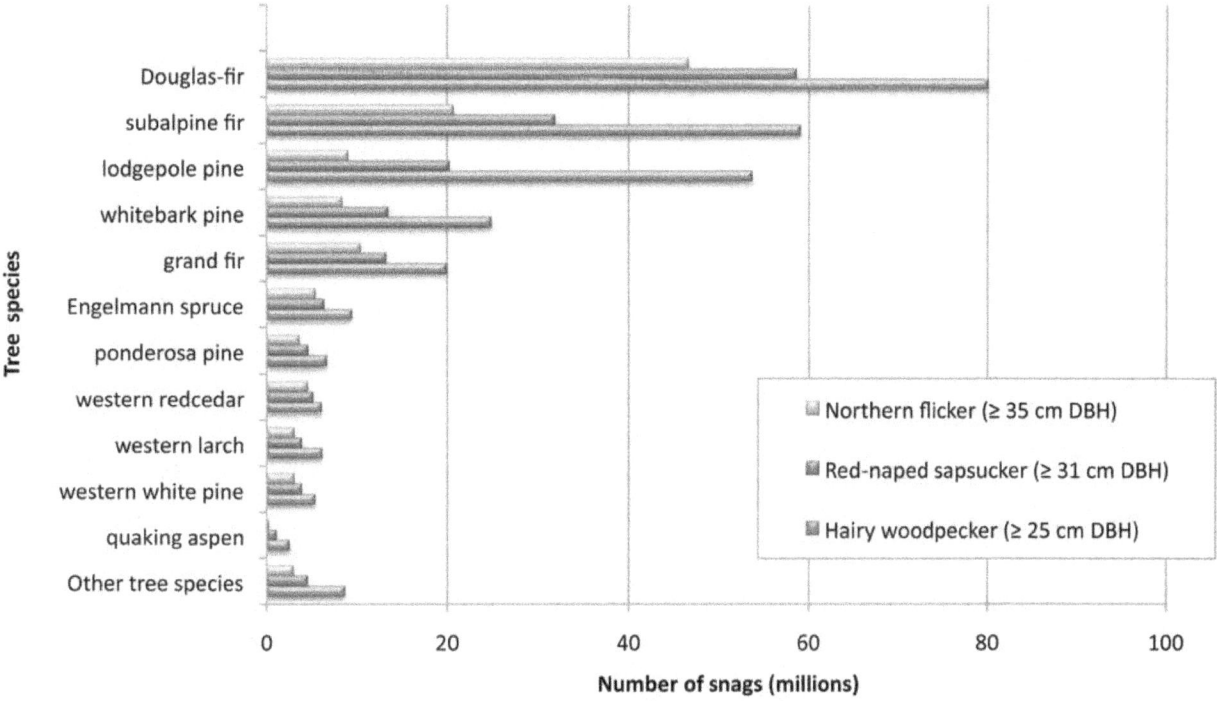

Figure 22: Number of snags meeting the preferences of three important cavity-excavating birds by tree species, Idaho, 2004-2009.

wildfire, disease, and insect infestations. These types of stands account for the high number of snags in this forest type.

Figure 23 shows the distribution of snags ≥35cm (13.8 in.) d.b.h. by stand-age. These snags are large enough to accommodate all three species of cavity excavators discussed here. For most forest type groups, the largest percentage of suitable snags for all three birds is found in the 51 to 100 and 101 to 151 age-classes. The zero age-class holds a large amount of suitable snags due to the large amount of disturbed forests in the non-stocked forest type. Another notable exception to the general age-class distribution is the aspen/ birch group. Aspen forests are particularly important for some primary and secondary nesting birds because of the relationship of diseased aspen, primary excavators, and secondary nesters (Hart and Hart 2001). Diseased trees provide a relatively soft substrate for primary excavators to build their nest cavities in. The secondary nesters then occupy many of these cavities in subsequent years. Few aspen trees live past 100 years in Idaho. Almost all (91 percent) snags found in aspen forests are found in the 1 to 50 year age-class.

Variables other than snag dimensions and numbers need to be considered when predicting suitable wildlife habitat for forest-dwelling species. Proximity to forest edge and stand density of live trees is important to many cavity-nesting birds. The state of decay of a tree and its distance to foraging also plays a role in nest site suitability. FIA data can address many of these factors and there are current efforts to build predictive models for these species by using data collected by our crews. These models can be valuable tools for Federal and State land managers; at least 92 percent of the forests in Idaho containing suitable snags occur on public lands.

USDA Forest Service Resour. Bull. RMRS-RB-14. 2012

39

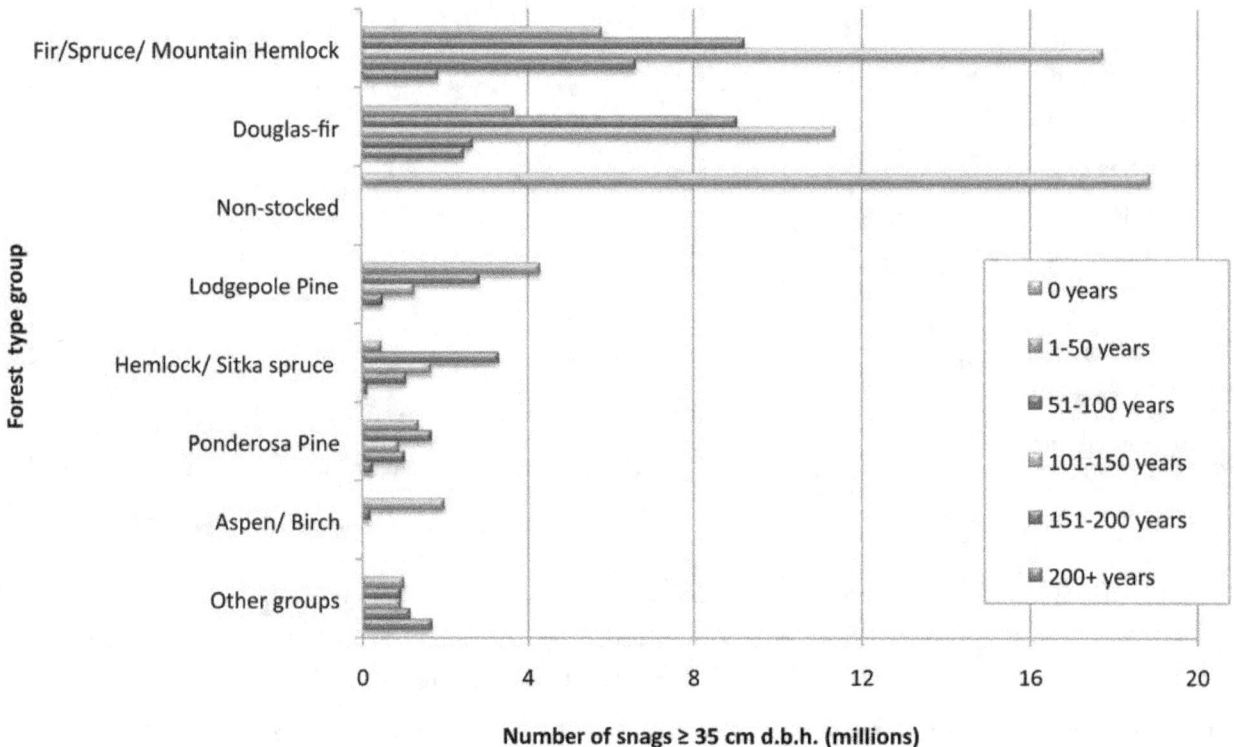

Figure 23: Number of snags meeting the preferences of three important cavity-excavating birds by stand-age class and forest type group, Idaho, 2004-2009.

Idaho Timber Harvest and Forest Products

The University of Montana Bureau of Business and Economic Research (BBER), in cooperation with the Interior West Forest Inventory and Analysis program, conducts periodic censuses of Idaho's timber processing facilities. The BBER conducted a statewide census of primary forest products facilities in Idaho for calendar year 2006 (Brandt and others 2011). This report updates key aspects of the 2006 census based on annual assessments and industry outlooks coordinated by the BBER in conjunction with the University of Idaho Forest Products Program in the College of Natural Resources.

Primary forest products facilities are firms that process timber into manufactured products such as lumber, and facilities such as pulp and paper mills and particleboard board plants that use wood fiber residue directly from timber processors. A total of 97 forest products plants were identified as active in Idaho during 2006, including 35 sawmills, 24 log home facilities, 16 Post, pole, and log furniture manufacturers, 12 residue related products facilities, 7 cedar product mills, and 3 plywood/veneer plants.

A strong economy, low interest rates, easy access to credit, and real estate speculation fostered more than two million U.S. housing starts in 2005 and record annual lumber consumption from 2003 to 2005. The year of the most recent census of the Idaho's forest products industry, 2006, was the beginning of what has been the most extended and severe economic downturn since the Great Depression. U.S. housing markets in 2006 dropped modestly to 1.8 million starts in 2006, and then with the onset of an official recession in 2007, the 2008 global financial crisis, and further weakening of the U.S. economy in 2009, housing starts fell to a post-World War II record low of 554,000, improving only to 587,000 in 2010.

With much weaker markets, wood product prices and outputs of Idaho's wood and paper products industry fell dramatically. In 2008, 2009, and 2010, virtually every major mill suffered curtailments and several large and numerous small mills closed permanently. Idaho mills' capacity to process timber dropped approximately 20 percent between 2006 and 2010, to just over one billion board feet, Scribner, while capacity utilization fell from nearly 80 percent during 2003 to an estimated 55 percent during 2010.

Wood and paper product output value dropped from $2 billion in 2004 to $1.8 billion in 2006 to under $1.5 billion in 2009 and 2010. The trend in lumber produced and volume of timber harvested in Idaho also reflects the current condition of the forest products industry. Lumber production, the major output of Idaho's industry and the component most impacted by weak housing markets, fell to 1,105 million board feet (MMBF) lumber tally in 2009 and 1,258 MMBF in 2010, the lowest 2 years on record since WWII (fig. 24).

Timber harvest for 2010 was 830 MMBF (Scribner), up about 10 percent from 2009 and approximately equal to 2008; the annual harvest each year for 2008-2010 were the three lowest harvest totals in Idaho since the second World War (fig. 25). Timber harvest on private lands accounted for 57 percent of the volume in 2010, down from 75 percent in 2006, and nearly one-third of Idaho's total harvest came from State lands in 2010, up from 18 percent in 2006. The share of harvest from Federal lands increased from 7 percent in 2006 to 11 percent in 2010. The number of forest industry workers declined by 4,000 workers since the stronger markets of mid-decade, dropping from approximately 14,500 to an estimated 10,500 in 2010.

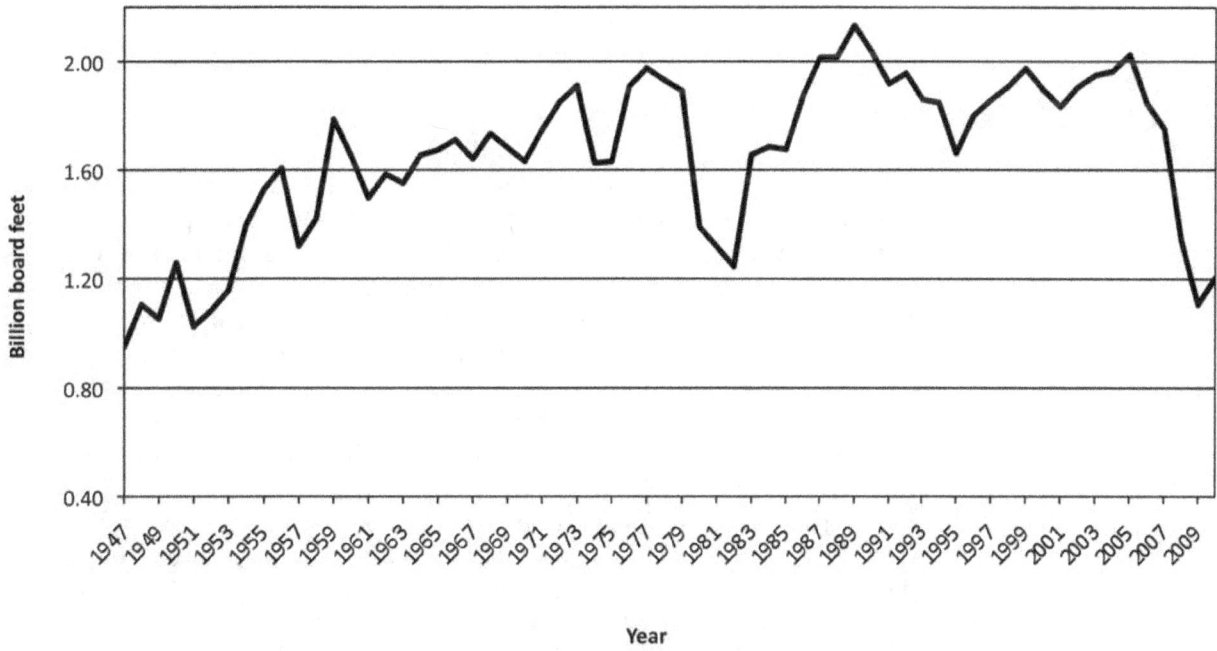

Figure 24: Idaho lumber production, 1947-2010 (sources: Bureau of Business and Economic Research, The University of Montana-Missoula; USDA Forest Service Region One, Missoula, Montana; Western Wood Products Association).

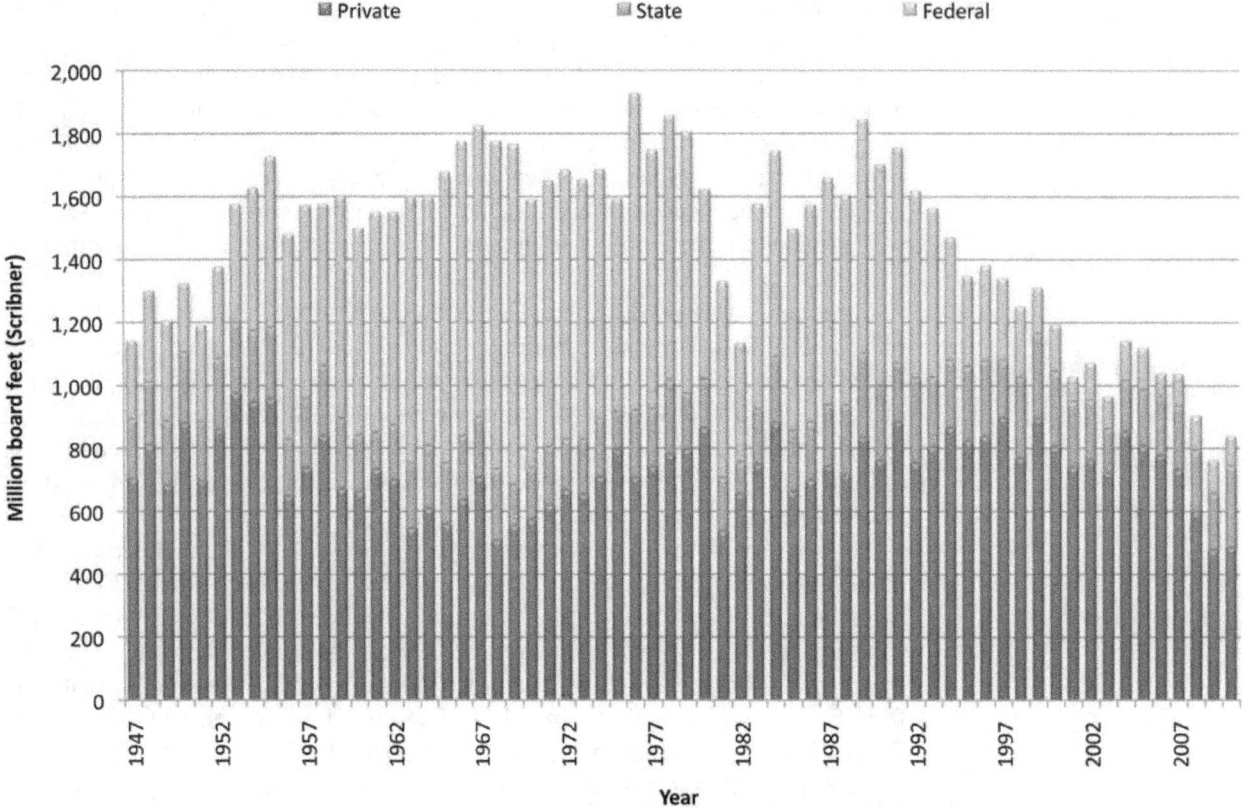

Figure 25: Idaho timber harvest by ownership, Idaho, 1947-2010 (sources: Bureau of Business and Economic Research, The University of Montana-Missoula; USDA Forest Service Region One, Missoula, Montana).

Issues in Idaho's Forests

Decline of Whitebark Pine

Whitebark pine has become recognized as an important component of high-elevation ecosystems in western North America. Its periodic crops of large wingless seeds provide a major food source for several species of birds and mammals including the black bear and grizzly bear (Schmidt and McDonald 1990). Wildlife biologists have noted that for several months after production of a large whitebark pine cone crop, bears concentrate their feeding on cone caches made by squirrels and tend to stay away from lower elevation encounters with humans and their habituations (Kendall 1980). Whitebark pine aids in the protection of watersheds by stabilizing soil and rock on the harshest sites and by catching and retaining snowpack. (Arno and Hoff 1989).

Compared to other conifer species in Idaho, whitebark pine is relatively uncommon. Whitebark pine forest types comprise about 297 thousand acres in Idaho or about 1.4 percent of total forest area in the State. The number of all live whitebark pine trees 1.0 inches d.b.h. and larger totals 190 million trees in Idaho or about 2.4 percent of all live trees in the State.

In many areas in the West, whitebark pine stands have experienced heavy mortality (Arno 1986). The principal agents named in the decline are the white pine blister rust (Cronartium ribicola), the mountain pine beetle (Dendroctonus ponderosae), and forest succession by shade-tolerant trees in the absence of fire.

To address the decline of whitebark pine in Idaho, an analysis of long-term trends was performed using remeasurement data from permanently established FIA plots. In the previous periodic inventory of Idaho, which occurred between 1990 and 1997, variable radius plots were the samples used to conduct the field inventory. When the annual inventory began in 2004, IWFIA changed the sampling design to the fixed-radius national mapped plot design. In addition to the initial establishment of the mapped plot, field crews were instructed to relocate and remeasure trees tallied on the previously established variable-radius plot. All trees measured in the previous inventory (time 1) were accounted for and current status recorded (live, dead, cut) in the current inventory (time 2). This remeasurement and accounting for trees on previously established plots provides an accurate measure of growth, removal, and mortality rates since the status of trees are known at both points in time. The procedures used to remeasure the previous variable-radius plot and a description of the plot layout is described in U.S. Forest Service 2011.

Remeasurement of permanent FIA plots can produce estimates of change that quantify the net change in inventory between two points in time. For this analysis, mean basal area per acre of whitebark pines 5.0 inches d.b.h. and larger was the attribute of interest. The following components were generated for the analysis:

- Initial Inventory—Basal area/acre of live whitebark pines 5.0 inches d.b.h. and larger measured at the previous visit.

- Survivor growth—Change in basal area/acre of live whitebark pine trees 5 inches d.b.h. and larger measured at the previous visit and the basal area/acre of live whitebark pine trees 5 inches d.b.h. and larger measured at the second visit.

- Ingrowth—Basal area/acre of live whitebark pine trees 5 inches d.b.h. and larger at time of second visit but were less than 5.0 inches d.b.h. at time of previous visit (trees that grew on to the inventory during the remeasurement period).

- Mortality—Basal area/acre of live whitebark pine trees 5 inches d.b.h. and larger measured at the previous visit that were dead due to natural causes at time of second visit.

- Removals—Basal area/acre of live whitebark pine trees 5 inches d.b.h. and larger measured at the previous visit that were cut at time of second visit.

- Terminal Inventory—Basal area/acre of live whitebark pines 5.0 inches d.b.h. and larger measured at the second or current visit.

For this analysis, only remeasured plots where at least one live whitebark pine 5.0 inches d.b.h. and larger measured in the initial inventory qualified as eligible for this analysis. A total of 50 remeasured plots in Idaho met the criteria. The initial inventory measurement years ranged from 1990 to 1997. The terminal inventory measurement years ranged from 2004 to 2009. Plots measured prior to 1993 were on non-National Forest Systems (NFS) land and those measured after 1992 were on NFS land. The average interval between plot measurements was 13.5 years. The procedure used to estimate the basal area per acre for the six components is described in Beers and Miller (1964).

Mean basal area per acre of whitebark pine for the six change components are illustrated in figure 26. Mean basal area per acre of whitebark pine in Idaho decreased 25 percent or by about 2.3 percent per year. Mortality reduced the estimate of initial inventory by 32 percent. Mortality rate of whitebark pine averaged 3 percent per year. The leading cause of death of the whitebark pines classified as

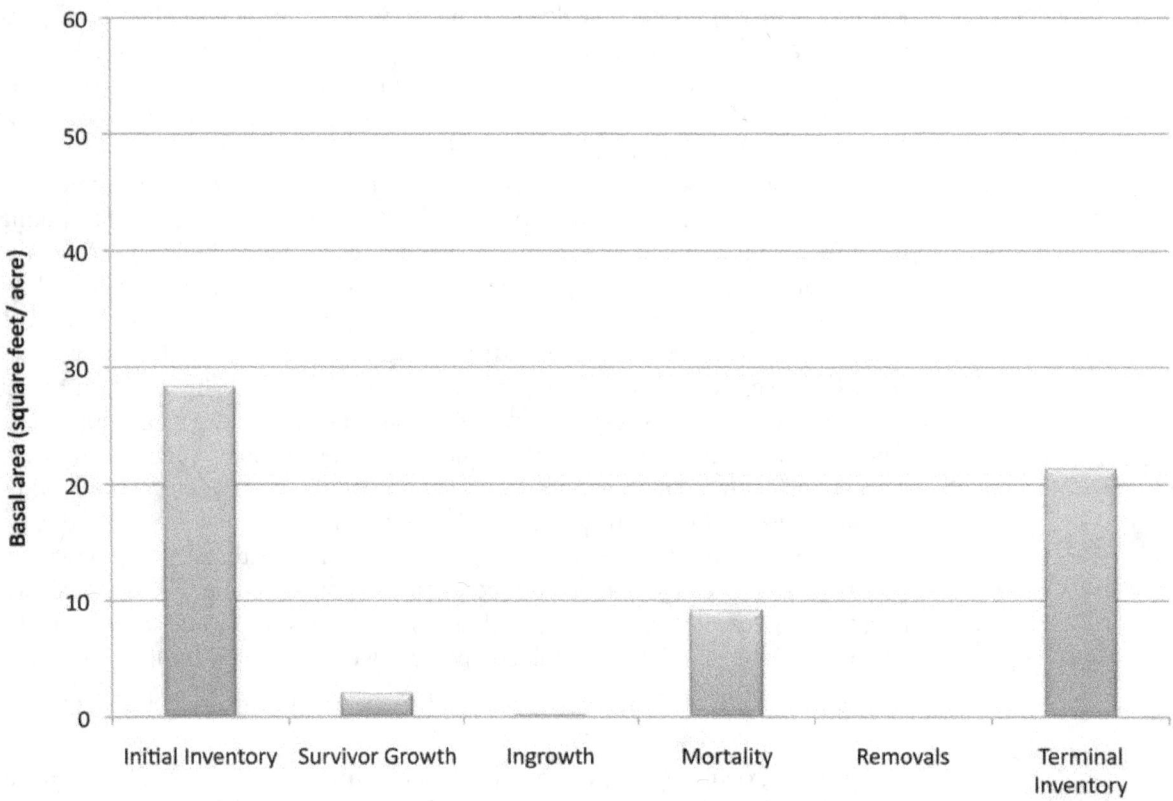

Figure 26: Periodic estimates of initial inventory, terminal inventory, and change components for whitebark pine in Idaho expressed as mean basal area per acre for remeasured plots.

mortality was insects, which accounted for 32 percent of the trees that died during the remeasurement interval. The second leading cause of death was attributed to unknown causes at 12 percent. Fire accounted for 11 percent of the whitebark pine mortality.

These results indicate a very significant decline in live basal area of whitebark pine. The annual level of mortality is greatly outpacing the combined annual basal area growth of survivor trees and ingrowth trees. Similar studies conducted in the early 1970s in western Montana also indicated significant basal area reductions in whitebark pine due to heavy mortality (Keane and Arno 1993). Figure 27 illustrates the numbers of live whitebark pine trees by diameter class. Numbers of 2- and 4-inch whitebark pines comprise almost 70 percent of all live whitebark pines in Idaho. The high proportion of sapling-size trees might suggest enough regeneration is occurring to offset losses due to mortality in the larger diameter classes. However, blister rust can cause mortality and top kill in whitebark pine seedlings and saplings resulting in fewer saplings reaching maturity. Blister rust incidence is particularly high in northern Idaho (Kegley and others 2011). Whitebark pine is a slow-growing tree. Depending on site conditions, the tree can attain small to moderately large size after 250 or more years, but may start producing cones as early as 70 years old.

This analysis underscores the need to use broad-scale inventory data for monitoring trends in whitebark pine. The power to detect significant effects related to whitebark pine mortality and other parameters of interest will increase substantially with estimates derived from the remeasurement (paired) plots that will be available as the IWFIA region begins to accumulate data from remeasured plots.

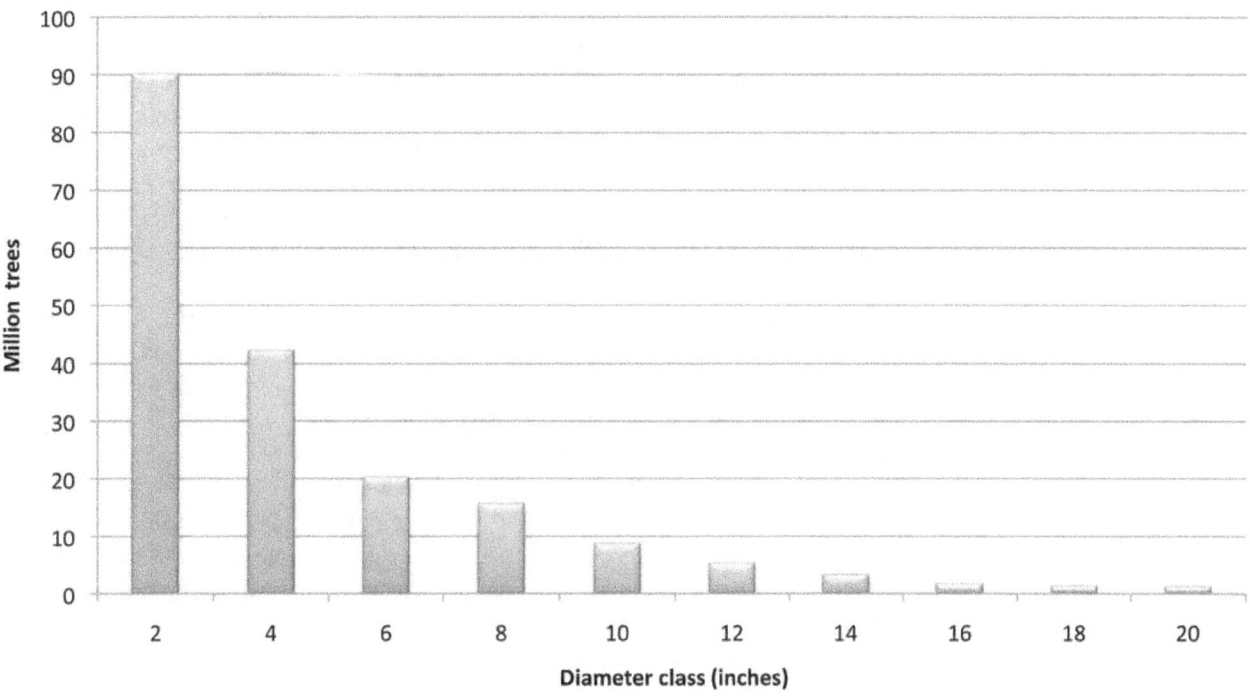

Figure 27: Numbers of live whitebark pines by diameter class in Idaho, 2004-2009.

Aspen Mortality

Aspen is the widest-ranging species in North America. It is present in all States in the Interior West and occupies a wide elevational range—from 2000 feet in northern Idaho to 11,700 feet in Colorado. It is also found on a wide range of sites, and occurs in 26 of the forest types that occur in the Interior West. The species is intolerant of shade and relatively short-lived, which makes it prone to replacement by conifers through successional change. In the Interior West, it also reproduces infrequently by seeding, relying mostly on root sprouting for reproduction. However, aspen responds well to fire and cutting, and it is able to dominate sites for many years following severe disturbance. In addition, there is some evidence that aspen is able to persist in conifer-dominated forests by exploiting gaps in the canopy that are caused by insects, disease, windthrow, and other smaller-scale disturbances.

In recent years there has been concern about the future of aspen on the landscape, primarily due to the characteristics of aspen and how they relate to changes in disturbance regimes. The earliest concerns were related to successional change in the Interior West, where fire suppression has decreased disturbance rates and, as a result, aspen regeneration rates. In addition, it has been shown that large populations of herbivores can inhibit aspen regeneration where it occurs spontaneously or after disturbance (e.g., Hessl and Graumlich 2002). The lack of disturbance allows conifers to gain dominance where they are present, and in pure aspen stands, consumption of regeneration by ungulates could lead to loss of senescing overstory trees without replacement. More recent concerns are related to a period of drought that has an impact on aspen and other forest types (e.g., Shaw and others 2005; Thompson 2009). Drought appears to have contributed to mortality in many low-elevation stands (Worrall and others 2008), and in some of these regeneration is either lacking or suppressed by herbivores.

Johnson (1994) suggested that the acreage of aspen-dominated stands had declined as much as 46 percent in Arizona since the 1960s, with most of these acres becoming dominated by mixed conifer forest types. Bartos (2001) suggested that similar changes—aspen acres decreasing by 61 percent—had occurred in Idaho. These assessments of "lost" aspen acres were based on the assumption that forested acres with a minority aspen component were, at one time in the recent past, dominated by aspen in pure or nearly pure stands. This assumption may not be reasonable because there are many situations where aspen may persist normally as a minor stand component.

It is not possible to estimate trends in the aspen forests of Idaho with great certainty because of the differences between the coverage of periodic and annual inventories. However, it is possible to make a limited set of comparisons when looking at certain characteristics that are indicative of aspen status, such as the proportion of aspen acreage to total forest acreage, number of acres with only dead aspen present, and number of acres with aspen reproduction present.

Current inventory data show that there are approximately 708,000 acres of the aspen forest type in Idaho, as compared to nearly 532,000 acres found during the previous inventory. When considering all acres where aspen is present, the current inventory data show that at least one live aspen stem is present on over 1.43 million acres, while the previous inventory showed live aspen present on just over 1.33 million acres.

Statistics on live trees may overlook "relict" aspen stands, and both inventories show that some stands had only dead aspen present at the time of inventory. The 1990s periodic inventory showed that only dead aspen 1.0 inch diameter and greater were found on approximately 64,000 acres, or about 4.6 percent of all acres with aspen present. The current inventory shows an apparent increase to over 101,000 acres, or about 6.6 percent of all acres with aspen present. However, when seedling-sized trees are taken into account the area with only dead aspen decreases substantially, and there are many more acres where only aspen seedlings (or suckers) are recorded. Of the plots where aspen is only found as seedlings or suckers, disturbances such as fire are frequently recorded (see the "Fire in Idaho Forests" section). The actual trends—whether the marginal aspen presence represents new establishment or fading remnants—will only be addressed through continuous monitoring.

Another way to compare the previous and current inventories is to normalize data on a common basis—for example, basal area per acre. During the 1990s periodic inventory in aspen-dominated stands (aspen forest type), the average basal area per acre of all aspen (live and standing dead) was just over 60 square feet per acre, with 49 square feet per acre in live aspen. In the current annual inventory, aspen-dominated stands averaged less than 42 square feet of live and dead basal aspen area, with just under 35 square feet per acre of live aspen. The results are similar for all stands with an aspen component of trees at least 1 inch diameter. Total aspen basal area in these stands averaged just under 34 square feet of basal area in the periodic inventory, with about 27 square feet of basal area in live aspen. As with the aspen-dominated acres, the numbers were lower in the annual inventory: slightly more than 26 square feet per acre of live and dead aspen, and slightly more than 21 square feet of live aspen. These data suggest that live aspen basal area has fallen approximately 30 percent on a per-acre basis since the periodic inventory. However, it is not yet possible to tell if this is a real decrease (for example, caused by successional changes and disturbances) or an apparent increase possibly caused by capturing a high proportion of regenerating aspen acres in the annual inventory that were not captured in the periodic inventory.

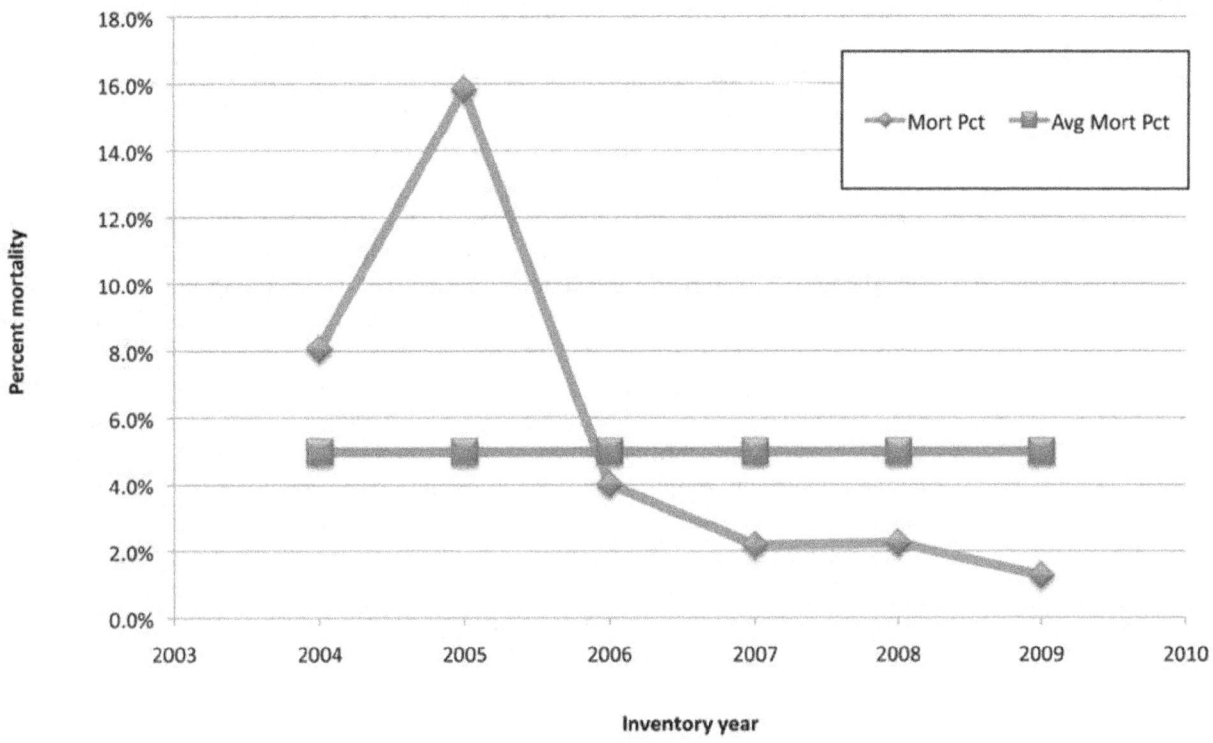

Figure 28: Estimated 5-year mortality rates of aspen for individual measurement years and average 5-year mortality, Idaho, 2004-2009.

In contrast with apparent trends in live aspen stocking, mortality rates do not appear to be increasing in recent years, at least in comparison to the mortality rates observed during the periodic inventory. Mortality is expressed here as the proportion of basal area estimated to have died in the 5 years prior to the plot visit. During the 1990s periodic inventory, mortality was estimated at almost 13 percent in aspen-dominated stands and almost 14 percent in stands with an aspen component. This equates to an average annual mortality of about 2.6 percent. During the annual inventory, mortality was estimated at almost 5 percent in aspen-dominated stands and 5 percent in stands with an aspen component. This equates to an average annual mortality of about 1.0 percent. Because the annual inventory is spatially unbiased over time, it is possible to look at year-by-year mortality estimates for possible trends. Figure 28 shows the mortality estimates for annual inventory years 2004-2009. Although the annual trend data might be somewhat noisy due to small sample size within any given year, it appears that there might have been some elevated mortality just prior to the initiation of the annual inventory. During the past few years of the inventory, mortality rates appear to have settled at relatively low levels, however, suggesting that mortality rate has not been increasing substantially, and may actually be decreasing.

Comparisons between the mid-1990s periodic inventory results and the current annual inventory data in Idaho give somewhat conflicting results, so aspen trends are difficult to interpret at this point in the inventory. Total acreage with aspen present appears to be somewhat higher than in the 1990s, but the aspen component appears to have decreased when considered on a basal area per acre basis. Several disturbance agents, including fire and drought, have apparently reduced aspen basal area. However, there are a substantial number of plots with aspen reproduction

USDA Forest Service Resour. Bull. RMRS-RB-14. 2012

47

present. On many of these plots there are no large, standing live or dead aspen, so it is difficult to ascertain whether these plots are capturing re-occupation of the sites by aspen or expansion of aspen into other forest types. However, continued monitoring of these plots in the future will tell whether or not the young aspen reproduction is able to persist.

There have been many studies that have shown aspen to be in decline at local scales (e.g., Bartos and Campbell 1998; Di Orio and others 2005; Worrall and others 2008), while other analyses have shown increased dominance of aspen in some landscapes (Kulakowski and others 2004). It is not surprising that studies documenting loss are more numerous, because unexplained or unexpectedly high mortality events tend to attract the attention of managers, researchers, and the public. Because these changes are evident to a wide range of observers, there is a tendency to extrapolate local conditions to larger areas. Aspen is found in many forest types with a wide variety of associate tree species, and the characteristics of aspen-dominated stands and stands with aspen as a minor component vary considerably over the range of the species. This makes generalization difficult. In addition, local or regional trends may differ from those of the population as a whole, because agents like drought and fire are not evenly distributed over the landscape. However, with continued monitoring under the annual inventory system, FIA will be able to assess regional- and population-scale trends in aspen.

Mountain Pine Beetle

High tree mortality rates associated with mountain pine beetle infestations have become a serious issue in many western forests. Since the primary host of mountain pine beetle is lodgepole pine, and lodgepole pine comprises a significant component of many western North American forests, recent epidemics of this insect have raised significant concerns about the health, stand structure, and composition of lodgepole pine stands.

The mountain pine beetle is a native insect to western pine forests in North America and innocuous populations are almost always present in forests. Transition to epidemic populations is a function of the beetle's capacity to locate, colonize, and reproduce within suitable host trees in a weather pattern conducive to overwintering survival, emergence, and dispersal (Carroll and Safranyik 2004). The reasons behind the recent outbreaks have received considerable discussion. Most bark beetles prefer to invade trees that are in poor physiological condition (Rudinsky 1962). Temperature is known to influence insect outbreaks, especially species such as the mountain pine beetle (Amman 1973). The effect of global warming is believed by some researchers to be a contributing factor in the severity of mountain pine beetle infestations (Logan and others 2003). Another significant factor is the presence of large areas of lodgepole pine stands comprised of ideal host trees homogeneous in age, composition, and structure.

Figure 29 illustrates the average annual volume of lodgepole trees killed by insects by measurement year in Idaho. The estimates in figure 27 illustrate a moving average trend that accumulates information from successive annual inventory measurements. The assumption is that most of the lodgepole classified as mortality and assigned a cause of death of insects is due to the mountain pine beetle. It is clearly evident that a pronounced upward trend has occurred during the 6 years of annual inventories in Idaho. As of 2009, the average annual volume of insect-killed lodgepole pines is 108 million cubic feet, which is double the 54 million cubic feet recorded in 2004.

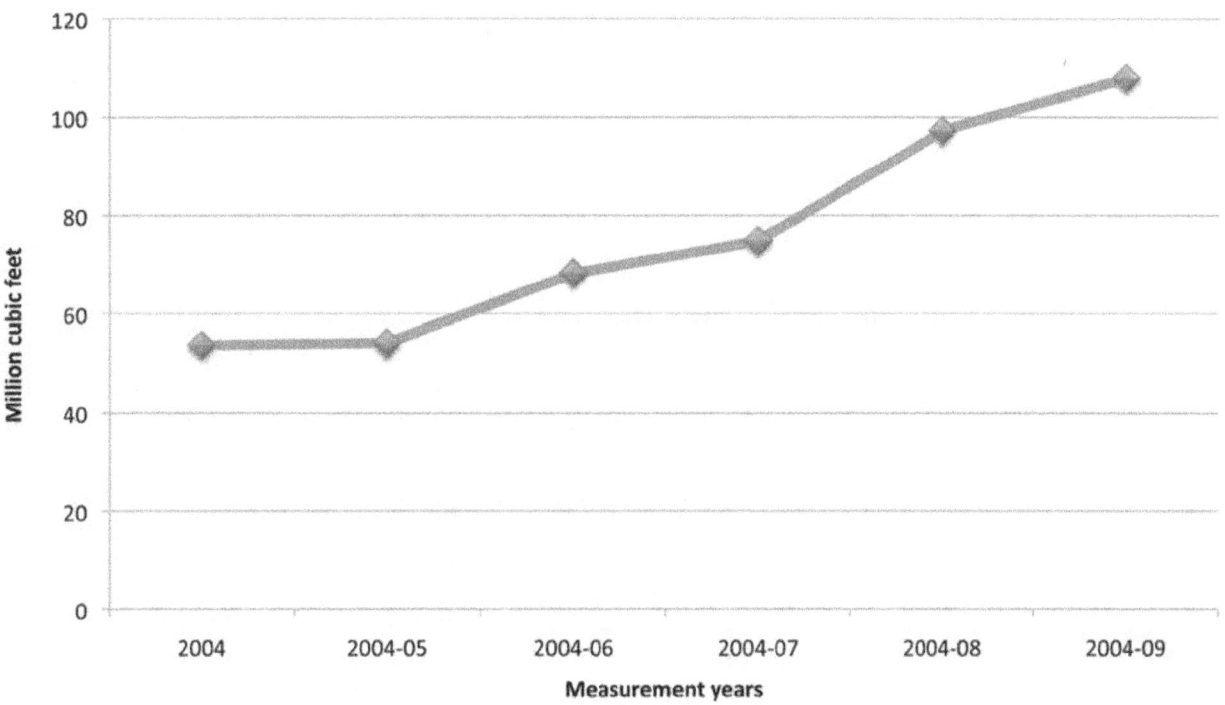

Figure 29: Moving average estimate of average annual volume of lodgepole pine killed by insects by measurement years, Idaho, 2004-2009.

Phase 2 Damage

The Interior West FIA program has used a regionally defined damage protocol for most of the periodic and annual inventories since 1981. Throughout this time, the protocol has remained consistent, with only a few modifications to the damage categories. Damages are assigned only to live trees, in contrast to mortality agents, which are only assigned to recently dead trees. Not all damaging agents are potential mortality agents, so there is only partial overlap in the two agent lists.

FIA currently has 50 damage codes representing a wide range of biotic, abiotic, and anthropogenic agents. Up to three damage agents may be assigned to a tree. However, less than a third of damaged trees have more than one agent assigned, and less than a 25 percent of trees with two damage agents will have a third agent assigned.

The protocol is based on a threshold system, where damage is only recorded if it is considered "serious." Although this is somewhat subjective, the general rules are that damage should be recorded when it will:

1. Prevent the tree from living to maturity, or surviving 10 more years if already mature.

2. Prevent the tree from producing marketable products.

3. Reduce (or has seriously reduced) the quality of the tree's products.

These rules roughly correspond to two main categories of damaging agents. Agents that are likely to prevent a tree from living to maturity or surviving for 10 years after the inventory date tend to be those related to insects, disease, fire, and atmospheric effects (drought, flooding, wind, etc.), whereas agents that preclude or reduce a tree's merchantability are more likely to be problems with form, such as forks, broken tops, or logging scars. The latter group may or may not affected a tree's survival. Therefore, not all trees with damages recorded are expected to die, and some of those with poor merchantability may live to typical upper ages for their species. A nationally consistent protocol for non-lethal damage to trees is scheduled to be implemented by the FIA program in 2013. A majority of the damage categories used in the national protocol crosswalk directly with the Interior West regional categories, ensuring that it will be possible to track trends in damaging agents over time.

Because earlier inventories of Idaho were done under the periodic system and parts of those inventories were spread over a wide range of years, it is difficult to compare earlier results to the current annual inventory. In order to keep the data as comparable as possible, damages are described as proportions of the trees tallied during the different time periods, that is, they are not expanded to make population-scale estimates.

There were 71,137 live trees tallied during the Idaho periodic inventory years (1981 to 2002), and 51,359 live trees tallied during the first 6 years of annual inventory (2004 to 2009). During the periodic inventories, 37.0 percent of trees were assigned one damage agent, 7.8 percent had two agents, and 1.2 percent had three. A smaller proportion of live trees (27.9%) were assigned one damage agent during the annual inventory, although the proportions of trees with secondary (7.3%) and tertiary (1.4%) damage agents were comparable to the periodic inventory proportions. The apparent reduction in the frequency of primary damage was spread across all major agent categories, with only the insect and fire categories showing increases (table VI).

Damage agents related to merchantability accounted for the majority of primary damage agents, with diseases being the second most frequently recorded damage (table VI). The lower rate of assignment of form damages accounted for about half of the overall decrease in primary damage agents. The next most frequent damage category was diseases, with the most frequently recorded agents within this category being stem and butt rots, cankers, and dwarf mistletoes. It should be noted that dwarf mistletoe is recorded for all infected trees using a separate variable, but only trees with a dwarf mistletoe rating (DMR) (Hawksworth 1977) of 4 to 6 are considered as "serious" for the purpose of damage agent assignment. Notable

Table VI—Distribution of primary damage agents by agent group, Idaho periodic (1981-2002) and annual (2004-2009) inventories.

Damage agent group (codes)	Periodic	Annual
	Percent	
No Damage (0)	63.00	72.10
Insects (10-16)	0.80	1.30
Diseases (20-29)	6.70	4.20
Fire (30-31)	0.40	0.50
Animals (40-48)	0.30	0.20
Atmosphere (50-59)	1.00	0.50
Suppression (61)	1.50	0.20
Form (71-79)	25.90	20.60
Human (80-85)	0.20	0.20
Unknown / Unidentified (70)	0.30	0.20

damage agents within the insect category were bark beetles (0.45% in periodic and 0.52% in annual) and defoliators (0.09% in periodic and 0.48% in annual). Within the animal category, the majority of damage was caused by big game (0.13% in periodic and 0.09% in annual), and within the atmosphere category, the most common sources of damage were snow (0.31% in periodic and 0.06% in annual) and frost (0.49% in periodic and 0.32% in annual).

While it is difficult to compare changes in damage rates between periodic and annual inventories with statistical certainty, it is possible to consider some of the expected patterns in comparison to the data. For example, it may seem reasonable that the decreases in form, suppression, and disease damages could be the result of fuel reduction and other silvicultural activities, which would tend to target trees in these categories disproportionally. However, this cannot be known with certainty until remeasurement occurs under the annual inventory system. On the other hand, the apparent increases in the insect categories of bark beetles and defoliators are consistent with aerial surveys and other information sources that show these agents have been on the increase in recent years. Damage from bark beetles shows a moderate increase compared to the known increase in mortality in many conifers (see the "Issues in Idaho's Forests" section of this document), but this is not surprising given that FIA crews are more likely to encounter a bark beetle-infested tree when it is dead, and not during the brief period when it is live and heavily infested. In the typical situation, bark beetles would be assigned as the mortality agent of a dead tree as opposed to the damaging agent of a live tree.

The comparison of damage frequency over time also illustrates a key difference between periodic and annual inventory data. Periodic data are intended to be taken together as a whole inventory, even though the plots may be spread out over several years. During a periodic inventory, it is not uncommon for the plots done in a given year to be concentrated in a particular part of the State. As a result, there is geographic bias when measurement years are considered separately. Under annual inventory, the plots are geographically distributed every year and there is no geographic bias. The end result is that apparent trend within the periodic inventory may actually be the result of geographic bias. Under annual inventory, any trend over time may be more reliably interpreted as real. This is apparent when total damage frequency is plotted by measurement year (fig. 30). Note that the proportion of damaged trees varies widely over the periodic inventory years (1990 to 2002), but remains relatively consistent (but with a slightly declining trend) over the annual inventory years (2004 to 2009). The variation among periodic years is likely due to plots being located in areas of relatively high or low damage (e.g., recent fires, areas with snow damage, or localized insect outbreaks) in any given year.

As noted above, assignment of damage does not necessarily imply impending death of a tree. The types of form damages most frequently recorded—lean, forks below or above merchantable top, broken or dead tops, and crook/sweep/taper—are unlikely to result in mortality, so few of those in the form damage group should be expected to die. If we assume that the form damage group is considered non-lethal and all other agents combined are considered as potentially lethal within a 10-year window, the numbers are probably within what would be expected for normal stand development. For example, form-damaged and undamaged trees account for 92.7% of all tally trees. Over a 10-year window this equates to 0.73 percent on an annual basis, which can easily be accounted for under normal stand dynamics. Of course, the damaged trees that are expected to die are in addition to the mortality trees encountered during the most recent plot visits, and mortality is elevated in

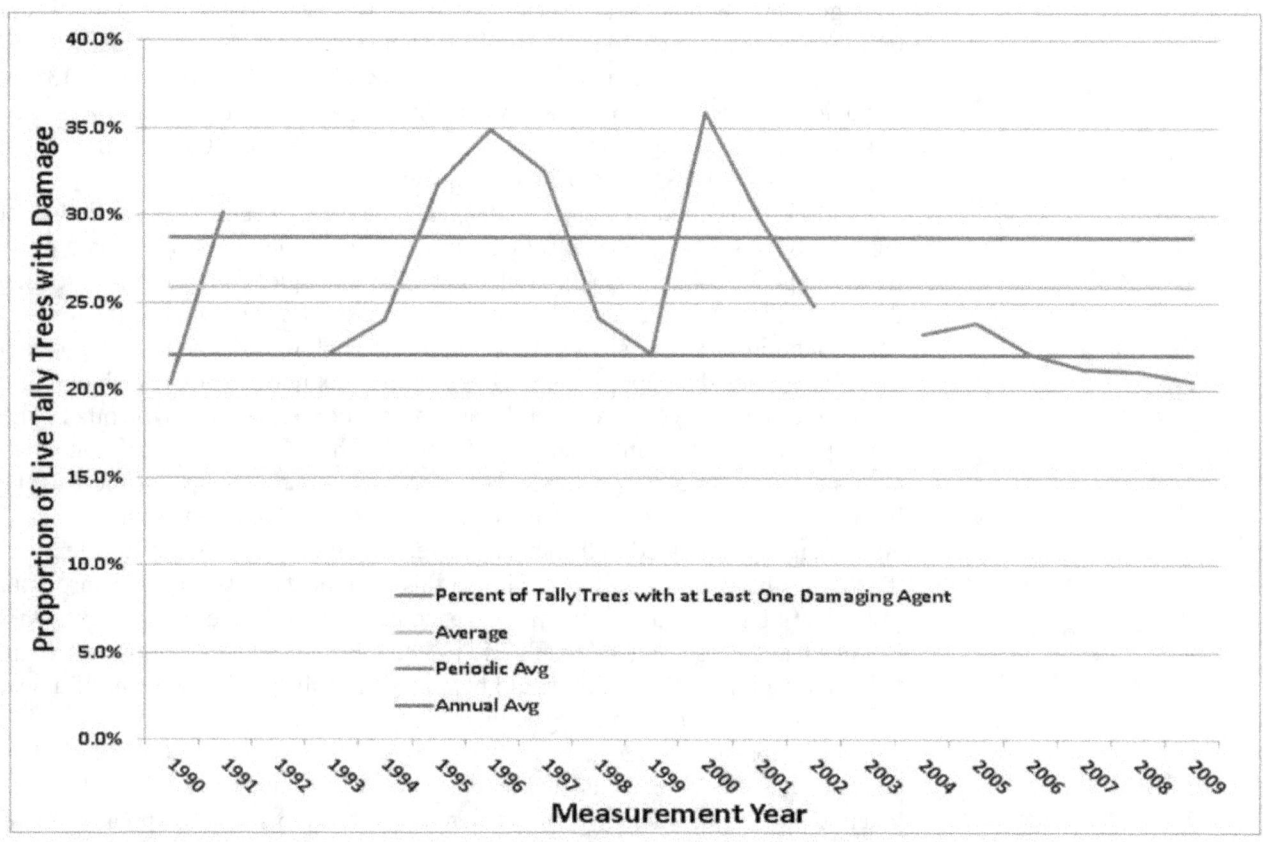

Figure 30: Variation of proportion of damage trees recorded by measurement year, 1990-2009. Years 1990 to 2002 were part of the Idaho periodic inventory; 2004 to 2009 were measured as part of the annual inventory system.

many species. This may suggest that damage frequencies are not greatly affected by elevated mortality rates, because for many agents the transition from "healthy" to dead may occur relatively quickly. It is possible that elevated mortality could partly explain the apparent decrease in many agent categories, because the damage variables identify trees that are predisposed to early mortality. Although this is the underlying assumption, it will not be conclusively demonstrable until annual remeasurement occurs.

Old Forests

An important aspect in managing for ecologically sustainable and diverse ecosystems is the maintenance of forest stands representing the full range of forest succession. The oldest stages of this range are of particular interest to forest managers. Historically, these last stages of forest growth have been difficult to define or describe. The terminology has included late seral, climax, mature, overmature, and old growth, among others. Generally, as forests mature, stand structure changes in ways that are important to ecological and habitat function. Some of the structural indicators proposed include the size (diameter) and age of the oldest trees, the number of large old trees per acre, and overall stand density (Green and others 1992; Hamilton 1993; Fiedler and others 2007). Standardized definitions are difficult because the final structure and age of a given forest stand depends on many biological and physical components: climate and geology, dominant tree species,

USDA Forest Service Resour. Bull. RMRS-RB-14. 2012

fire regimes, and others (Kaufmann and others 2007; Vosick and others 2007). The forest structural indicators used to assess old forests will change with changes in these components. In addition, the characteristics of old growth can change with the scale of observation, from patches to stands and landscapes (Kaufmann and others 2007).

One method of assessing old forests is simply to use the stand age of 150 years or greater as a surrogate for old forests. Another method uses a minimum density of trees with individual ages of at least 150 years. These approaches were recently used in assessing old forests in Utah (DeBlander and others 2010). These same criteria, as well as a minimum tree diameter and a minimum density (basal area per acre), were used for this analysis. It should be noted that these criteria are not those used by any of Idaho's National Forests to define old forest.

Almost 12 percent (2.5 million acres) of Idaho's forest land has a stand age of 150 years or older. Figure 31 shows this distribution by forest type. The Douglas-fir and subalpine fir types have the most acres 150 years and greater based on stand age, while the highest proportions are found in the limber pine (72%), whitebark pine (61%), and Engelmann spruce (33%) types. Common types with lower than average proportions of area with stand age of at least 150 years include lodgepole pine (5%) and grand fir (4%). The western larch type had not only the least acres with a stand age of at least 150 years; it also had the smallest proportion of any type with older stands (2%).

Stand age is generally calculated as the mean age of trees from the stand-size class that has the plurality of stocking. This tends to diminish the significance of older trees by averaging tree ages of both old and young trees. Another method

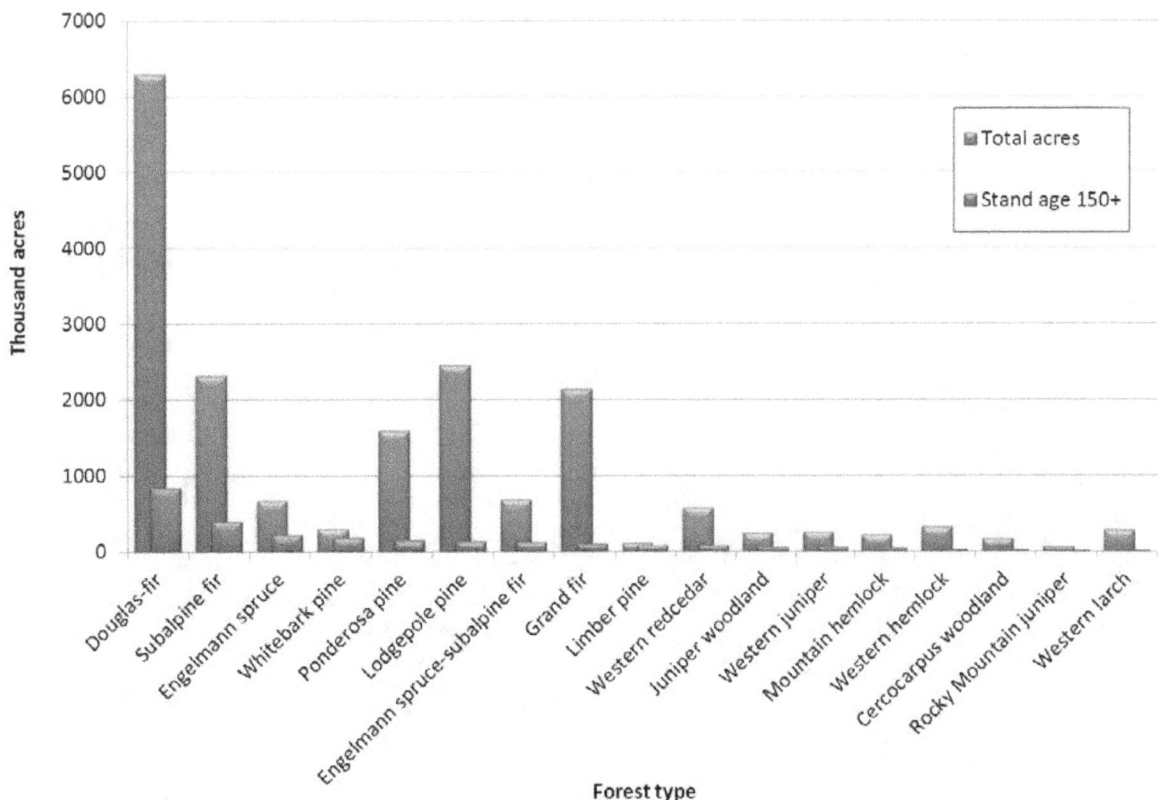

Figure 31: Total area of forest land and area of forest land with stand age of 150 years or more by forest type (types with stand age of 150 years or more), Idaho, 2004-2009.

of using FIA data for describing stand structure is by calculating the number of trees per acre that are at least 150 years old, based on sample core trees. Core ages were adjusted, based on the height of the core, and assigned to other trees of the same species and diameter class; essentially the same procedure as used in assigning stand age. Area of old forest using thresholds of 10 trees per acre and 5 trees per acre at least 150 years old were determined in order to illustrate differences in methods for assessing old forests. In addition, since most sources recommend minimum stand densities and tree diameters to define old forest, 80 square feet per acre of total live basal area and 18 inches diameter (d.b.h./d.r.c.) were somewhat arbitrarily chosen; again to illustrate differences in assessment methods. Area of old forest meeting this minimum density and with either 5 or 10 trees per acre meeting both the age (150 years) and diameter (18 inches) thresholds was also determined. The area of forest land meeting four combinations of criteria are shown by forest type in figure 32.

While an estimated 12 percent (2.5 million acres) of Idaho's forests are "old" based on stand age alone, by using a minimum tree age criteria, 24 percent (5.1 million acres) of all forest land acreage in Idaho could qualify as old forest at 10 old trees per acre, and 32 percent at 5 old trees per acre. This increase in acreage is reflected differently by forest type; notice the very large increase in grand fir compared to the smaller change in Engelmann spruce. One drawback of using only tree age criteria is that only one or two trees measured on an FIA plot expand to over five or ten trees per acre. Therefore, very sparse stands with only old trees may meet these criteria: very unproductive sites, like scree slopes, or seed-tree

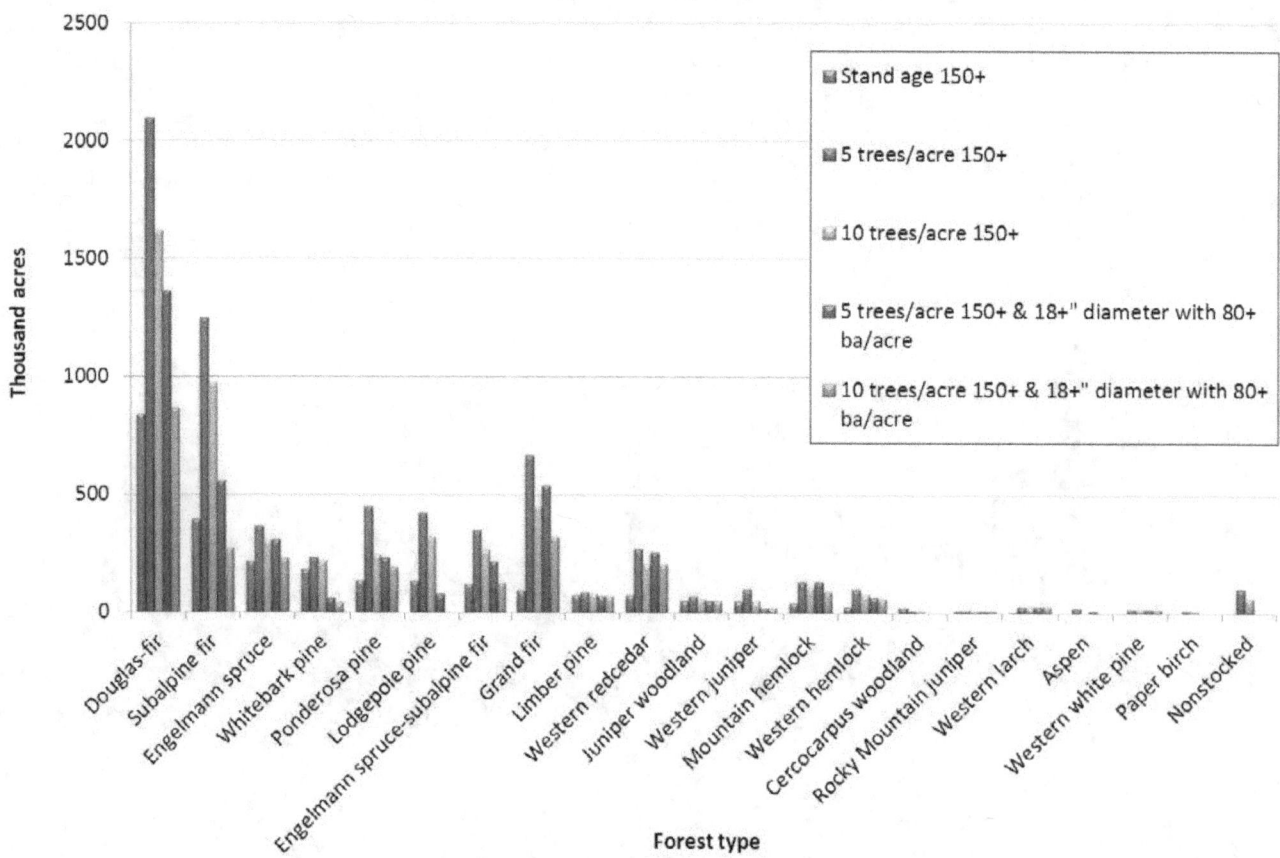

Figure 32: Area of old forest stand structure by forest type and stand age method (types with old forest structure by any method), Idaho, 2004-2009.

cuts. This is illustrated by the inclusion of nonstocked stands meeting the tree age criteria, at both 5 and 10 old trees per acre. If we include a basal area requirement, along with adding a diameter to the tree age requirement, the sparse stands can be eliminated.

With all three criteria, 12 percent (2.6 million acres) of Idaho forest land meet the old forest criteria at 10 large old trees per acre and 19 percent at 5 large old trees per acre. Although the acreage for 10 large and old trees per acre with at least 80 square feet per acre of basal area of all live trees is similar to the area meeting the stand age requirement, the overlap between the two is just over 50 percent. That is, about 1.3 million acres of forest land meet both criteria. Comparing stand age with the 10 trees per acre age/diameter/basal area criteria by forest type, some types show little overall difference (Douglas-fir and Engelmann spruce). Other types have relatively more area meeting the age/diameter/basal area minima (grand fir and western redcedar), while others have less (whitebark pine and lodgepole pine). Notice that no acres of the nonstocked forest type meet the age/diameter/basal area criteria.

The large differences between the area meeting different criteria by forest type illustrate the need for individual definitions for determining old forest structure. Some tree species are longer lived, or typically grow larger than others. Life histories of different species may affect how much area would be expected to be dominated by large, old trees of a given species: a larger proportion of old forest might be expected in Engelmann spruce than in lodgepole pine, for example.

As discussed in the previous section on Quality Assurance Analysis, tree age is an important but sometimes difficult variable to collect accurately. This analysis depended on individual tree ages as well as stand ages, which are derived from them. An option for future research is that the FIA database could be used to validate or even help to establish surrogate measurements to define old forest structure in different regions, for different forest types, and under different growth potential conditions, so that FIA data could be more effectively used to assess various old forest conditions. Since the surrogates used to categorize old forest structure can give varying results for different forest types it is important to align size/age structure definitions with the methods or variables intended for monitoring them. It is also important that the desired measure for monitoring be able to address the full range of size/age structural categories included in the definitions, in order that categories are mutually exclusive and cumulative.

Fire in Idaho Forests

Fire is an important disturbance in Idaho forests. In some forest types, like ponderosa pine, fire can maintain open stands and promote grasses and forbs growth in the understory. For other forest types, such as aspen and lodgepole pine, fire plays an important role in stand regeneration. In some areas, a century of fire suppression has led to a buildup of fuels and stand density. In these areas there can be uncharacteristically intense fires. Some areas that are intensely burned may experience slow regeneration, but others may recover relatively quickly. For example, the area inside the boundary of the large 1910 fires in Idaho and Montana (Cohen and Miller 1978; Pyne 2008; Egan 2009) now carries about the same amount of live tree volume per acre as areas outside the fires, although the mean stand age is somewhat lower and the volume is generally distributed among smaller trees (Wilson and others 2010).

Assessment of fire effects without a complete cycle of FIA data is not straight-forward. During the period covered by this report there were many fires in Idaho. Some FIA plots within fire boundaries were measured before the fire occurred in that area, and some were measured after. As a result, within the perimeter of a large fire there may be pre- and post-fire data, or a plot within the perimeter of a small fire may represent only pre-fire conditions. This means that normal data compilation methods cannot be used without introducing some element of temporal bias – that is, plots measured earlier in the inventory will tend to underestimate the effect of fire because they might have been affected by fire after they were measured. These limitations on analysis will be reduced as the current inventory cycle is completed and remeasurement data are acquired during the next cycle. However, there are some general analyses that can be conducted with the current data. These results should be considered preliminary.

We used data from the Monitoring Trends in Burn Severity (MTBS) project, which is an interagency effort being conducted and maintained by the USDA Forest Service Remote Sensing Applications Center and the US Geological Survey National Center for Earth Resources Observation and Science (EROS). The purpose of the MTBS project is to consistently map the burn perimeters and severity of fires across all lands of the United States. The multi-year project was designed to "assesses the frequency, extent, and magnitude (size and severity) of all large wildland fires (includes wildfire, wildland fire use, and prescribed fire) in the conterminous United States (CONUS), Alaska, Hawaii, and Puerto Rico for the period of 1984 through 2010" (Eidenshenk and others 2007). The analysis presented here is based on burned area perimeters of wildland fires identified by the MTBS program between 2003 and 2009 and FIA plot data for 2004-2009.

MTBS data showed 342 fires and fire complexes (hereafter, fires) burned 4.17 million acres in Idaho between 2003 and 2009. The size of these fires ranged from about 1000 acres (the minimum size mapped by the MTBS project) to nearly 460,000 acres, with an average of 12,183 acres. Forested plots measured during the same period occurred within the boundaries 74 of the fires. The remaining 268 fires encompassed only non-forested plots, encompassed plots that have not yet been measured on the current cycle, or the fires did not encompass an FIA plot location. Two of the largest fires, the Cascade Complex and the East Zone Complex, encompassed 31 and 32 measured plots, respectively. In contrast, only one measured plot was located within the Murphy Complex, which was the largest fire of the period at 458,542 acres. The average number of forested plots within a sampled fire boundary was just under three, and about half of the fires that were sampled by FIA plots encompassed only one plot.

For large fires, a comparison of the estimate of forested acres to the total number of acres within the MTBS boundaries gives some indication of the proportion of forest and non-forest acres within the burned area. For example, the occurrence of a single forested plot within the Murphy complex indicates that the fire was largely limited to non-forest. In contrast, the plot-based forest acreage estimates for the Cascade and the East Zone Complexes are 302,000 and 290,000 acres, very close to the 317,156 and 318,723 acres included, respectively, within the MTBS boundaries. This indicates that these two large fires primarily affected forest land. Although the plot-based and MTBS-based acreage estimates for smaller fires can be similar, it is not appropriate to draw inference about the mixture of forest and nonforest for small, individual fires. At this point in the inventory, the scaling factor for a single plot is approximately 10,000 acres, which is larger than most of the

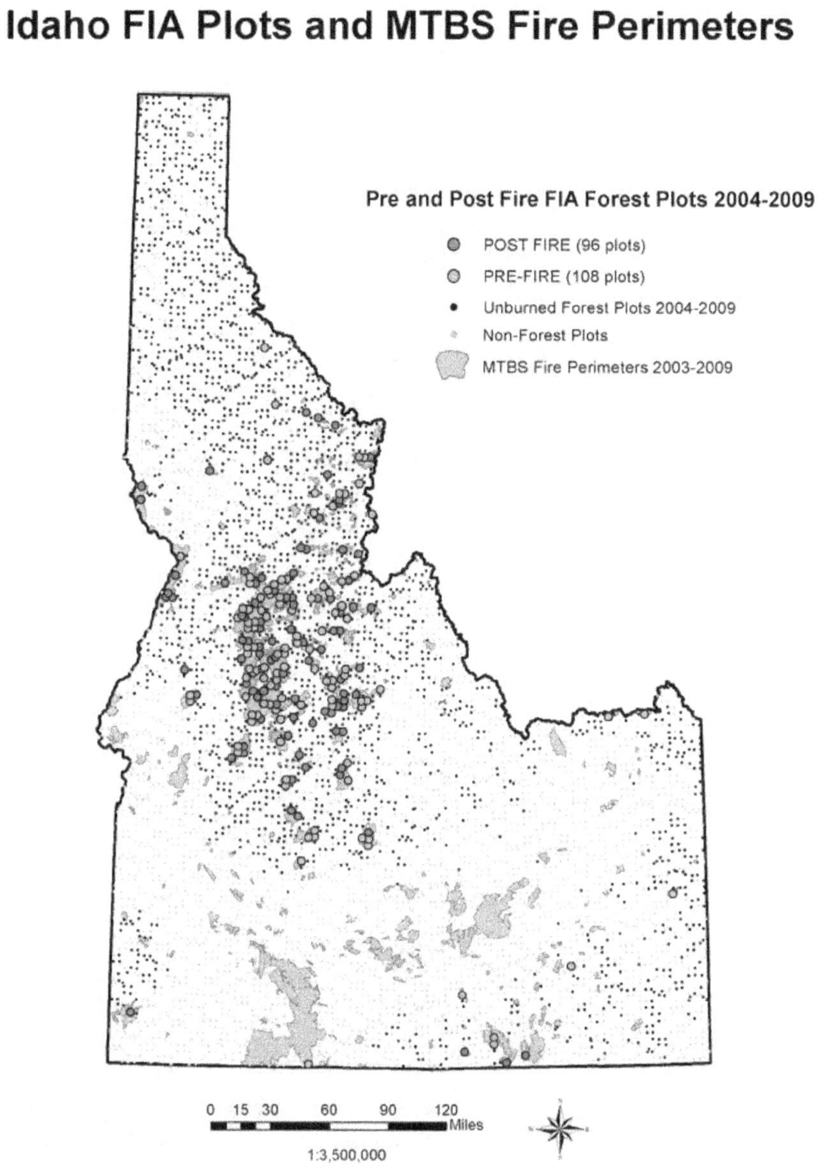

Idaho FIA Plots and MTBS Fire Perimeters

Pre and Post Fire FIA Forest Plots 2004-2009

- ◉ POST FIRE (96 plots)
- ◯ PRE-FIRE (108 plots)
- • Unburned Forest Plots 2004-2009
- ∘ Non-Forest Plots
- ▒ MTBS Fire Perimeters 2003-2009

Figure 33: FIA plots measured in Idaho, 2004-2009, and fire areas from the Monitoring Trends in Burn Severity (MTBS) program, 2003-2009. Pre-fire plots are those that are located within a fire perimeter, but were measured before the fire occurred. Post-fire plots are those that were measured at some time after the fire occurred. Plots identified as non-forest were either classified as non-forest from aerial imagery or verified as non-forest with a plot visit. Some forest plots can include multiple forest conditions or non-forest conditions.

```
0   15  30      60      90      120
                                   Miles
        1:3,500,000
```

fires in the MTBS database. As a result, the proportion of burned area in forest vs. nonforest must be done by aggregating a large number of plots and burned area.

Given that population-scale estimates are difficult to produce with a partial inventory, another way to look at the data is to examine per-acre estimates. There were 2,482 forested conditions measured in Idaho between 2004 and 2009. Of these, 2,262 were located outside the MTBS fire boundaries and 220 were located inside (fig. 33). Of the 220 located inside, 117 were measured prior to the fire in which they were located and 103 were measured after the fire. Conditions located outside the burned areas had an average of 119 square feet of basal area per acre in live and dead trees, with 97 square feet of that in live trees. Conditions within the burned areas that were measured before the fires occurred averaged 116 square feet of total basal area per acre and 89 square feet per acre of live trees. While the unburned conditions within the fires appear to have slightly less basal area than conditions outside the burned areas, the ratio of live basal area to total basal area (live + dead) was similar for both groups (81% and 77% respectively). This would suggest that the burned areas did not have extraordinarily large amounts of standing dead trees prior to the fires, but the lower standing basal area might indicate that the stands were more open or that there was more down wood in these stands.

When comparing within-fire, pre-burn conditions to within-fire, post-burn conditions, it is possible to estimate the proportion of trees killed within burned areas. Conditions located within fire boundaries and measured after the fires averaged 104 total square feet of basal area per acre, with only 40 square feet of basal area remaining in live trees. The lower average total basal area found in within-fire, post-burn conditions as compared to within-fire, pre-burn conditions (104 vs. 116 sq. ft. per acre) is consistent with the expectation that fire would result in some basal area being consumed and/or falling down. Likewise, the lower ratio of live to total basal area (39%) is consistent with the expectation that only partial mortality of trees located within the fire boundaries would occur. If it is assumed that the pre-burn conditions are representative of the post-burn conditions, then it would appear that the average fire-caused mortality was about 50 square feet per acre, or about 55 percent of the pre-fire live basal area.

One of the potential beneficial effects of fire includes the stimulation of aspen regeneration. Although there are only about 708,000 acres of the aspen forest type in Idaho, approximately 1.5 million acres have some aspen component (see the "Aspen Mortality" section). Of the 191 conditions measured with some aspen component, only six were located within MTBS fire boundaries and only one was measured after the fire had burned. Although this sample is very small, it suggests that the number of potentially fire-disturbed acres with aspen present is around 51,000 acres, or about 3.3 percent of all acres with an aspen component. Converting this figure to an annual rate and assuming that fire will be evenly distributed over time and area, it implies that it would take approximately 210 years for all acres with aspen present to be disturbed by fire. This rate may be lower than would be necessary to maintain aspen across the Idaho landscape, but it will only be possible to establish long-term trend with continued monitoring.

The analysis in this section should be considered only a first approximation of fire effects on Idaho forests. Although the results are generally consistent with expectations, the magnitude of fire-related mortality cannot be stated with precision at this point in the inventory. However, the data confirm that within fire boundaries there has been only partial mortality. Additional data and analysis will be required to determine whether, for example, mortality is more-or-less evenly distributed among plots within the burned areas or mortality tends to be all-or-none at the plot scale. Remeasurement data will be necessary to confirm the portions of standing live and dead trees that are consumed by fire and converted to the down woody material pool. Also, given the short time period over which the estimate of aspen stand disturbance has been made, it should be considered with a great deal of caution. However, future measurements will not only enable analysis of fires effects on aspen, they will also provide important information on the amount and rate of recovery in all burned areas over time.

Noxious Weeds

Noxious weeds are invasive species of plants that have been identified and targeted by a state for monitoring, control, and eradication. Many of Idaho's noxious plant species can have negative effects on forest communities. Noxious species can displace native flora, alter fire regimes, reduce diversity in the plant and pollinator communities, and generally reduce the diversity and resiliency of forest ecosystems. FIA field crews record any instance where a noxious weed is found

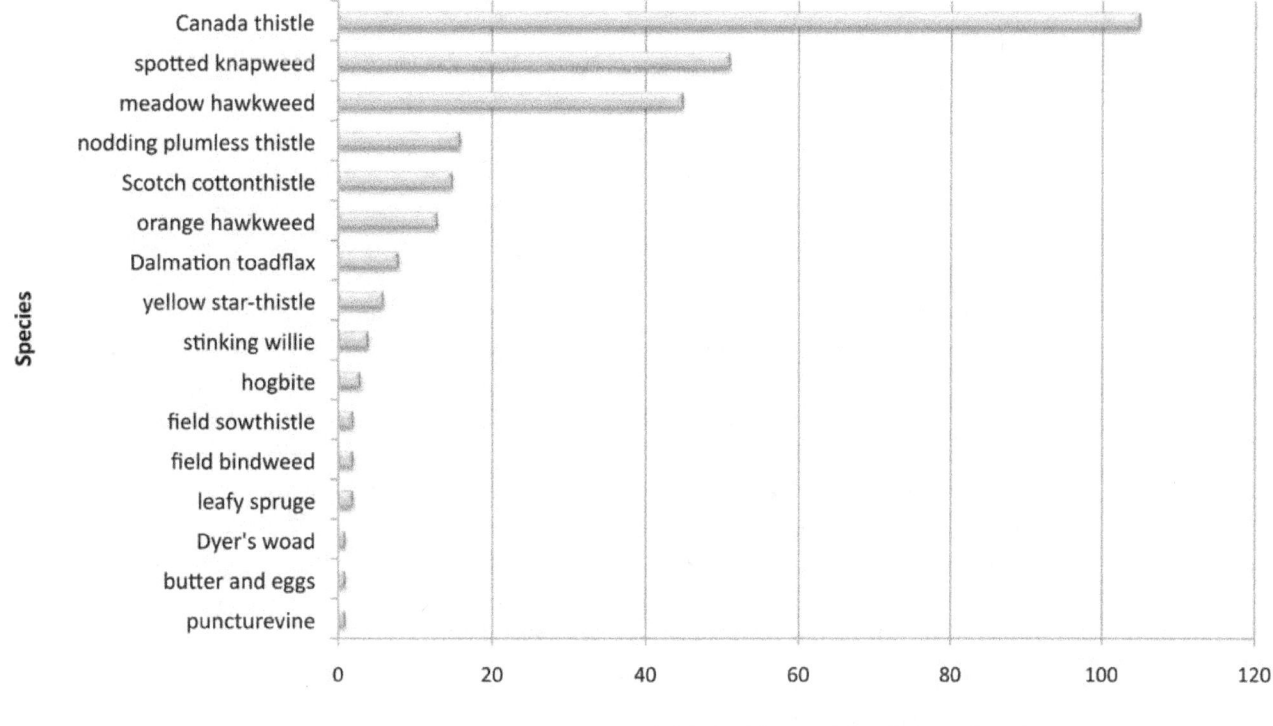

Figure 34: Number of forested conditions infested by each State-listed noxious plant, Idaho, 2004-2009.

on a plot that contains a forested condition. This allows the spatial and temporal extent of these species to be documented as plots are revisited. A total of 2,541 sample conditions were used to assess the occurrence of noxious plants in Idaho. These samples represent plots that had a forested condition recorded somewhere within the boundaries of the four subplots.

Sixteen different species were documented on forested plots in Idaho, with one or more found on 207 (9%) of the sampled plots (fig. 34). Canada thistle (*Cirsium arvence*), spotted knapweed (*Centaurea biebersteinii*), and meadow hawkweed (*Hieracium caespitosum*) were the most common species by a large margin. These three species accounted for 73% of the weed occurrences. It appears that Idaho's cottonwood and those types found in the hemlock/ sitka spruce forest type group are most prone to noxious plant infestation. This may be due to one or more factors, including soil conditions, accessibility to livestock grazing, road and foot traffic, and/or high frequency of both natural and man-induced disturbance. The cottonwood forest type has the highest percentage of its area infested with at least one noxious species (fig. 35). However, a low sample size (n = 8) needs to be considered in this instance. Conversely, one of the most abundant forest types in Idaho, the subalpine fir type, had a smaller proportion of infested locations (0.4%) than any other group.

Multiple conditions on a plot often indicate transition zones between forest types and between forest and non-forest conditions. These "edge" areas are often dynamic in terms of site occupation, utilization, and species composition. This makes them more susceptible to occupation by noxious plants than the more stable interior of the stands. Plots in Idaho that had more than one condition (more than one forest type or a portion of the plot was non-forest) had almost twice the

USDA Forest Service Resour. Bull. RMRS-RB-14. 2012

59

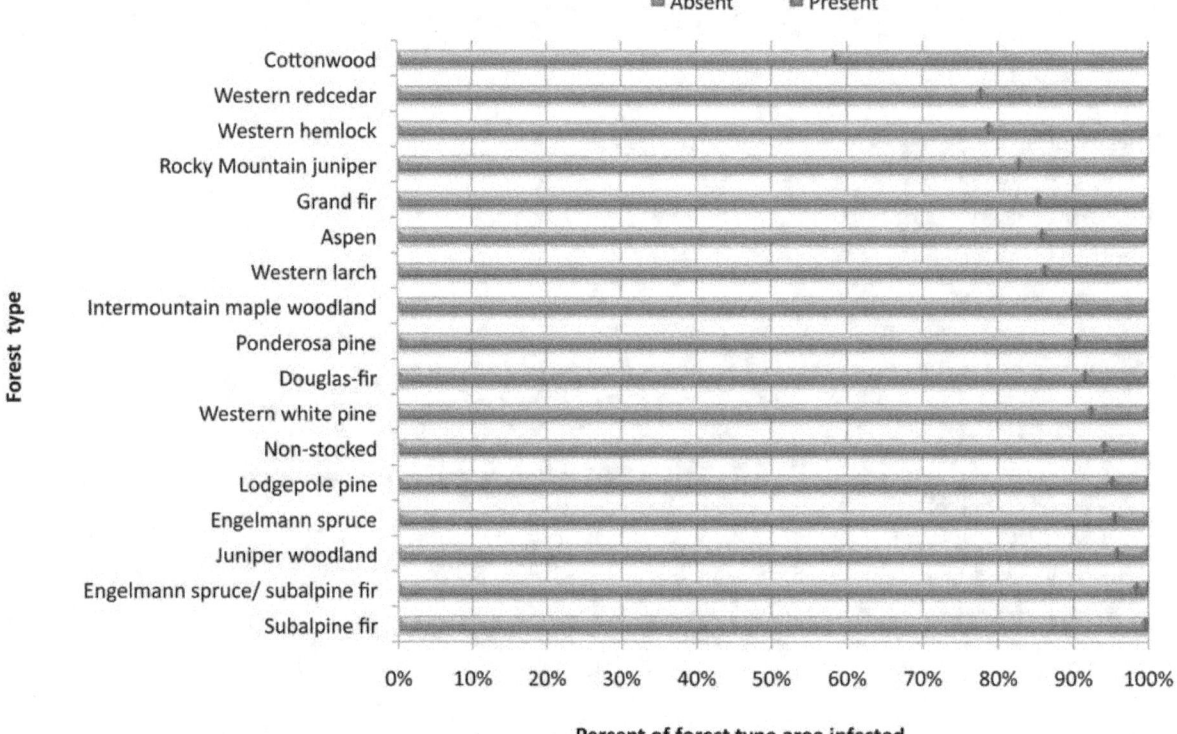

Figure 35: Percentage of forest area infested with one or more noxious plant species by forest type, Idaho, 2004-2009.

occurrence of noxious species than did those locations where only a single forested condition represented the entire plot (12% and 7% respectively). Sixteen percent of all sampled plots in Idaho had multiple conditions

Special Topic—Bridging the Gap Between Periodic and Annual Forest Inventories: Caveats and Limitations

When Idaho's annual forest inventory began in 2004, a new inventory design replaced that which was used to produce several periodic inventories that were summarized in 1990 and 1991 reports, as well as 1997 and 2007 RPA assessments. The discrepancies between the periodic and annual inventories can be attributed to inconsistencies in sample design, field methods, and procedures for calculating statewide forest metrics such as biomass, carbon, and forest land area. The FIA sample design, plot design, and estimation procedures changed with the implementation of the annual inventory. Attempts to clarify trends between Idaho's periodic and annual inventories show that comparisons of only plots common to both inventories yield trends that differ from those produced by direct periodic-to-annual comparisons. For example, figure 36 illustrates the effect of comparing tree volume estimates from each inventory in its entirety versus comparing only plots that are common to both inventories. The spatial distributions of both annual and periodic plots are displayed in figures 37a-c. Several reasons why direct comparisons between periodic and annual inventory data may be misleading are summarized below.

Sample Design: Spatial and Temporal Consistency—The FIA annual inventory is based on a spatially systematic grid. Ten percent of all plots in the grid are

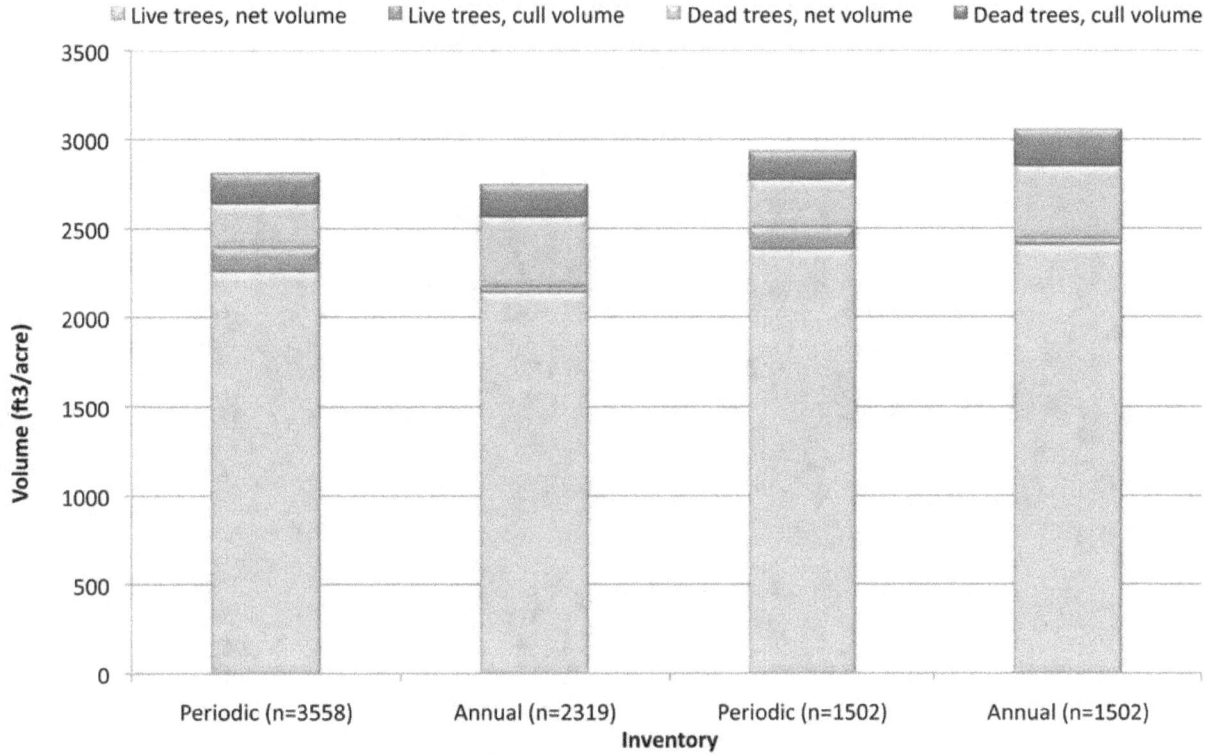

Figure 36: Mean volume (cubic feet per acre) represented by each plot in both periodic and annual inventories for live and standing dead trees 5.0 inches diameter and greater. The 3rd and 4th bars represent mean volume for plots that were surveyed during both periodic and annual inventories. Note that a direct comparison of all periodic plots to all annual plots shows a slight decrease in both live and dead volume, while a comparison of only plots in common to both inventories shows a steady trend in live volume and an increase in dead volume.

sampled each year, and each year's 10 percent sample is geographically distributed across the State; therefore, the annual inventory design is considered to be both spatially and temporally balanced.

In contrast, the various sample designs for the Idaho periodic inventories were both spatially and temporally inconsistent. Periodic inventories prior to 1992 did not include National Forest lands, while beginning in 1993 they consisted almost exclusively of National Forest lands. The pre-1993 inventory relied on a combination of field data and aerial photograph interpretation of plots that were measured during the 1981 Idaho woodland inventory. If no change was observed on aerial photographs of woodland plots, then the 1981 data were merged with the data collected during the 1990s field inventory. During the post-1993 inventory, each National Forest was responsible for conducting its own inventory, and the inventory methods, sample designs, and the actual inventory year(s) varied among Forests. For example, large areas of the Payette and Targhee National Forests were not sampled at all, and thus these areas are under-represented in statewide forest metrics from this period (figs. 37a,b).

Due to these spatial and temporal inconsistencies in the periodic inventory design, it is likely that forest metrics from the periodic inventory are neither spatially representative of the entire State or nor temporally representative of a single point in time. Direct comparisons with the annual inventory estimates are even more incongruous and should not be made without accounting for these inconsistencies.

Field Methods: Changes in Definitions and Field Procedures—While there are many minor differences between the methods used during the periodic and annual

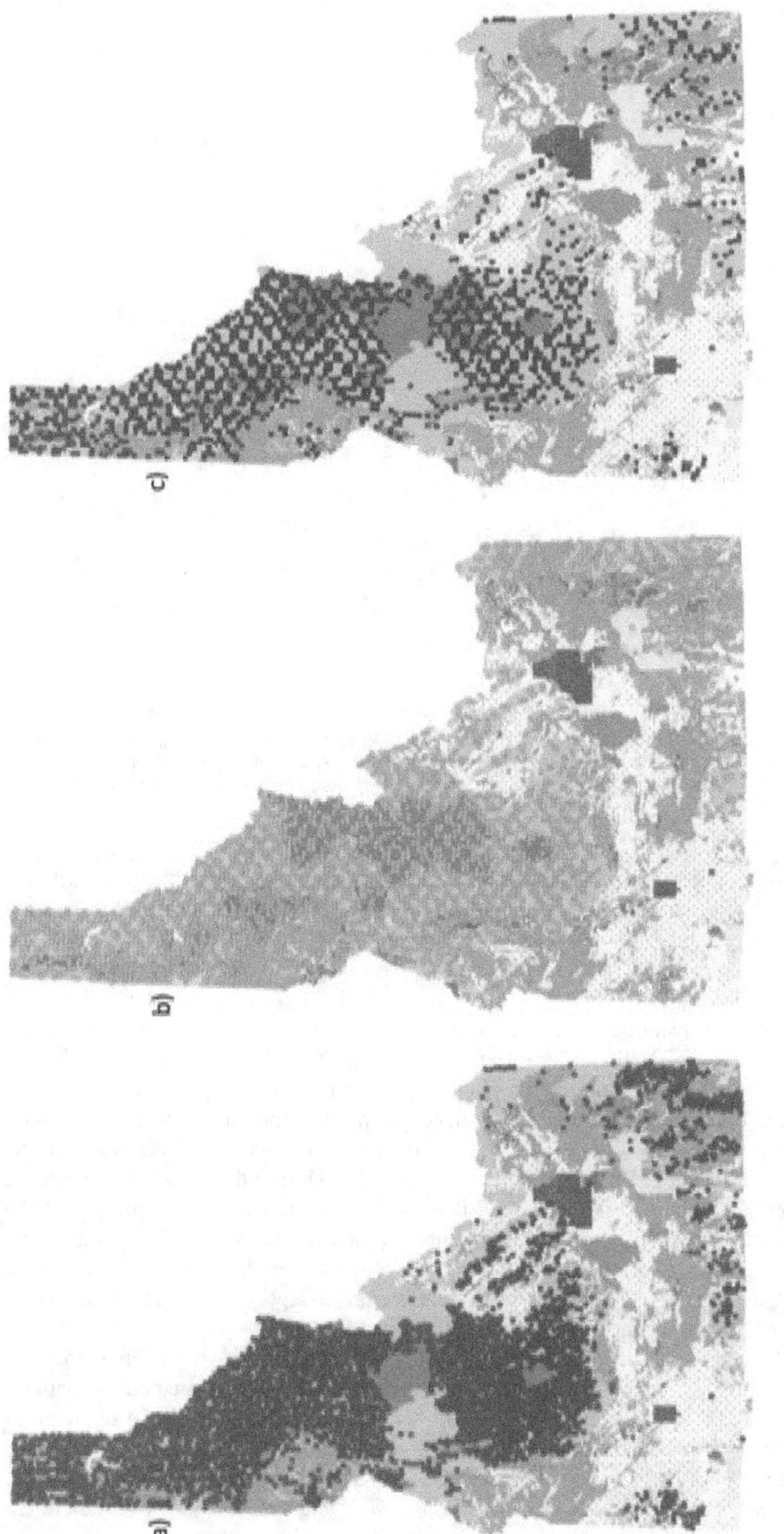

Forest inventory plots

- Periodic inventory plots (a)
- Annual inventory plots (b)
- Plots from both inventories (c)

Ownership categories

National Forest	USFWS	Private
National Forest - Wilderness Areas	BLM	State
National Parks/Monuments	Other Federal	Tribal Lands

Figure 37: Map showing the fuzzed locations of all periodic plots inventoried prior to 2004, by ownership category, in (a) the periodic inventory, (b) the annual inventory, and (c) both inventories.

inventories, there are two major differences that affect how forest land is identified in the field. The first is the definition of "tree," which in turn defines canopy cover and thus forest land. The second is the protocol for defining forest land in heterogeneous areas.

The field manuals for both periodic and annual inventories in Idaho specify that tree canopy cover of 5 percent or greater qualifies a condition as forest land. (Although national manuals prescribe a stocking-based definition, the Idaho forest inventory has consistently used percent canopy cover as a surrogate for stocking.) The periodic inventory's definition of a tree was dependent not only on the species but also on the growth form at the plot. At each plot, woodland trees were classified as either "tree form" or "shrub form," based on their height and crown width. For example, a woodland species such as Rocky Mountain juniper that was found to be growing horizontally and under a minimum height threshold would be classified as "shrub form." In this example, the "shrub form" junipers would not count toward the definition of forest land, and an entire stand of "shrub form" junipers would not be considered forest land. In contrast, the annual inventory's definition of a tree is solely determined by its inclusion on a list of species, and growth form is not considered. Under the annual inventory, the stand of "shrub form" junipers in the example above would be sampled as forest land provided the tree canopy cover was 5 percent or greater. Therefore, it is possible that plots that were deemed to be nonforest land during the periodic inventory would now be sampled as forest land.

The periodic and annual inventories also differ in their treatment of areas with a mixture of forest and nonforest land, which affects their procedures for estimating forest area. During most periodic inventories in Idaho, the land class status at plot center, i.e., forest or nonforest, determined the single land class that would be assigned to the entire plot. In contrast, annual inventory procedures allow for multiple land classes on each plot. For example, for plots where the center point was nonforest but forest land occurs nearby, periodic field procedures stipulated that the entire plot would be treated as nonforest. Conversely, for plots where the center point occurred in forest land and portions of the plot were nonforest, the periodic inventory would treat the entire plot as forest land when producing statewide estimates. In contrast, the annual inventory includes field procedures for delineating condition classes, which allows both forest and nonforest portions of sample plots to contribute to statewide forest estimates and, therefore, produces more precise estimates of forest area.

Procedures for Calculating Statewide Estimates—The procedures for calculating statewide forest metrics have also changed between the periodic and annual forest inventories. One of these changes pertains to the statistical methods used to estimate forest land area in specific ownership categories, and another is related to how those ownership categories are determined for each plot.

Although FIA attempts to obtain data from every plot in the sample grid, not every plot is actually sampled. Nonsampled plots are defined as those that cannot be sampled by a field crew, either because access to the plot location is denied by land owners or managers, or because the plot is deemed too hazardous to safely survey due to terrain or other environmental factors. Between 2004 and 2009, about 15 percent of all potentially forested private land plots were not sampled due to denial of access by private landowners. Less than 3 percent of all field plots, among all owner classes, were nonsampled for other reasons (i.e., hazardous, denial of access on non-private lands, etc.). Therefore, nonsampled plots occurred at a higher rate on private lands than on any other ownership category.

The inability to sample every plot affects statewide estimates of forest land area, and the periodic and annual inventories use different statistical methods to account for nonsampled plots. The periodic inventory relied on area control procedures, wherein the relative contribution of each sampled plot was weighted with respect to the total number of acres in each ownership group across the entire State. Nonsampled plots were not included in estimates of forest area, and the weights assigned to sampled plots were adjusted accordingly. Under the annual inventory, the statistical methods for estimating forest area assume that all plots have an equal chance of being nonsampled (Patterson and others 2012). However, we know this assumption is not true because nearly all denied-access plots occur on private lands. In an investigation of the effect that nonsampled plots can have on estimates of forest land area, Patterson and others (2012) found that a failure to account for the fact that certain subpopulations have different proportions of nonsampled plots (e.g., private versus public forest lands) can lead to considerable under-estimation of forest area in the subpopulations where a relatively high proportion of plots are nonsampled. They recommended that FIA estimation procedures be revised to account for different rates of nonsampled plots among subpopulations. FIA's current statistical estimation procedures may be underestimating the area of private forest land in Idaho due to the underlying assumptions about nonsampled plots.

Changes in the methods for determining plot ownership have also confounded trends in forest land area, as reported by ownership class. During the periodic inventory, the ownership status of each plot was assigned using 1:100,000 BLM surface management maps. The annual inventory procedure combines the most current GIS layers and county plat maps to verify the ownership class assigned to each plot, and several errors in previous plot ownership attributes have been discovered and corrected using this procedure. In general, previous errors in ownership class assignments were biased against private forest lands.

Implications for Interpreting Long-Term Trends in Volume, Biomass, Carbon, and Forest Land Area—As mentioned above, the periodic inventory metrics alone are likely not representative of the State of Idaho as a whole, yet data from the early 1990s is often used as a baseline and annual inventory data are compared to this baseline. Figure 36 illustrates the possibility that erroneous conclusions may be drawn by making such comparisons. The first two bars show mean volume per acre based on the entire periodic and the entire annual inventory, respectively, and it appears that the total volume and live volume both decreased substantially. The third and fourth bars show volume based only on plots that were sampled during both inventories, for periodic and annual inventories, respectively. Based on this apples-to-apples comparison, live volume has only slightly decreased and total volume has increased. Therefore, directly comparing periodic versus annual inventory data produces trends that are either more substantial or in opposition to those observed by comparing only remeasured plots.

Despite these caveats, scientists and policy-makers often rely on forest inventory data to quantify long-term trends in metrics such as volume, standing forest biomass, forest carbon, and forest land area. In their analysis of forest carbon for the U.S. greenhouse gas inventory, Heath and others (2011) specifically mentioned that observed changes in Idaho's forest carbon since 1990 were likely due to changes in forest inventory methods. Any future analyses of long-term trends in forest metrics that utilize Idaho's periodic forest inventory data should not consist of direct comparisons of summary statistics, but rather must account for the many differences in inventory methods described here.

Conclusions

Idaho's forests include a variety of tree and understory species, age-classes, and disturbance dynamics that together create a multitude of complex ecosystems. These forests provide an abundance of services, including timber products, recreational opportunities, air and water quality, wildlife habitat, and scenic beauty. The tree species of Idaho are adapted to a wide range of soils, moisture, and topography, from low-elevation juniper woodlands, to wildlife-rich aspen stands in moisture-trapping snow pockets, to the massive fir and hemlock forests of the northern mountains.

Most of the forests in Idaho are administered by Federal agencies, primarily the Forest Service and the Bureau of Land Management. These forests are to be managed to meet the multiple-use objectives defined in statutes and to provide a sustained flow of outputs that meet the expectations of an ever-growing public as well as industries that support Idaho's rural economies.

As the number of people living in and using Idaho's forests increases, so does the challenge of providing a variety of quality experiences and products derived from the forest. Furthermore, the dynamic nature of Idaho's forest ecosystems dictates ever-changing conditions and management strategies. Extensive wildfires, mountain pine beetle infestations, aspen decline, whitebark pine mortality, and noxious weeds are a few of the factors addressed in this report that currently affect Idaho's forests. The issues of the future might be different and it is important to have the tools to identify potential issues as soon as possible. In addition, the application of data for down woody material, understory vegetation, standing dead trees, damage indicators, and others have only been briefly addressed in this report. Many of the analyses performed for this report demonstrate both the utility of FIA data as an analysis tool and the potential for further, more in-depth analysis of a wide range of topics. Data from FIA's annualized inventory will continue to provide valuable information to resource managers and researchers who are interested in the quantity and condition of resources provided by Idaho's forests.

Standard Forest Inventory and Analysis Terminology

Average annual mortality—The average annual volume of trees 5.0 inches d.b.h./ d.r.c. and larger that died from natural causes.

Average net annual growth—Average annual net change in volume of trees 5.0 inches d.b.h./d.r.c. and larger in the absence of cutting (average annual gross growth minus average annual mortality).

Basal area (BA)—The cross-sectional area of a tree stem/bole (trunk) at the point where diameter is measured, inclusive of bark. BA is calculated for trees 1.0-inch and larger in diameter, and is expressed in square feet. For timber species, the calculation is based on diameter at breast height (d.b.h.); for woodland species, it is based on diameter at root collar (d.r.c.).

Biomass—The quantity of wood fiber, for trees 1.0-inch d.b.h./d.r.c. and larger, expressed in terms of oven-dry weight. It includes above-ground portions of trees: bole/stem (trunk), bark, and branches. Biomass estimates can be computed for live and/or dead trees.

Board-foot volume—A board-foot is a unit of measure indicating the amount of wood contained in an unfinished board 1-foot wide, 1-foot long, and 1-inch thick. Board-foot volume is computed for the sawlog portion of a sawtimber-size tree; the sawlog portion includes the part of the bole on sawtimber-size tree from a 1-foot stump to a minimum sawlog top of 7-inches diameter outside bark (d.o.b.) for softwoods, or 9-inches d.o.b. for hardwoods. **Net board-foot volume** is calculated as the gross board-foot volume in the sawlog portion of a sawtimber-size tree, less deductions for cull (note: board-foot cull deductions are limited to rotten/missing material and form defect—referred to as the **merchantability factor—board-foot**). Board-foot volume estimates are computed in both Scribner and International ¼-inch rule, and can be calculated for live and/or dead (standing or down) trees.

Census water—Streams, sloughs, estuaries, canals, and other moving bodies of water 200 feet wide and greater, and lakes, reservoirs, ponds, and other permanent bodies of water 4.5 acres in area and greater.

Coarse woody debris—Down pieces of wood leaning more than 45 degrees from vertical with a diameter of at least 3.0 inches and a length of at least 3.0 feet.

Condition class—The combination of discrete landscape and forest attributers that identify, define, and stratify the area associated with a plot. Examples of such attributes include condition status, forest type, stand origin, stand size, owner group, and stand density.

Crown class—A classification of trees based on dominance in relation to adjacent trees in the stand as indicated by crown development and amount of sunlight received from above and the sides.

Crown cover (Canopy cover)—The percentage of the ground surface area covered by a vertical projection of plant crowns. Tree crown cover for a sample site includes the combined cover of timber and woodland trees 1.0-inch d.b.h./d.r.c. and larger. Maximum crown cover for a site is 100 percent; overlapping cover is not double counted.

Cubic-foot volume (merchantable)—A cubic-foot is a unit of measure indicating the amount of wood contained in a cube 1 by 1 by 1 foot. Cubic-foot volume is computed for the merchantable portion of timber and woodland species; the merchantable portion for timber species includes that part of a bole from a 1-foot stump to a minimum 4-inch top d.o.b, or above the place(s) of diameter measurement for any woodland tree with a single 5.0-inch stem or larger or a cumulative (calculated) d.r.c. of at least 5.0 inches to the 1.5-inch ends of all branches. **Net cubic-foot volume** is calculated as the gross cubic-foot volume in the merchantable portion of a tree, less deductions for cull.

Diameter at breast height (d.b.h.)—The diameter of a tree bole/stem (trunk) measured at breast height (4.5 feet above ground), measured outside the bark. The point of diameter measurement may vary for abnormally formed trees.

Diameter at root collar (d.r.c.)—The diameter of a tree stem(s) measured at root collar or at the point nearest the ground line (whichever is higher) that represents the basal area of the tree, measured outside the bark. For multistemmed trees, d.r.c. is calculated from an equation that incorporates the individual stem diameter measurements. The point of diameter measurement may vary for woodland trees with stems that are abnormally formed. With the exception of seedlings, woodland stems qualifying for measurement must be at least 1.0-inch in diameter or larger and at least 1.0-foot in length.

Diameter class—A grouping of tree diameters (d.b.h. or d.r.c.) into classes of a specified range. For some diameter classes, the number referenced (e.g., 4", 6", 8") is designated as the midpoint of an individual class range. For example, if 2-inch classes are specified (the range for an individual class) and even numbers are referenced, the 6-inch class would include trees 5.0- to 6.9-inches in diameter.

Diameter outside bark (d.o.b.)—Tree diameter measurement inclusive of the outside perimeter of the tree bark. The d.o.b. measurement may be taken at various points on a tree (e.g., breast height, tree top) or log, and is sometimes estimated.

Field plot/location—A reference to the sample site or plot; an area containing the field location center (LC) and all sample points. A field location consists of four subplots and four microplots.

- **Subplot**—A 1/24-acre fixed-radius area (24-foot horizontal radius) used to sample trees 5.0-inches d.b.h./d.r.c. and larger and understory vegetation.

- **Microplot**—A 1/300-acre fixed-radius plot (6.8-foot radius), located at the center of each subplot, used to inventory seedlings and saplings.

Fixed-radius plot—A circular sample plot of a specified horizontal radius: 1/300 acre = 6.8-foot radius (microplot); 1/24 acre = 24.0-foot radius (subplot).

Forest industry land—Land owned by a company or an individual(s) operating a primary wood-processing plant.

Forest land—Land that has at least 10 percent cover of live tally tree species of any size, or land formerly having such tree cover, and not currently developed for a nonforest use. The minimum area for classification as forest land is one acre. Roadside, stream-side, and shelterbelt strips of trees must be at least 120 feet wide to qualify as forest land. Unimproved roads and trails, streams and other bodies of water, or natural clearings in forested areas are classified as forest, if less than 120 feet in width or one acre in size. Grazed woodlands, reverting fields, and pastures that are not actively maintained are included if above qualifications are satisfied.

Forest type—A classification of forest land based on the species forming a plurality of live-tree stocking.

Gross growth—The annual increase in volume of trees 5.0 inches d.b.h. and larger in absence of cutting and mortality. Gross growth includes survivor growth, ingrowth, growth on ingrowth, growth on removals before removal, and growth on mortality prior to death.

Growing-stock trees—A live timber species, 5.0-inches d.b.h. or larger, with less than 2/3 (67 percent) of the merchantable volume cull, and containing at least one solid 8-foot section, now or prospectively, reasonably free of form defect, on the merchantable portion of the tree.

Growing-stock volume—the cubic-foot volume of sound wood in growing-stock trees at least 5.0 inches d.b.h. from a 1-foot stump to a minimum 4-inch top d.o.b. to the central stem.

Hardwoods—Dicotyledonous trees, usually broadleaf and deciduous.

Hexagonal grid (Hex)—A hexagonal grid formed from equilateral triangles for the purpose of tessellating the FIA inventory sample. Each hexagon in the base grid has an area of 5,937 acres (2,403.6 ha) and contains one inventory plot. The base grid can be subdivided into smaller hexagons to intensify the sample.

Indian Trust lands—American Indian lands held in fee, or trust, by the Federal Government, but administered for tribal groups or as individual trust allotments.

Land use—The classification of a land condition by use or type.

Litter—The uppermost layer of organic debris on a forest floor; that is, essentially the freshly fallen, or only slightly decomposed material, mainly foliage, but also bark fragments, twigs, flowers, fruits, and so forth. Humus is the organic layer, unrecognizable as to origin, immediately beneath the litter layer from which it is derived. Litter and humus together are often termed duff.

Logging residue/products—

- **Bolt**—A short piece of pulpwood; a short log.

- **Industrial wood**—All commercial roundwood products, excluding fuelwood.

- **Logging residue**—The unused sections within the merchantable portions of sound (growing-stock) trees cut or killed during logging operations.

- **Mill or plant residue**—Wood material from mills or other primary manufacturing plants that is not used for the mill's or plant's primary products. Mill or plant residue includes bark, slabs, edgings, trimmings, miscuts, sawdust, and shavings. Much of the mill and plant residue is used as fuel and as the raw material for such products as pulp, palletized fuel, fiberwood, mulch, and animal bedding. Mill or plant residue includes bark and the following components:

- **Coarse residue**—Wood material suitable for chipping, such as slabs, edgings, and trim.

- **Fine residue**—Wood material unsuitable for chipping, such as sawdust and shavings.

- **Pulpwood**—Roundwood, whole-tree chips, or wood residues that are used for the production of wood pulp.

- **Roundwood**—Logs, bolts, or other round sections cut from trees.

Mapped-plot design—A sampling technique that identifies (maps) and separately classifies distinct "conditions" on the field location sample area. Each condition must meet minimum size requirements. At the most basic level, condition class delineations include forest land, nonforest land, and water. Forest land conditions can be further subdivided into separate condition classes if there are distinct variations in forest type, stand-size class, stand origin, and stand density, given that each distinct area meets minimum size requirements.

Merchantable portion—For trees measured at d.b.h. and 5.0-inches d.b.h. and larger, the merchantable portion (or "merchantable bole") includes the part of the tree bole from a 1-foot stump to a 4.0-inch top (d.o.b.). For trees measured at d.r.c., the merchantable portion includes all qualifying segments above the place(s) of diameter measurement for any tree with a single 5.0-inch stem or larger or a cumulative (calculated) d.r.c. of at least 5.0 inches to the 1.5-inch ends of all branches; sections below the place(s) of diameter measurement are not included. Qualifying segments are stems or branches that are a minimum of 1 foot in length and at least 1.0 inch in diameter; portions of stems or branches smaller than 1.0 inch in diameter, such as branch tips, are not included in the merchantable portion of the tree.

Miscellaneous Federal lands—Public lands administered by Federal agencies other than the Forest Service, U.S. Department of Agriculture, or the Bureau of Land Management, U.S. Department of the Interior.

Mortality tree—All standing or down dead trees 5.0-inches d.b.h./d.r.c. and larger that were alive within the previous 5 years.

National Forest System (NFS) lands—Public lands administered by the Forest Service, U.S. Department of Agriculture, such as National Forests, National Grasslands, and some National Recreation Areas.

National Park lands—Public lands administered by the Park Service, U.S. Department of the Interior, such as National Parks, National Monuments, National Historic Sites (such as National Memorials and National Battlefields), and some National Recreation Areas.

Noncensus water—Portions of rivers, streams, sloughs, estuaries, and canals that are 30 to 200 feet wide and at least 1 acre in size; and lakes, reservoirs, and ponds 1 to 4.5 acres in size. Portions of rivers and streams not meeting the criteria for census water, but at least 30 feet wide and 1 acre in size, are considered noncensus water. Portions of braided streams not meeting the criteria for census water, but at least 30 feet in width and 1 acre in size, and more than 50 percent water at normal high-water level are also considered noncensus water.

Nonforest land—Land that does not support, or has never supported, forests, and lands formerly forested where tree regeneration is precluded by development for other uses. Includes areas used for crops, improved pasture, residential areas, city parks, improved roads of any width and adjoining rights-of-way, power line clearings of any width, and noncensus water. If intermingled in forest areas, unimproved roads and nonforest strips must be more than 120 feet wide, and clearings, etc., more than 1 acre in size, to qualify as nonforest land.

Nonindustrial private lands—Privately owned land excluding forest industry land.

Unreserved forest land—Forest land not withdrawn from management for production of wood products through statute or administrative designation.

Other private lands—Privately owned lands other than forest industry or Indian Trust.

Other public lands—Public lands administered by agencies other than the Forest Service, U.S. Department of Agriculture. Includes lands administered by other Federal, State, county, and local government agencies, including lands leased by these agencies for more than 50 years.

Other wooded land—Land that has 5 to 10 percent cover of live tally tree species of any size, or land formerly having such tree cover, and not currently developed for a nonforest use. The minimum area for classification as forest land is one acre. Roadside, stream-side, and shelterbelt strips of trees must be at least 120 feet wide to qualify as forest land. Unimproved roads and trails, streams and other bodies of water, or natural clearings in forested areas are classified as forest, if less than 120 feet wide or one acre in size. Grazed woodlands, reverting fields, and pastures that are not actively maintained are included if above qualifications are satisfied.

Poletimber-size trees—For trees measured at d.b.h, softwoods 5.0 to 8.9 inches d.b.h. and hardwoods 5.0 to 10.9 inches d.b.h. For trees measured at d.r.c., all live trees 5.0 to 8.9 inches d.r.c.

Primary wood-processing plants—An industrial plant that processes roundwood products, such as sawlogs, pulpwood bolts, or veneer logs.

Productive forest land—Forest land capable of producing 20 cubic feet per acre per year of wood from trees classified as a timber species (see Appendix A) on forest land classified as a timber forest type (see Appendix B).

Productivity—The potential yield capability of a stand calculated as a function of site index (expressed in terms of cubic-foot growth per acre per year at age of culmination of MAI). Productivity values for forest land provide an indication of biological potential. Timberland stands are classified by the potential net annual growth attainable in fully stocked natural stands. For FIA reporting, Productivity Class is a variable that groups stand productivity values into categories of a specified range. Productivity is sometimes referred to as "Yield" or "Mean annual increment (MAI)."

Removals—The net volume of sound (growing-stock) trees removed from the inventory by harvesting or other cultural operations (such as timber-stand improvement), by land clearing, or by changes in land use (such as a shift to wilderness).

Reserved land—Land withdrawn from management for production of wood products through statute or administrative designation; examples include Wilderness areas and National Parks and Monuments.

Sampling error—A statistical term used to describe the accuracy of the inventory estimates. Expressed on a percentage basis in order to enable comparisons between the precision of different estimates, sampling errors are computed by dividing the estimate into the square root of its variance.

Sapling—A live tree 1.0-4.9-inches d.b.h./d.r.c.

Sawlog portion—The part of the bole of sawtimber-size trees between a 1-foot stump and the sawlog top.

Sawlog top—The point on the bole of sawtimber-size trees above which a sawlog cannot be produced. The minimum sawlog top is 7 inches d.o.b. for softwoods, and 9 inches d.o.b. for hardwoods.

Sawtimber-size trees—Softwoods 9.0 inches d.b.h. and larger and hardwoods 11.0 inches and larger.

Sawtimber volume—The growing-stock volume in the saw-log portion of sawtimber-size trees in board feet.

Seedlings—Live trees less than 1.0 inch d.b.h./d.r.c.

Site index—A measure of forest productivity for a timberland tree/stand. Expressed in terms of the expected height (in feet) of trees on the site at an index age of 50 (or 80 years for aspen and cottonwood). Calculated from height-to-age equations.

Site tree—A tree used to provide an index of site quality. Timber species selected for site index calculations must meet specified criteria with regards to age, diameter, crown class, and damage.

Snag—A standing-dead tree.

Softwood trees—Coniferous trees, usually evergreen, having needle- or scale-like leaves.

Stand—A community of trees that can be distinguished from adjacent communities due to similarities and uniformity in tree and site characteristics, such as age-class distribution, species composition, spatial arrangement, structure, etc.

Stand density—A relative measure that quantifies the relationship between trees per acre, stand basal area, average stand diameter, and stocking of a forested stand.

Stand density index (SDI)—A widely used measure developed by Reineke (1933), and is an index that expresses relative stand density based on a comparison of measured stand values with some standard condition; **relative stand density** is the ratio, proportion, or percent of absolute stand density to a reference level defined by some standard level of competition. For FIA reporting, the SDI for a site is usually presented as a percentage of the maximum SDI for the forest type. Site SDI values are sometimes grouped into SDI classes of a specified percentage range. Maximum SDI values vary by species and region.

Standing tree—To qualify as a standing dead tally tree, dead trees must be at least 5.0 inches in diameter, have a bole that has an unbroken actual length of at least 4.5 feet, and lean less than 45 degrees from vertical as measured from the base of the tree to 4.5 feet. Portions of boles on dead trees that are separated greater than 50 percent (either above or below 4.5 feet), are considered severed and are included in Down Woody Material (DWM) if they otherwise meet DWM tally criteria. For western woodland species with multiple stems, a tree is considered down if more than 2/3 of the volume is no longer attached or upright; do not consider cut and removed volume. For western woodland species with single stems to qualify as a standing dead tally tree, dead trees must be at least 5.0 inches in diameter, be at least 1.0 foot in unbroken actual length, and lean less than 45 degrees from vertical.

Stand-size class—A classification of forest land based on the predominant diameter size of live trees presently forming the plurality of live-tree stocking. Classes are defined as follows:

- **Sawtimber stand (Large-tree stand)**—A stand at least 10 percent stocked with live trees, in which half or more of the total stocking is from live trees 5.0-inches or larger in diameter, and with sawtimber (large tree) stocking equal to or greater than poletimber (medium tree) stocking.

- **Poletimber stand (Medium-tree stand)**—A stand at least 10 percent stocked with live trees, in which half or more of the total stocking is from live trees 5.0-inches or larger in diameter, and with poletimber (medium tree) stocking exceeding sawtimber (large tree) stocking.

- **Sapling/seedling stand**—A stand at least 10 percent stocked with live trees, in which half or more of the total stocking is from live trees less than 5.0-inches in diameter.

- **Nonstocked stand**—A formerly stocked stand that currently has less than 10 percent stocking, but has the potential to again become 10 percent stocked. For example, recently harvested, burned, or windthrow-damaged areas.

Stockability (Stockability factor)—An estimate of the stocking potential of a given site; for example, a stockability factor of 0.8 for a given site indicates that the site is capable of supporting only about 80 percent of "normal" stocking as indicated by yield tables. Stockability factors (maximum site value of 1.0) are assigned to sites based on habitat type/plant associations.

Stocking—An expression of the extent to which growing space is effectively utilized by live trees.

Timber species—Tally tree species traditionally used for industrial wood products. These include all species of conifers, except pinyon and juniper. Timber species are measured at d.b.h.

Timber stand improvement—A term comprising all intermediate cuttings or treatments, such as thinning, pruning, release cutting, girdling, weeding, or poisoning, made to improve the composition, health, and growth of the remaining trees in the stand.

Timberland—Unreserved forest land capable of producing 20 cubic feet per acre per year of wood from trees classified as a timber species (see Appendix A) on forest land designated as a timber forest type (see Appendix B)..

USDA Forest Service Resour. Bull. RMRS-RB-14. 2012

71

Unproductive forest land—Forest land not capable of producing 20 cubic feet per acre per year of wood from trees classified as a timber species (see Appendix A) on forest land designated as a timber forest type and all forest lands designated as a woodland forest type (see Appendix B).

Wilderness area—An area of undeveloped land currently included in the Wilderness System, managed to preserve its natural conditions and retain its primeval character and influence.

Woodland species—Tally tree species that are not usually converted into industrial wood products. Common uses of woodland trees are fuelwood, fenceposts, and Christmas trees. These species include pinyon, juniper (except Western juniper), mesquite, locust, mountain-mahogany (*Cercocarpus* spp.), Rocky Mountain maple, bigtooth maple, desert ironwood, and most oaks (note: Bur oak and Chinkapin oak are classified as timber species). Because most woodland trees are extremely variable in form, diameter is measured at d.r.c.

Note: For the FIA national glossary please go to:

http://socrates.lv-hrc.nevada.edu/fia/ab/issues/pending/glossary.html.

References

Amacher, M. C.; Perry, C. H. 2011. Background technical report for Criterion 4. Conservation and maintenance of soil water resources: Indicator 19. Area and percent of forest land with significant soil degradation. National Report on Sustainable Forests—2010. FS-979. Washington, DC: U.S. Department of Agriculture, Forest Service.

Amman, G. D. 1973. Population changes of the mountain pine beetle in relation to elevation. Environ. Entomol. 2: 541-547.

Arno, S. F. 1986. Whitebark pine cone crops: A diminishing source of wildlife food? Western Journal of Applied Forestry 1(3): 92-94.

Arno, S. F.; Hoff, R. J. 1989. Silvics of whitebark pine (*Pinus albicaulis*). Gen. Tech. Rep. INT-253. Ogden, UT: U.S. Department of Agriculture, Forest Service, Intermountain Research Station. 14 p.

Bailey, R. G. 1995. Descriptions of the ecoregions of the United States. (2nd ed. rev. and expanded). Misc. Publ. No. 1391. Washington, DC: U.S. Department of Agriculture, Forest Service. Online: http://csfs.colostate.edu/foresttypes.htm#ecoregions. [June 10 2011].

Bartos, Dale L. 2001. Landscape dynamics of aspen and conifer forests. In: Shepperd, Wayne D.; Binkley, Dan; Bartos, Dale L.; Stohlgren, Thomas J.; Eskew, Lane G., comps. Sustaining aspen in western landscapes: Symposium proceedings; 13-15 June 2000; Grand Junction, CO. Proceedings RMRS-P-18. Fort Collins, CO: U.S. Department of Agriculture, Forest Service, Rocky Mountain Research Station: 5-14.

Bartos, D. L.; Campbell, R. B., Jr. 1998. Decline of quaking aspen in the Interior West— examples from Utah. Rangelands 20(1): 17-24.

Bechtold, W. A.; Patterson, P. L., eds. 2005. The enhanced Forest Inventory and Analysis program—national sampling design and estimation procedures. Gen. Tech. Rep. SRS-80. Asheville, NC: U.S. Department of Agriculture, Forest Service, Southern Research Station. 85 p.

Beers, T. W.; Miller, C. I. 1964. Point sampling; research results, theory and applications. Res. Bull. 786. Purdue University Agricultural Experiment Station. 55 p.

Benson, R. E.; Green, A. W.; Van Hooser, D. D. 1987. Idaho's forest resources. Resour. Bull. INT-39. Ogden, UT: U.S. Department of Agriculture, Forest Service, Intermountain Research Station. 114 p.

Brandt, J. P.; Morgan, T. A.; Keegan, C. E., III.; [and others]. 2011. Idaho's forest products industry and timber harvest, 2006. Resour. Bull. RMRS-RB-12. Fort Collins, CO: U.S. Department of Agriculture, Forest Service, Rocky Mountain Research Station. 45 p.

Brown, M. J.; Chojnacky, D. C. 1996. Idaho's Forests, 1991. Resour. Bull. INT-RB-88. Ogden, UT: U.S. Department of Agriculture, Forest Service, Intermountain Research Station. 63 p.

Carroll, A. L.; Safranyik, L. 2004. The bionomics of the mountain pine beetle in lodgepole pine forests: establishing a context. In: Shore, T. L.; Brooks, J. E.; Stone, J. E., editors. Mountain pine beetle symposium: Challenges and solutions; October 30-31, 2003; Kelowna, BC, Canada. Infor. Rep. BC-X-399. Victoria, BC: Natural Resources Canada, Canadian Forest Service, Pacific Forestry Centre: 19-30.

Cohen, S.; Miller, D. 1978. The big burn: The Northwest's fire of 1910. Missoula, MT: Pictorial Histories Publishing Co. 96 p.

DeBlander, L. T.; Shaw, J. D.; Witt, C.; [and others]. 2010. Utah's Forest resources, 2000-2005. Resour. Bull. RMRS-RB-10. Fort Collins, CO: U.S. Department of Agriculture, Forest Service, Rocky Mountain Research Station. 144 p.

Di Orio, A. P.; Callasa, R.; Schaefer, R. J. 2005. Forty-eight year decline and fragmentation of aspen (*Populus tremuloides*) in the South Warner Mountains of California. Forest Ecology and Management 206(1-3): 307-313.

Dobkin, D. S.; Rich, A. C.; Pretare, J. A.; Pyle, W. H. 1995. Nest-site relationships among cavity-nesting birds of riparian and snowpocket aspen woodlands in the northwestern Great Basin. The Condor 97: 694-707.

Egan, T. 2009. The Big Burn: Teddy Roosevelt and the fire that saved America. Boston: Houghton Mifflin Harcourt. 324 p.

Eidenshenk, J.; Schwind, B.; Brewer, K.; [and others]. (2007). A project for monitoring trends in burn severity. *Fire Ecology Special Issue*. 3(1).

Fiedler, C. E.; Friederici, P.; Petruncio, M. 2007. Monitoring old growth in frequent-fire landscapes. Ecology and Society 12(2): 22. [online] http://www.ecologyandsociety.org/vol12/iss2/art22/ [January 15, 2012].

Flack, J. A. D. 1976. Bird population s of aspen forests in western North America. Ornithological Monographs 19. Washington, DC: American Ornithologist's Union.

Gillespie, A. J. R. 1999. Rationale for a national annual forest inventory program. Journal of Forestry 97(12): 16-20.

Gingrich, S. F. 1967. Measuring and evaluating stocking and stand density in Upland Hardwood forests in the Central States. Forest Science 13: 38-53.

Green, P.; Joy, J.; Sirucek, D.; [and others]. 1992. Old-growth forest types of the northern region. R-1 SES 4/92. Missoula, MT: U.S. Department of Agriculture, Forest Service, Northern Region. 62 p.

Hamilton, R. G., comp. 1993. Characteristics of old-growth forests in the intermountain region. Unpublished report on file at: U.S. Department of Agriculture, Forest Service, Intermountain Region, Ogden, Utah.

Hart, J. H.; Hart, D. L. 2001. Heartrot fungi's role in creating Picid nesting sites in living aspen. In: Sheppard, W. D., Binkley, D., Bartos, D. L., [and others], ed. Sustaining aspen in western landscapes: symposium proceedings; 13-15 June 2000; Grand Junction, CO. Proc. RMRS-P-18. Fort Collins, CO: U.S. Department of Agriculture, Forest Service, Rocky Mountain Research Station: 207-214.

Hawksworth, F. G. 1977. The 6-class dwarf mistletoe rating system. Gen. Tech. Rep. RM-48. Fort Collins, CO: U.S. Department of Agriculture, Forest Service, Rocky Mountain Forest and Range Experiment Station.

Heath, L. S.; Smith, J. E.; Skog, K. E.; [and others]. 2011. Managed forest carbon estimates for the US greenhouse gas inventory, 1990-2008. Journal of Forestry 109: 167-173.

Hessl, A. E.; Graumlich, L. J. 2002. Interactive effects of human activities, herbivory and fire on quaking aspen (*Populus tremuloides*) age structures in western Wyoming. Journal of Biogeography 29: 889902.

Jenny, H. 1994. Factors of soil formation—a system of quantitative pedology. Dover Edition. New York: Dover Publications. 191 p.

Johnson, M. 1994. Changes in Southwestern forests: Stewardship implications. Journal of Forestry 92: 16-19.

Kaufmann, M. R.; Binkley, D.; Fulé, P. Z.; [and others]. 2007. Defining old growth for fire-adapted forests of the western United States. Ecology and Society 12(2): 15. [online] http://www.ecologyandsociety.org/vol12/iss2/art15/ [January 15, 2012].

Kay, C. E. 1997. Is aspen doomed? Journal of Forestry 95(5): 4-11.

Keane, R. E.; Arno, S. F. 1993. Rapid decline of whitebark pine in western Montana: Evidence from 20-year remeasurements. Western Journal of Applied Forestry 8(2): 44-46.

Kegley, Sandra; Schwandt, John; Gibson, Ken; Perkins, Dana. 2011. Health of whitebark pine forests after mountain pine beetle outbreaks. In: Keane, Robert E.; Tomback, Diana F.; Murray, Michael P.; Smith, Cyndi M., eds. The future of high-elevation, five-needle white pines in Western North America: Proceedings of the High Five Symposium; 28-30 June 2010; Missoula, MT. Proc. RMRS-P-63. Fort Collins, CO: U.S. Department of Agriculture, Forest Service, Rocky Mountain Research Station: 85-93.

Kendall, K. C. 1980. Use of pine nuts by grizzly and black bears in the Yellowstone area. Int. Conf. Bear Res. Manage. 5: 166-173.

Kulakowski, D.; Veblen, T. T.; Drinkwater, S. 2004. The persistence of quaking aspen (*Populus tremuloides*) in the Grand Mesa area, Colorado. Ecological Applications 14 (5): 1603-1614.

Lilieholm, R. J.; Long, J. N.; Patla, S. 1994. Assessing goshawk nest stand habitat using stand density index. Cooper Ornithological Society. Studies in Avian Biology 16: 18-24.

Logan, J. A.; Regniere, J.; Powell, J. A. 2003 Assessing the impacts of global warming on forest pest dynamics. Frontiers in Ecology and the Environment 1: 130-137.

Long, J. N. 1985. A practical approach to density management. Forest Chronicle 61: 23-37.

Long, J. N.; Daniel, T. W. 1990. Assessment of growing stock in uneven-aged stands. Western Journal of Applied Forestry 5: 93-96.

Long, J. N.; Shaw, J. D. 2005. A density management diagram for even-aged ponderosa pine stands. Western Journal of Applied Forestry 20: 205-215.

Lutes, D. C.; Keane, R. E.; Caratti, J. F. 2009. A surface fuel classification for estimating fire effects. International Journal of Wildland Fire. 18: 802-814.

Martin, K.; Aitken, K. E. H.; Wiebe, K. L. 2004. Nest sites and nest webs for cavity-nesting communities in British Columbia, Canada: Nest characteristics and niche partitioning. Condor 106(1): 5-19.

McClelland, R. B.; Frissell, S. S.; Fischer, W. C.; Halvorson C. H. 1979. Habitat management for hole-nesting birds in forests of western larch and Douglas-fir. Journal of Forestry 77: 480-483.

Patterson, P. L.; Coulston, J. W.; Roesch, F. A.; [and others]. 2012. A primer for nonresponse in the US forest inventory and analysis program. Environmental Monitoring and Assessment 184(3): 1423-1433.

Pollard, J. E.; Westfall, J. A.; Patterson, P. L.; [and others]. 2006. Forest inventory and analysis national data quality assessment report 2000 to 2003. Gen. Tech. Rep. RMRS-GTR-181. Fort Collins, CO: U.S. Department of Agriculture, Forest Service, Rocky Mountain Research Station. 43 p.

Pyne, S. J. 2008. Year of the fires: The story of the great fires of 1910. Revised Ed. Missoula, MT: Mountain Press Publishing Company. 320 p.

Reineke, L. H. 1933. Perfecting a stand density index for even-aged forests. Journal of Agricultural Research 46(7): 627-638.

Rudinsky, J. A. 1962. Ecology of Scolytidae. Annu. Rev. Entomol. 7: 327-348.

Schmidt, W. C.; McDonald, K. J. 1990. Proceedings: Symposium on whitebark pine ecosystems: Ecology and management of a high-mountain resource. Gen. Tech. Rep. INT-270. Ogden, UT: U.S. Department of Agriculture, Forest Service, Intermountain Research Station. 386 p.

Shaw, J. D. 2000. Application of stand density index to irregularly structured stands. Western Journal of Applied Forestry 15: 40-42.

Shaw, J. D.; Steed, B. E.; DeBlander, L. T. 2005. Forest Inventory and Analysis (FIA) annual inventory answers the question: What is happening to pinyon-juniper woodlands? Journal of Forestry 103(6): 280-285.

Shaw, J. D.; Long, J. N. [In prep]. Consistent definition and use of stand density index.

Shinneman, D.; McClellan, R.; Smith, R. 2000. The state of the Southern Rockies Ecoregion. Nederland, CO: Southern Rockies Ecosystem Project. Online: http://csfs. colostate.edu/foresttypes htm#ecoregions.

Smith, F. W.; Long, J. N. 1987. Elk hiding and thermal cover guidelines in the context of lodgepole pine stand density. Western Journal of Applied Forestry 2: 6-10.

Thompson, M. T. 2009. Analysis of conifer mortality in Colorado using Forest Inventory and Analysis's annual forest inventory. Western Journal of Applied Forestry. 24(4): 193-197.

Thompson, M. T.; Duda, J. A.; DeBlander, L. T.; [and others]. 2010. Colorado's forest resources, 2002-2006. Resour. Bull. RMRS-RB-11. Fort Collins, CO: U.S. Department of Agriculture, Forest Service, Rocky Mountain Research Station. 108 p.

U.S. Forest Service. 2011. Interior West Forest Inventory and Analysis Forest Survey field procedures, Ver. 5.0. Online: http://fsweb.ogden rmrs.fs fed.us/manual/pdf/iwfia_ p2_50.pdf. U.S [Accessed August 2011].

U.S. Department of Agriculture, Forest Service. 2006-2009. Forest survey field procedures. Unpublished field guide on file at: U.S. Department of Agriculture, Forest Service, Rocky Mountain Research Station, Forestry Sciences Laboratory, Interior West Forest Inventory and Analysis Program, Ogden, UT. Online: http://fsweb.ogden rmrs.fs fed.us/ manual/manual html [December 1 2011].

Vosick, D.; Ostergren, D. M.; Murfitt, L. 2007. Old-growth policy. 2007. Ecology and Society 12(2): 19. Online: http://www.ecologyandsociety.org/vol12/iss2/art19/ [January 15 2012].

Wilson, M. J.; Deblander, L. T.; Halverson, K. A. 2010. Resource impacts of the 1910 fires: A Forest Inventory and Analysis (FIA) perspective. Powerpoint presentation given at: 1910 Fires: A Century Later. Wallace, Idaho, May 20-22, 2010. Unpublished document on file at: U.S. Department of Agriculture, Forest Service, Intermountain Region, Ogden, UT.

Woodall, C. W.; Monleon, V. J. 2008. Sampling protocol, estimation, and analysis procedures for the down woody materials indicator of the FIA program. Gen. Tech. Rep. NRS-22. Newtown Square, PA: U.S. Department of Agriculture, Forest Service, Northern Research Station. 68 p.

Worrall, J. J.; Egeland, L.; Eager, T.; [and others]. 2008. Rapid mortality of *Populus tremuloides* in southwestern Colorado, USA. Forest Ecology and Management 255(3-4): 686-696.

USDA Forest Service Resour. Bull. RMRS-RB-14. 2012

75

Appendix A: Species Group, Common Name, Scientific Name, and Timber (T) or Woodland (W) Designation for Trees Measured in Idaho's Annual Inventory.

Cottonwood and aspen
  Black cottonwood (*Populus balsamifera* ssp. *trichocarpa*) T
  Narrowleaf cottonwood (*Populus angustifolia*) T
  Quaking aspen (*Populus tremuloides*) T
Douglas-fir
  Douglas-fir (*Pseudotsuga menziesii*) T
Engelmann and other spruces
  Engelmann spruce (*Picea engelmannii*) T
Lodgepole pine
  Lodgepole pine (*Pinus contorta*) T
Other western hardwoods
  Paper birch (*Betula papyrifera*) T
  Water birch (*Betula occidentalis*) T
Other western softwoods
  Limber pine (*Pinus flexilis*) T
  Mountain hemlock (*Tsuga mertensiana*) T
  Pacific yew (*Taxus brevifolia*) T
  Subalpine larch (*Larix lyallii*) T
  Whitebark pine (*Pinus albicaulis*) T
Ponderosa and Jeffrey pines
  Ponderosa pine (*Pinus ponderosa*) T
Red alder
  Red alder (*Alnus rubra*) T
True fir
  Grand fir (*Abies grandis*) T
  Subalpine fir (*Abies lasiocarpa*) T
Western hemlock
  Western hemlock (*Tsuga heterophylla*) T
Western larch
  Western larch (*Larix occidentalis*) T
Western redcedar
  Western redcedar (*Thuja plicata*) T
Western white pine
  Western white pine (*Pinus monticola*) T
Western woodland hardwoods
  Bigtooth maple (*Acer grandidentatum*) W
  Curlleaf mountain-mahogany (*Cercocarpus ledifolius*) W
Western woodland softwoods
  Rocky Mountain juniper (*Juniperus scopulorum*) W
  Singleleaf pinyon (*Pinus monophylla*) W
  Western juniper (*Juniperus occidentalis*) W
  Utah juniper (*Juniperus osteosperma*) W

76

USDA Forest Service Resour. Bull. RMRS-RB-14. 2012

Appendix B: Forest Type Groups, Forest Type Names, and Timber (T) or Woodland (W) Designation for Forest Type.

Alder-maple group
Red alder T
Aspen-birch group
Aspen T
Paper birch T
Douglas-fir group
Douglas-fir T
Elm-ash-cottonwood group
Cottonwood T
Fir-spruce-mountain hemlock group
Engelmann spruce T
Engelmann spruce-subalpine fir T
Grand fir T
Mountain hemlock T
Subalpine fir T
Hemlock-Sitka spruce group
Western hemlock T
Western redcedar T
Lodgepole pine group
Lodgepole pine T
Nonstocked
Nonstocked (only as stand-size class) T or W
Other hardwoods group
Other hardwoods W
Other western softwoods group
Limber pine T
Whitebark pine T
Western juniper W
Pinyon-juniper group
Juniper woodland W
Pinyon-juniper woodland W
Rocky Mountain juniper W
Ponderosa pine group
Ponderosa pine T
Western white pine group
Western white pine T
Western larch group
Western larch T
Woodland hardwoods group
Cercocarpus (mountain brush) woodland W
Intermountain maple woodland W

USDA Forest Service Resour. Bull. RMRS-RB-14. 2012

77

Appendix C: Volume, Biomass, and Site Index Equation Sources.

Volume

Chojnacky (1985) was used for curlleaf mountain-mahogany volume estimation.

Chojnacky (1994) was used for Rocky Mountain juniper and Utah juniper volume estimation.

Kemp (1956) was used for black cottonwood, Engelmann spruce, mountain hemlock, narrowleaf cottonwood, paper birch, plains cottonwood, quaking aspen, red alder, subalpine fir, water birch, western hemlock, and western redcedar volume estimation.

Volume equations provided by the USDA Forest Service's Northern Research Station were used for American elm, boxelder, and green ash volume estimation. [Documentation on file at Rocky Mountain Research Station, Ogden, UT.]

Biomass

Chojnacky (1984) was used for curlleaf mountain mahogany biomass estimation.

Chojnacky and Moisen (1993) was used for Rocky Mountain juniper and Utah juniper biomass estimation.

Van Hooser and Chojnacky (1983) was used for all timber (T) species biomass estimation.

Site Index

Brickell (1970) was used for Douglas-fir, Engelmann spruce, limber pine, lodgepole pine, Pacific yew, ponderosa pine, and subalpine fir, subalpine larch, western larch, western white pine, and whitebark pine site index estimation.

Edminster and others (1985) was used for American elm, black cottonwood, boxelder, green ash, narrowleaf cottonwood, paper birch, plains cottonwood, quaking aspen, red alder, and water birch site index estimation.

Stage (1966, 1969) was used for grand fir site index estimation. [Original equations were reformulated by J. Shaw; documentation on file at Rocky Mountain Research Station, Ogden, UT.]

Equations from RMSTAND (USDA 1993) were used for mountain hemlock, western hemlock, and western redcedar site index estimation.

Stage (1966, 1969) was used for white fir site index estimation. [Original equations were reformulated by J. Shaw; documentation on file at U.S. Department of Agriculture, Forest Service, Rocky Mountain Research Station, Inventory Monitoring, Ogden, UT.]

Appendix D: Standard Reporting Tables.

Table 1: Percentage of area by land status.
Table 2: Area of accessible forest land by owner class and forest land status.
Table 3: Area of accessible forest land by forest type group and productivity class.
Table 4: Area of accessible forest land by forest type group, ownership group, and land status.
Table 5: Area of accessible forest land by forest type group and stand-size class.
Table 6: Area of accessible forest land by forest type group and stand-age class.
Table 7: Area of accessible forest land by forest type group and stand origin.
Table 8: Area of forest land by forest type group and primary disturbance class.
Table 9: Area of timberland by forest type group and stand-size class.
Table 10: Number of live trees on forest land by species group and diameter class.
Table 11: Number of growing stock trees on timberland by species group and diameter class.
Table 12: Net volume of all live trees by owner class and forest land status.
Table 13: Net volume of all live trees on forest land by forest type group and stand-size class.
Table 14: Net volume of all live trees on forest land by species group and ownership group.
Table 15: Net volume of all live trees on forest land by species group and diameter class.
Table 16: Net volume of all live trees on forest land by forest type group and stand origin.
Table 17: Net volume of growing stock trees on timberland by species group and diameter class.
Table 18: Net volume of growing stock trees on timberland by species group and ownership group.
Table 19: Net volume of sawtimber trees (International 1/4 inch rule) on timberland by species group and diameter class.
Table 20: Net volume of sawtimber trees on timberland by species group and ownership group.
Table 21: Average annual net growth of all live trees by owner class and forest land status.
Table 22: Average annual net growth of all live trees on forest land by forest type group and stand-size class.
Table 23: Average annual net growth of all live trees on forest land by species group and ownership group.
Table 24: Average annual net growth of growing stock trees on timberland by species group and ownership group.
Table 25: Average annual mortality of all live trees by owner class and forest land status.
Table 26: Average annual mortality of all live trees on forest land by forest type group and stand-size class.
Table 27: Average annual mortality of all live trees on forest land by species group and ownership group.
Table 28: Average annual mortality of growing stock trees on timberland by species group and ownership group.
Table 29a: Aboveground dry weight (regional equation method) of all live trees by owner class and forest land status.
Table 29b: Aboveground dry weight (component ratio method) of all live trees by owner class and forest land status.
Table 30a: Aboveground dry weight (regional equation method) of all live trees on forest land by species group and diameter class.
Table 30b: Aboveground dry weight (component ratio method) of all live trees on forest land by species group and diameter class.
Table 31: Area of accessible forest land by Forest Survey Unit, county and forest land status.
Table 32: Area of accessible forest land by Forest Survey Unit, county, ownership group and forest land status.
Table 33: Area of timberland by Forest Survey Unit, county and stand-size class.
Table 34: Area of timberland by Forest Survey Unit, county and stocking class.
Table 35: Net volume of growing stock and sawtimber (International 1/4 inch rule) on timberland by Forest Survey Unit, county, and major species group.
Table 36: Average annual net growth of growing stock and sawtimber (International 1/4 inch rule) on timberland by Forest Survey Unit, county, and major species group.
Table 37: Sampling errors by Forest Survey Unit and county for area of timberland, volume, average annual net growth, average annual removals, and average annual mortality on timberland.

Table 1—Percentage of area by land status, Idaho, cycle 2, 2004-2009.

Land status	Percentage of area
Accessible forest land	
Unreserved forest land	
Timberland	29.9
Unproductive	2.2
Total unreserved forest land	32.1
Reserved forest land	
Productive	6.2
Unproductive	0.2
Total reserved forest land	6.3
All accessible forest land	38.4
Nonforest and other land	
Nonforest land	58.0
Water	
Census	1.1
Non-Census	0.1
All nonforest and other land	59.1
Nonsampled land	
Access denied	1.2
Hazardous conditions	1.0
Other	0.2
All land	100.0
Total area (thousands of acres)	53,485

All table cells without observations in the inventory sample are indicated by --. Table value of 0.0 indicates the percentage rounds to less than 0.1 percent. Columns and rows may not add to their totals due to rounding.

80

USDA Forest Service Resour. Bull. RMRS-RB-14. 2012

Table 2—Area of accessible forest land by owner class and forest land status, Idaho, cycle 2, 2004-2009.
(In thousand acres)

Owner class	Unreserved forests			Reserved forests			All forest land
	Timberland	Unproductive	Total	Productive	Unproductive	Total	
Forest Service							
National forest	12,226.7	539.9	12,766.6	3,388.2	68.1	3,456.3	16,222.9
Other Federal							
National Park Service	--	--	--	61.6	19.1	80.6	80.6
Bureau of Land Management	613.8	330.3	944.1	--	--	--	944.1
Department of Defense or Energy	21.5	10.1	31.7	--	--	--	31.7
State and local government							
State	1,183.2	85.0	1,268.2	31.4	--	31.4	1,299.5
Private							
Undifferentiated private	2,571.6	239.2	2,810.8	--	--	--	2,810.8
All owners	16,616.8	1,204.5	17,821.3	3,481.1	87.2	3,568.3	21,389.6

All table cells without observations in the inventory sample are indicated by --. Table value of 0.0 indicates the acres round to less than 0.1 thousand acres. Columns and rows may not add to their totals due to rounding.

Table 3—Area of accessible forest land by forest type group and productivity class, Idaho, cycle 2, 2004-2009. (In thousand acres).

Forest-type group	Site productivity class (cubic feet/acre/year)							All classes
	0-19	20-49	50-84	85-119	120-164	165-224	225+	
Pinyon / juniper group	306.5	--	--	--	--	--	--	306.5
Douglas-fir group	35.2	2,023.3	2,207.6	1,368.8	569.3	84.3	--	6,288.5
Ponderosa pine group	--	284.0	807.6	393.3	105.2	--	--	1,590.2
Western white pine group	--	10.8	--	14.8	19.7	9.8	--	55.1
Fir / spruce / mountain hemlock group	10.6	1,608.1	2,187.1	1,387.2	722.0	100.9	--	6,015.9
Lodgepole pine group	110.5	1,528.1	677.8	124.5	14.9	--	--	2,455.8
Hemlock / Sitka spruce group	--	9.9	252.2	397.2	217.7	10.6	--	887.5
Western larch group	--	1.9	44.5	100.4	32.5	--	--	279.3
Other western softwoods group	249.3	400.0	6.6	--	--	--	--	655.9
Elm / ash / cottonwood group	--	10.0	23.2	39.9	--	--	--	73.0
Aspen / birch group	126.1	492.1	159.1	17.2	--	--	--	794.5
Alder / maple group	--	6.8	--	--	--	--	--	6.8
Other hardwoods group	2.8	--	--	--	--	--	--	2.8
Woodland hardwoods group	279.0	--	--	--	--	--	--	279.0
Nonstocked	171.7	904.8	391.5	161.7	55.8	13.3	--	1,698.9
All forest-type groups	1,291.7	7,279.7	6,872	4,004.9	1,737.0	219.0	--	21,389.6

All table cells without observations in the inventory sample are indicated by --. Table value of 0.0 indicates the acres round to less than 0.1 thousand acres. Columns and rows may not add to their totals due to rounding.

USDA Forest Service Resour. Bull. RMRS-RB-14. 2012

Table 4—Area of accessible forest land by forest type group, ownership group, and land status, Idaho, cycle 2, 2004-2009. (In thousand acres)

Forest-type group	Forest Service		Other Federal		State and local government		Undifferentiated private		All forest land
	Timber-land	Other forest land	Timber-land	Other forest land	Timber-land	Other forest land	Timber-land	Other forest land	
Pinyon / juniper group	--	67.2	--	120.8	--	--	--	118.5	306.5
Douglas-fir group	3,964.5	990.4	260.7	10.0	299.7	--	763.1	--	6,288.5
Ponderosa pine group	893.1	200.6	30.4	--	126.9	--	339.2	--	1,590.2
Western white pine group	35.4	--	--	--	--	9.8	9.9	--	55.1
Fir / spruce / mountain hemlock group	3,909.7	957.1	88.1	10.3	406.8	21.5	622.3	--	6,015.9
Lodgepole pine group	1,552.4	704.0	--	61.6	38.5	--	92.5	6.8	2,455.8
Hemlock / Sitka spruce group	430.3	21.2	19.6	--	99.8	--	316.6	--	887.5
Western larch group	139.7	--	--	--	57.9	--	81.7	--	279.3
Other western softwoods group	211.5	175.4	64.7	100.3	44.7	37.1	--	22.3	655.9
Elm / ash / cottonwood group	--	--	10.4	--	2.5	--	60.1	--	73.0
Aspen / birch group	407.6	84.5	62.5	12.2	35.8	18.0	139.3	34.7	794.5
Alder / maple group	--	--	--	--	--	--	6.8	--	6.8
Other hardwoods group	--	--	--	--	--	--	--	2.8	2.8
Woodland hardwoods group	--	147.0	--	74.0	--	20.1	--	37.9	279.0
Nonstocked	682.4	648.9	99.0	31.8	70.6	9.9	140.2	16.1	1,698.9
All forest-type groups	12,226.7	3,996.3	635.3	421.0	1,183.2	116.3	2,571.6	239.2	21,389.6

All table cells without observations in the inventory sample are indicated by --. Table value of 0.0 indicates the acres round to less than 0.1 thousand acres. Columns and rows may not add to their totals due to rounding.

Table 5—Area of accessible forest land by forest type group and stand-size class, Idaho, cycle 2, 2004-2009. (In thousand acres).

Forest-type group	Stand-size class					All size classes
	Large diameter	Medium diameter	Small diameter	Chaparral	Nonstocked	
Pinyon / juniper group	283.2	20.5	2.8	--	--	306.5
Douglas-fir group	5,191.0	401.4	696.1	--	--	6,288.5
Ponderosa pine group	1,407.3	27.3	155.6	--	--	1,590.2
Western white pine group	33.7	10.6	10.8	--	--	55.1
Fir / spruce / mou tain hemlock group	4,291.3	543.8	1,180.8	--	--	6,015.9
Lodgepole pine group	1,044.8	789.6	621.5	--	--	2,455.8
Hemlock / Sitka spruce group	710.7	78.7	98.1	--	--	887.5
Western larch group	167.4	59.7	52.1	--	--	279.3
Other western softwoods group	486.3	35.2	134.4	--	--	655.9
Elm / ash / cottonwood group	73.0	--	--	--	--	73.0
Aspen / birch group	117.9	283.9	392.7	--	--	794.5
Alder / maple group	--	--	6.8	--	--	6.8
Other hardwoods group	--	--	2.8	--	--	2.8
Woodland hardwoods group	126.6	55.4	97.0	--	--	279.0
Nonstocked	--	--	--	--	1,698.9	1,698.9
All forest-type groups	13,933.0	2,306.1	3,451.6	--	1,698.9	21,389.6

All table cells without observations in the inventory sample are indicated by --. Table value of 0.0 indicates the acres round to less than 0.1 thousand acres. Columns and rows may not add to their totals due to rounding.

Table 6—Area of accessible forest land by forest type group and stand-age class, Idaho, cycle 2, 2004-2009. (In thousand acres).

Forest-type group	Non stocked	Stand-age class (years)											All classes
		1-20	21-40	41-60	61-80	81-100	101-120	121-140	141-160	161-180	181-200	201+	
Pinyon / juniper group	--	--	2.8	52.1	56.0	66.2	50.2	17.8	20.5	7.6	20.3	12.7	306.5
Douglas-fir group	--	555.7	188.8	456.1	1,096.0	1,389.0	1,103.1	507.9	343.2	214.9	149.7	284.1	6,288.5
Ponderosa pine group	--	148.2	24.4	240.4	380.4	315.3	184.8	111.4	71.3	20.5	39.2	54.1	1,590.2
Western white pine group	--	10.8	9.9	10.6	9.8	--	4.2	--	9.8	--	--	--	55.1
Fir / spruce / mountain hemlock group	--	840.9	365.2	270.1	734.7	1,038.6	876.2	792.1	450.7	262.9	181.4	203.2	6,015.9
Lodgepole pine group	--	536.4	105.1	176.3	448.9	569.2	263.6	183.7	114.7	36.8	21.0	--	2,455.8
Hemlock / Sitka spruce group	--	78.1	22.6	68.5	191.5	193.9	112.3	116.9	34.9	26.3	21.9	20.6	887.5
Western larch group	--	52.1	--	33.4	114.0	29.8	33.9	10.8	5.3	--	--	--	279.3
Other western softwoods group	--	67.6	57.2	9.9	19.8	67.3	49.7	51.5	57.7	75.8	64.6	134.8	655.9
Elm / ash / cottonwood group	--	--	--	--	40.5	22.8	9.7	--	--	--	--	--	73.0
Aspen / birch group	--	307.9	80.3	113.4	201.0	78.4	13.5	--	--	--	--	--	794.5
Alder / maple group	--	6.8	--	--	--	--	--	--	--	--	--	--	6.8
Other hardwoods group	--	2.8	--	--	--	--	--	--	--	--	--	--	2.8
Woodland hardwoods group	--	36.4	55.6	20.8	20.4	46.2	24.6	51.9	5.2	7.9	--	10.2	279.0
Nonstocked	1,698.9	--	--	--	--	--	--	--	--	--	--	--	1,698.9
All forest-type groups	1,698.9	2,643.7	911.9	1,451.5	3,312.9	3,816.9	2,725.8	1,844.0	1,113.4	652.7	498.1	719.7	21,389.6

All table cells without observations in the inventory sample are indicated by --. Table value of 0.0 indicates the acres round to less than 0.1 thousand acres. Columns and rows may not add to their totals due to rounding.

Table 7—Area of accessible forest land by forest type group and stand origin, Idaho, cycle 2, 2004-2009. (In thousand acres).

Forest-type group	Stand origin		All forest land
	Natural stands	Artificial regeneration	
Pinyon / juniper group	306.5	- -	306.5
Douglas-fir group	6,237.3	51.2	6,288.5
Ponderosa pine group	1,482.0	108.2	1,590.2
Western white pine group	55.1	- -	55.1
Fir / spruce / mountain hemlock group	5,995.4	20.5	6,015.9
Lodgepole pine group	2,436.6	19.2	2,455.8
Hemlock / Sitka spruce group	887.5	- -	887.5
Western larch group	268.2	11.1	279.3
Other western softwoods group	655.9	- -	655.9
Elm / ash / cottonwood group	73.0	- -	73.0
Aspen / birch group	784.2	10.3	794.5
Alder / maple group	6.8	- -	6.8
Other hardwoods group	2.8	- -	2.8
Woodland hardwoods group	279.0	- -	279.0
Nonstocked	1,689.5	9.4	1,698.9
All forest-type groups	21,159.8	229.8	21,389.6

All table cells without observations in the inventory sample are indicated by --. Table value of 0.0 indicates the acres round to less than 0 1 thousand acres Columns and rows may not add to their totals due to rounding

Table 8—Area of forest land by forest type group primary disturbance class, Idaho, cycle 2, 2004-2009. (In thousand acres)

Forest-type group	Disturbance class									All forest land
	None	Insects	Disease	Weather	Fire	Domestic animals	Wild animals	Human	Other	
Pinyon / juniper group	278.9	--	--	--	7.3	20.3	--	--	--	306.5
Douglas-fir group	5,419.6	252.2	232.0	--	237.7	115.2	5.0	--	19.7	6,288.5
Ponderosa pine group	1,368.7	19.3	29.7	--	149.8	14.1	--	8.6	--	1,590.2
Western white pine group	55.1	--	--	--	--	--	--	--	--	55.1
Fir / spruce / mountain hemlock group	5,400.2	246.6	124.9	11.3	134.8	38.4	--	10.8	15.1	6,015.9
Lodgepole pine group	1,997.4	172.0	57.1	--	175.4	53.8	--	--	--	2,455.8
Hemlock / Sitka spruce group	837.4	--	28.7	10.6	--	--	--	--	--	887.5
Western larch group	268.9	--	--	--	10.4	--	--	--	--	279.3
Other western softwoods group	527.3	57.3	--	21.0	15.6	29.8	--	--	--	655.9
Elm / ash / cottonwood group	70.5	--	--	--	--	2.5	--	--	--	73.0
Aspen / birch group	724.0	--	17.5	--	33.9	9.2	--	--	--	794.5
Alder / maple group	6.8	--	--	--	--	--	--	--	--	6.8
Other hardwoods group	2.8	--	--	--	--	--	--	--	--	2.8
Woodland hardwoods group	271.7	--	--	--	--	7.3	--	--	--	279.0
Nonstocked	1,010.2	42.0	10.7	--	590.0	43.1	--	--	--	1,698.9
All forest-type groups	18,239.5	789.5	500.5	42.9	1,355.0	333.8	5.0	19.4	34.7	21,389.6

All table cells without observations in the inventory sample are indicated by --. Table value of 0.0 indicates the acres round to less than 0.1 thousand acres. Columns and rows may not add to their totals due to rounding.

USDA Forest Service Resour. Bull. RMRS-RB-14. 2012

87

Table 9—Area of timberland by forest type group and stand-size class, Idaho, cycle 2, 2004-2009. (In thousand acres).

Forest-type group	Stand-size class					All size classes
	Large diameter	Medium diameter	Small diameter	Chaparral	Nonstocked	
Douglas-fir group	4,448.4	315.8	523.7	--	--	5,288.0
Ponderosa pine group	1,209.3	27.3	153.0	--	--	1,389.6
Western white pine group	23.9	10.6	10.8	--	--	45.3
Fir / spruce / mou tain hemlock group	3,605.8	466.9	954.3	--	--	5,027.0
Lodgepole pine group	764.3	585.9	333.2	-	--	1,683.4
Hemlock / Sitka spruce group	689.5	78.7	98.1	--	--	866.3
Western larch group	167.4	59.7	52.1	--	--	279.3
Other western softwoods group	267.6	10.0	43.2	--	--	320.8
Elm / ash / cottonwood group	73.0	--	--	--	--	73.0
Aspen / birch group	117.9	223.6	303.6	--	--	645.1
Alder / maple group	--	--	6.8	--	--	6.8
Nonstocked	--	--	--	--	992.2	992.2
All forest-type groups	11,367.1	1,778.6	2,479.0	--	992.2	16,616.8

All table cells without observations in the inventory sample are indicated by --. Table value of 0.0 indicates the acres round to less than 0.1 thousand acres. Col mns and rows may not add to their totals due to rounding.

Table 10—Number of live trees on forest land by species group and diameter class, Idaho, cycle 2, 2004-2009. (In thousand trees).

| Species group | Diameter class (inches) | | | | | | | | | | | | | | | All classes |
	1.0-2.9	3.0-4.9	5.0-6.9	7.0-8.9	9.0-10.9	11.0-12.9	13.0-14.9	15.0-16.9	17.0-18.9	19.0-20.9	21.0-24.9	25.0-28.9	29.0-32.9	33.0-36.9	37.0+	
Softwood species groups																
Western softwood species groups																
Douglas-fir	462,333	213,425	143,142	111,957	97,979	80,244	61,181	44,723	28,021	21,981	24,087	10,847	3,705	2,779	864	1,307,268
Ponderosa and Jeffrey pines	58,548	29,618	21,597	15,567	13,531	10,315	8,273	7,470	4,928	4,667	6,372	4,018	1,894	635	435	187,867
True fir	1,433,498	514,848	265,531	168,671	107,889	68,173	43,911	29,498	18,985	11,629	12,756	4,971	2,390	1,356	1,075	2,685,182
Western hemlock	141,595	50,113	24,689	16,585	9,148	5,524	3,843	2,194	1,041	430	1,278	245	241	122	--	257,046
Western white pine	38,990	17,671	5,673	3,285	1,465	1,172	860	667	545	302	605	190	59	--	--	71,486
Engelmann and other spruces	120,644	57,155	32,672	24,731	17,191	15,194	11,863	8,043	6,931	4,441	6,777	2,745	849	816	249	310,300
Western larch	17,075	7,459	10,369	9,378	8,260	5,899	4,572	3,556	1,718	1,100	1,378	553	380	124	--	71,821
Lodgepole pine	463,326	269,995	206,961	154,539	89,211	44,768	20,337	8,689	3,290	1,373	680	--	--	--	--	1,263,170
Western redcedar	233,820	80,495	42,518	23,900	16,262	10,577	6,310	5,760	5,303	2,179	3,498	2,082	1,458	627	1,760	436,549
Western woodland softwoods	19,502	10,117	9,883	7,978	6,580	4,073	3,230	2,641	1,900	1,001	697	620	261	122	--	68,603
Other western softwoods	226,299	96,696	44,316	33,258	20,843	13,356	8,376	5,741	5,054	2,304	3,269	901	365	122	121	461,019
All softwoods	3,215,629	1,347,593	807,349	569,849	388,359	259,295	172,757	118,982	77,714	51,405	61,398	27,172	11,603	6,702	4,503	7,120,312
Hardwood species groups																
Western hardwood species groups																
Cottonwood and aspen	216,317	54,603	23,726	20,258	10,571	6,331	2,188	989	620	299	311	304	122	--	--	336,638
Red alder	6,720	739	648	254	59	194	194	65	--	65	--	--	--	--	--	8,939
Other western hardwoods	12,830	4,670	9,995	3,941	2,113	1,202	246	127	64	--	--	--	--	--	--	35,188
Western woodland hardwoods	176,168	57,198	19,473	12,512	5,597	2,664	1,312	400	242	239	197	--	--	--	--	276,002
All hardwoods	412,036	117,210	53,843	36,964	18,340	10,391	3,940	1,581	926	603	508	304	122	--	--	656,767
All species groups	3,627,665	1,464,803	861,192	606,814	406,699	269,686	176,698	120,563	78,640	52,009	61,906	27,476	11,725	6,702	4,503	7,777,079

All table cells without observations in the inventory sample are indicated by --. Table value of 0 indicates the number of trees rounds to less than 1 thousand trees. Columns and rows may not add to their totals due to rounding.

Table 11—Number of growing stock trees on timberland by species group and diameter class, Idaho, cycle 2, 2004-2009. (In thousand trees).

Species group	Diameter class (inches)													All classes
	5.0-6.9	7.0-8.9	9.0-10.9	11.0-12.9	13.0-14.9	15.0-16.9	17.0-18.9	19.0-20.9	21.0-24.9	25.0-28.9	29.0-32.9	33.0-36.9	37.0+	
Softwood species groups														
Western softwood species groups														
Douglas-fir	117,970	90,330	82,452	66,892	52,619	39,274	24,128	18,662	19,695	9,453	3,150	2,588	674	527,886
Ponderosa and Jeffrey pines	19,434	13,934	12,458	9,492	7,270	6,769	4,292	3,710	5,672	3,321	1,319	379	309	88,360
True fir	219,000	137,756	89,904	57,768	37,547	26,020	16,762	9,845	10,533	4,398	1,880	1,042	1,011	613,466
Western hemlock	24,263	16,520	9,083	5,524	3,778	2,129	1,041	430	1,278	245	241	122	--	64,654
Western white pine	5,609	3,226	1,465	1,172	860	667	545	302	487	190	--	--	--	14,524
Engelmann and other spruces	25,710	19,988	13,349	11,794	8,832	5,464	5,489	3,245	5,441	2,308	663	373	188	102,844
Western larch	10,304	9,378	8,196	5,899	4,572	3,556	1,718	1,100	1,378	553	380	124	--	47,159
Lodgepole pine	149,525	118,784	64,951	34,209	16,153	6,531	2,716	1,060	556	--	--	--	--	394,485
Western redcedar	41,307	23,403	16,134	10,513	6,119	5,444	5,175	2,051	3,052	2,017	1,331	627	1,505	118,680
Other western softwoods	29,091	22,315	14,571	9,238	6,094	4,058	3,845	1,507	2,503	546	365	122	--	94,255
All softwoods	642,213	455,635	312,565	212,502	143,844	99,913	65,712	41,911	50,595	23,030	9,329	5,377	3,686	2,066,312
Hardwood species groups														
Western hardwood species groups														
Cottonwood and aspen	15,922	15,347	9,085	5,422	1,883	873	378	299	311	304	122	--	--	49,945
Red alder	648	254	59	194	194	65	--	65	--	--	--	--	--	1,480
Other western hardwoods	9,562	3,941	2,113	1,202	246	127	64	--	--	--	--	--	--	17,255
All hardwoods	26,132	19,541	11,257	6,818	2,324	1,065	441	364	311	304	122	--	--	68,679
All species groups	668,345	475,176	323,823	219,320	146,168	100,978	66,153	42,276	50,905	23,333	9,451	5,377	3,686	2,134,992

All table cells without observations in the inventory sample are indicated by --. Table value of 0 indicates the number of trees rounds to less than 1 thousand trees. Columns and rows may not add to their totals due to rounding.

90

USDA Forest Service Resour. Bull. RMRS-RB-14. 2012

Table 12—Net volume of all live trees by owner class and forest land status, Idaho, cycle 2, 2004-2009. (In million cubic feet).

Owner class	Unreserved forests			Reserved forests			All forest land
	Timberland	Unproductive	Total	Productive	Unproductive	Total	
Forest Service							
National forest	30,911.7	353.0	31,264.7	6,486.9	26.5	6,513.3	37,778.0
Other Federal							
National Park Service	- -	- -	- -	55.2	5.2	60.4	60.4
Bureau of Land Management	1,061.6	119.0	1,180.6	- -	- -	- -	1,180.6
Department of Defense or Energy	144.8	12.3	157.2	- -	- -	- -	157.2
State and local government							
State	3,126.7	36.2	3,162.9	52.9	- -	52.9	3,215.8
Private							
Undifferentiated private	4,709.9	103.7	4,813.6	- -	- -	- -	4,813.6
All owners	39,954.8	624.2	40,579.0	6,594.9	31.7	6,626.6	47,205.6

All table cells without observations in the inventory sample are indicated by --. Table value of 0.0 indicates the volume rounds to less than 0.1 million cubic feet. Columns and rows may not add to their totals due to rounding.

Table 13—Net volume of all live trees on forest land by forest type group and stand-size class, Idaho, cycle 2, 2004-2009. (In million cubic feet).

Forest-type group	Large diameter	Medium diameter	Small diameter	Chaparral	Nonstocked	All size classes
Pinyon / junipe group	165.9	3.6	0.8	--	--	170.3
Douglas-fir g oup	14,383.8	500.3	295.1	--	--	15,179.2
Ponderosa pine group	3,084.0	16.8	28.9	--	--	3,129.7
Western white pine group	103.9	7.8	0.8	--	--	112.5
Fir / spruce / mountai hemlock group	15,870.4	821.5	573.6	--	--	17,265.6
Lodgepole pi e group	2,809.6	1,618.1	158.4	--	--	4,586.2
Hemlock / Sitka sp uce group	4,041.9	181.7	21.0	--	--	4,244.7
Western la ch group	716.3	124.6	24.2	--	--	865.2
Other western softwoods group	500.8	16.9	26.9	--	--	544.6
Elm / ash / cottonwood group	165.6	--	--	--	--	165.6
Aspen / birch group	233.4	349.3	87.1	--	--	669.8
Alder / maple group	--	--	6.0	--	--	6.0
Woodland hardwoods group	55.6	21.0	17.9	--	--	94.5
Nonstocked	--	--	--	--	171.8	171.8
All forest-type groups	42,131.3	3,661.7	1,240.8	--	171.8	47,205.6

All table cells without observations in the inventory sample are indicated by --. Table value of 0.0 indicates the volume rounds to less than 0.1 million cubic feet. Columns and rows may not add to their totals due to rounding.

Table 14—Net volume of all live trees on forest land by species group and ownership group, Idaho, cycle 2, 2004-2009. (In million cubic feet).

Species group	Forest Service	Other Federal	Ownership group State and local government	Undifferentiated private	All owners
Softwood species groups					
Western softwood species groups					
Douglas-fir	10,916.4	549.8	678.1	1,339.2	13,483.6
Ponderosa and Jeffrey pines	2,240.8	35.3	178.9	559.6	3,014.5
True fir	10,375.3	244.2	1,110.0	1,180.5	12,910.0
Western hemlock	642.5	35.5	84.0	238.9	1,001.0
Western white pine	178.1	11.0	85.2	53.0	327.3
Engelmann and other spruces	3,570.0	19.3	245.2	78.2	3,912.8
Western larch	806.5	32.2	158.8	220.5	1,218.0
Lodgepole pine	5,222.7	60.7	135.3	205.0	5,623.7
Western redcedar	2,063.8	35.2	392.0	557.6	3,048.6
Western woodland softwoods	61.0	70.8	0.7	75.5	207.9
Other western softwoods	1,341.6	178.3	61.9	19.9	1,601.7
All softwoods	37,418.6	1,272.3	3,130.1	4,528.0	46,349.1
Hardwood species groups					
Western hardwood species groups					
Cottonwood and aspen	275.6	76.8	65.2	191.3	608.8
Red alder	5.7	17.0	--	1.9	24.6
Other western hardwoods	31.9	5.3	14.1	81.7	132.9
Western woodland hardwoods	46.3	26.7	6.5	10.7	90.2
All hardwoods	359.4	125.8	85.7	285.6	856.5
All species groups	37,778.0	1,398.1	3,215.8	4,813.6	47,205.6

All table cells without observations in the inventory sample are indicated by --. Table value of 0.0 indicates the volume rounds to less than 0.1 million cubic feet. Columns and rows may not add to their totals due to rounding.

Table 15—Net volume of all live trees on forest land by species group and diameter class, Idaho, cycle 2, 2004-2009. (In million cubic feet).

Species group	Diameter class (inches)													All classes
	5.0-6.9	7.0-8.9	9.0-10.9	11.0-12.9	13.0-14.9	15.0-16.9	17.0-18.9	19.0-20.9	21.0-24.9	25.0-28.9	29.0-32.9	33.0-36.9	37.0+	
Softwood species groups														
Western softwood species groups														
Douglas-fir	329	622	1,024	1,387	1,581	1,573	1,318	1,331	1,888	1,188	521	517	206	13,484
Ponderosa and Jeffrey pines	31	62	106	146	177	242	227	288	556	494	371	147	167	3,015
True fir	886	1,183	1,365	1,413	1,366	1,312	1,169	898	1,324	742	499	322	431	12,910
Western hemlock	57	102	113	111	125	98	62	34	160	39	52	48	--	1,001
Western white pine	13	19	18	28	31	33	39	28	76	32	12	--	--	327
Engelmann and other spruces	101	168	219	310	370	349	410	349	727	439	169	216	88	3,913
Western larch	31	70	118	145	163	161	108	87	144	83	73	34	--	1,218
Lodgepole pine	672	1,193	1,277	1,049	662	414	196	99	63	--	--	--	--	5,624
Western redcedar	143	148	175	184	164	206	263	126	298	252	235	145	711	3,049
Western woodland softwoods	9	15	22	25	22	30	27	17	13	14	10	4	--	208
Other western softwoods	67	139	168	177	160	142	191	106	225	95	74	34	23	1,602
All softwoods	2,337	3,720	4,606	4,974	4,822	4,559	4,008	3,362	5,474	3,377	2,017	1,467	1,626	46,349
Hardwood species groups														
Western hardwood species groups														
Cottonwood and aspen	53	107	110	111	54	35	25	23	24	42	24	--	--	609
Red alder	1	1	1	5	8	4	--	4	--	--	--	--	--	25
Other western hardwoods	33	31	30	24	7	5	3	--	--	--	--	--	--	133
Western woodland hardwoods	18	22	15	12	9	4	3	3	4	--	--	--	--	90
All hardwoods	106	161	155	153	78	47	32	31	27	42	24	--	--	857
All species groups	2,443	3,882	4,761	5,126	4,900	4,607	4,040	3,393	5,501	3,419	2,041	1,467	1,626	47,206

All table cells without observations in the inventory sample are indicated by --. Table value of 0 indicates the volume rounds to less than 1 million cubic feet. Columns and rows may not add to their totals due to rounding.

94

USDA Forest Service Resour. Bull. RMRS-RB-14. 2012

Table 16—Net volume of all live trees on forest land by forest type group and stand origin, Idaho, cycle 2, 2004-2009.

(In million cubic feet).

| | Stand origin | | |
Forest-type group	Natural stands	Artificial regeneration	All forest land
Pinyon / junipe group	170.3	- -	170.3
Douglas-fir g oup	15,148.2	31.0	15,179.2
Ponderosa pine group	3,071.1	58.5	3,129.7
Western white pin group	112.5	- -	112.5
Fir / spruc / mounta n hemlock group	17,265.0	0.5	17,265.6
Lodgepole pi e group	4,579.9	6.3	4,586.2
Hemlock / Sitka sp uce group	4,244.7	- -	4,244.7
Western larch group	863.1	2.1	865.2
Other western softwoods group	544.6	- -	544.6
Elm / ash / cottonwood group	165.6	- -	165.6
Aspen / birch group	667.1	2.7	669.8
Alder / maple group	6.0	- -	6.0
Woodland hardwoods group	94.5	- -	94.5
Nonstocked	171.8	- -	171 8
All forest-type groups	47,104.3	101.2	47,205.6

All table cells without observations in the inventory sample are indicated by --. Table value of 0.0 indicates the volume rounds to less than 0.1 million cubic feet. Columns and rows may not add to their totals due to rounding.

Table 17—Net volume of growing stock trees on timberland by species group and diameter class, Idaho, cycle 2, 2004-2009. (In million cubic feet).

Species group	Diameter class (inches)													All classes
	5.0-6.9	7.0-8.9	9.0-10.9	11.0-12.9	13.0-14.9	15.0-16.9	17.0-18.9	19.0-20.9	21.0-24.9	25.0-28.9	29.0-32.9	33.0-36.9	37.0+	
Softwood species groups														
Western softwood species groups														
Douglas-fir	273	509	866	1,145	1,362	1,396	1,135	1,148	1,545	1,045	461	489	171	11,544
Ponderosa and Jeffrey pines	28	54	95	132	156	216	194	223	496	407	260	79	124	2,464
True fir	722	973	1,151	1,226	1,191	1,178	1,058	767	1,132	664	418	252	424	11,157
Western hemlock	56	102	112	111	123	97	62	34	160	39	52	48	--	998
Western white pine	13	19	18	28	31	33	39	28	61	32	--	--	--	301
Engelmann and other spruces	80	135	169	245	275	231	326	249	582	363	128	93	73	2,949
Western larch	31	70	117	145	163	161	108	87	144	83	73	34	--	1,217
Lodgepole pine	478	912	935	813	536	316	164	82	52	--	--	--	--	4,288
Western redcedar	139	145	174	183	160	194	256	118	256	248	211	145	590	2,818
Other western softwoods	43	98	124	136	127	117	163	79	196	71	74	34	--	1,261
All softwoods	1,862	3,016	3,761	4,164	4,124	3,940	3,504	2,815	4,625	2,951	1,677	1,175	1,382	38,996
Hardwood species groups														
Western hardwood species groups														
Cottonwood and aspen	40	88	100	103	51	32	17	23	24	42	24	--	--	545
Red alder	1	1	1	5	8	4	--	4	--	--	--	--	--	25
Other western hardwoods	32	31	30	24	7	5	3	--	--	--	--	--	--	132
All hardwoods	74	121	131	133	65	41	20	27	24	42	24	--	--	701
All species groups	1,935	3,137	3,892	4,297	4,189	3,980	3,524	2,842	4,648	2,994	1,702	1,175	1,382	39,697

All table cells w/hout observations in the inventory sample are indicated by --. Table value of 0 indicates the volume rounds to less than 1 million cubic feet. Columns and rows may not add to their totals due to rounding.

Table 18—Net volume of growing stock trees on timberland by species group and ownership group, Idaho, cycle 2, 2004-2009. (In million cubic feet).

Species group	Ownership group				All owners
	Forest Service	Other Federal	State and local government	Undifferentiated private	
Softwood species groups					
Western softwood species groups					
Douglas-fir	9,003.8	535.1	673.6	1,331.4	11,543.9
Ponderosa and Jeffrey pines	1,692.2	35.2	178.3	558.7	2,464.3
True fir	8,649.7	236.7	1,091.0	1,179.2	11,156.6
Western hemlock	642.2	35.5	82.3	237.6	997.6
Western white pine	177.7	11.0	58.8	53.0	300.5
Engelmann and other spruces	2,618.6	14.1	238.0	78.2	2,949.0
Western larch	805.4	32.2	158.8	220.5	1,216.9
Lodgepole pine	3,933.8	15.3	134.7	204.4	4,288.2
Western redcedar	1,838.8	35.2	391.7	552.6	2,818.3
Other western softwoods	1,061.9	151.4	36.0	11.5	1,260.8
All softwoods	30,424.1	1,101.7	3,043.2	4,427.1	38,996.1
Hardwood species groups					
Western hardwood species groups					
Cottonwood and aspen	241.0	72.1	59.8	171.8	544.7
Red alder	5.7	17.0	- -	1.9	24.6
Other western hardwoods	31.2	5.3	13.8	81.6	131.8
All hardwoods	277.8	94.4	73.6	255.3	701.1
All species groups	30,702.0	1,196.1	3,116.8	4,682.4	39,697.2

All table cells without observations in the inventory sample are indicated by --. Table value of 0.0 indicates the volume rounds to less than 0.1 million cubic feet. Columns and rows may not add to their totals due to rounding.

Table 19—Net volume of sawtimber trees (International 1/4 inch rule) on timberland by species group and diameter class, Idaho, cycle 2, 2004-2009. (In million board feet).

Species group	Diameter class (inches)											All classes
	9.0-10.9	11.0-12.9	13.0-14.9	15.0-16.9	17.0-18.9	19.0-20.9	21.0-24.9	25.0-28.9	29.0-32.9	33.0-36.9	37.0+	
Softwood species groups												
Western softwood species groups												
Douglas-fir	3,410	5,316	6,915	7,522	6,366	6,683	9,318	6,604	3,011	3,286	1,169	59,601
Ponderosa and Jeffrey pines	190	571	846	1,333	1,276	1,529	3,499	3,086	2,154	663	1,108	16,256
True fir	5,561	6,537	6,728	6,953	6,453	4,822	7,334	4,378	2,811	1,782	3,112	56,471
Western hemlock	488	569	686	565	368	207	1,011	248	338	315	--	4,796
Western white pine	90	155	181	200	246	181	402	221	--	--	--	1,677
Engelmann and other spruces	936	1,397	1,588	1,349	1,904	1,446	3,497	2,328	822	623	481	16,370
Western larch	633	799	924	936	637	521	871	496	428	199	--	6,443
Lodgepole pine	5,318	4,495	2,947	1,722	869	430	276	--	--	--	--	16,057
Western redcedar	848	947	869	1,061	1,434	663	1,456	1,428	1,228	823	3,411	14,167
Other western softwoods	564	678	673	636	930	449	1,194	428	477	217	--	6,246
All softwoods	18,038	21,464	22,357	22,277	20,482	16,932	28,857	19,217	11,269	7,910	9,280	198,084
Hardwood species groups												
Western hardwood species groups												
Cottonwood and aspen	--	524	261	166	86	118	129	213	117	--	--	1,614
Red alder	--	29	44	23	--	14	--	--	--	--	--	111
Other western hardwoods	--	126	37	23	15	--	--	--	--	--	--	201
All hardwoods	--	679	342	213	101	132	129	213	117	--	--	1,926
All species groups	18,038	22,142	22,699	22,490	20,583	17,065	28,986	19,430	11,386	7,910	9,280	200,010

All table cells wihout observations in the inventory sample are indicated by --. Table value of 0 indicates the volume rounds to less than 1 million board feet. Columns and rows may not add to their totals due to rounding.

Table 20—Net volume of sawtimber trees on timberland by species group and ownership group, Idaho, cycle 2, 2004-2009. (In million cubic feet).

Species group	Forest Service	Other Federal	State and local government	Undifferentiated private	All owners
Softwood species groups					
Western softwood species groups					
Douglas-fir	7,687.6	450.9	547.5	1,071.2	9,757.2
Ponderosa and Jeffrey pines	1,526.8	31.8	151.6	476.6	2,186.8
True fir	6,615.9	194.4	863.2	842.1	8,515.6
Western hemlock	488.3	27.8	59.1	132.7	707.9
Western white pine	150.6	10.4	52.3	40.7	254.1
Engelmann and other spruces	2,208.3	12.0	203.0	54.6	2,477.8
Western larch	684.6	28.4	127.7	163.6	1,004.3
Lodgepole pine	2,403.7	7.0	106.1	136.0	2,652.8
Western redcedar	1,504.9	29.9	295.3	355.8	2,185.7
Other western softwoods	813.2	130.3	32.6	9.3	985.4
All softwoods	24,083.8	922.9	2,438.5	3,282.7	30,727.8
Hardwood species groups					
Western hardwood species groups					
Cottonwood and aspen	78.1	39.0	23.7	104.2	245.0
Red alder	3.3	12.6	--	--	15.9
Other western hardwoods	9.8	--	1.7	16.9	28.3
All hardwoods	91.2	51.7	25.3	121.1	289.2
All species groups	24,175.0	974.5	2,463.8	3,403.8	31,017.1

All table cells without observations in the inventory sample are indicated by --. Table value of 0.0 indicates the volume rounds to less than 0.1 million cubic feet. Columns and rows may not add to their totals due to rounding.

USDA Forest Service Resour. Bull. RMRS-RB-14. 2012

99

Table 21—Average annual net growth of all live trees by owner class and forest land status, Idaho, cycle 2, 2004-2009. (In million cubic feet).

Owner class	Unreserved forests			Reserved forests			All forest land
	Timberland	Unproductive	Total	Productive	Unproductive	Total	
Forest Service							
National forest	247.3	-3.0	244.4	-138.9	-3.2	-142.2	102.2
Other Federal							
National Park Service	- -	- -	- -	0.9	0.2	1.1	1.1
Bureau of Land Management	18.9	-0.2	18.7	- -	- -	- -	18.7
Department of Defense or Energy	4.3	0.0	4.3	- -	- -	- -	4.3
State and local government							
State	80.3	0.6	80.9	0.1	- -	0.1	80.9
Private							
Undifferentiated private	167.2	1.7	168.8	- -	- -	- -	168.8
All owners	518.0	-0.8	517.1	-138.0	-3.0	-141.0	376.2

All table cells without observations in the inventory sample are indicated by --. Table value of 0.0 indicates the volume rounds to less than 0.1 million cubic feet. Columns and rows may not add to their totals due to rounding.

Table 22—Average annual net growth of all live trees on forest land by forest type group and stand-size class, Idaho, cycle 2, 2004-2009. (In million cubic feet).

Forest-type group	Stand-size class					All size classes
	Large diameter	Medium diameter	Small diameter	Chaparral	Non stocked	
Pinyon / juniper group	1.4	0.1	0.0	--	--	1.5
Douglas-fir g oup	176.9	16.7	4.1	--	--	197.6
Ponderosa pine group	40.9	1.4	-1.3	--	--	41.0
Western white pine group	2.3	1.1	0.1	--	--	3.6
Fir / spruce / mountai hemlock group	183.5	25.6	7.1	--	--	216.1
Lodgepole pi e group	11.5	14.2	-25.5	--	--	0.3
Hemlock / Sitka sp uce group	64.2	10.7	-3.0	--	--	71.8
Western la ch group	13.2	6.9	0.0	--	--	20.1
Other western softwoods group	0.2	0.1	-1.3	--	--	-1.0
Elm / ash / cottonwood group	3.9	--	--	--	--	3.9
Aspen / birch group	7.4	11.1	-6.1	--	--	12.4
Alder / maple group	--	--	0.7	--	--	0.7
Woodland hardwoods group	0.9	0.3	0.6	--	--	1.9
Nonstocked	--	--	--	--	-193.8	-193.8
All forest-type groups	506 2	88 1	-24.4	--	-193.8	376.2

All table cells without observations in the inventory sample are indicated by --. Table value of 0.0 indicates the volume rounds to less than 0.1 million cubic feet. Columns and rows may not add to their totals due to rounding.

Table 23—Average annual net growth of all live trees on forest land by species group and ownership group, Idaho, cycle 2, 2004-2009. (In million cubic feet).

Species group	Ownership group				
	Forest Service	Other Federal	State and local government	Undifferentiated private	All owners
Softwood species groups					
Western softwood species groups					
Douglas-fir	-14.8	10.0	13.7	47.3	56.3
Ponderosa and Jeffrey pines	12.0	0.5	5.7	16.2	34.4
True fir	96.5	6.6	35.1	49.7	188.0
Western hemlock	15.7	0.9	3.0	10.4	30.0
Western white pine	0.1	-0.1	0.2	2.6	2.8
Engelmann and other spruces	31.2	0.2	4.8	3.2	39.5
Western larch	10.6	0.3	3.3	5.3	19.6
Lodgepole pine	-80.1	0.5	0.3	3.9	-75.3
Western redcedar	30.1	1.2	12.4	20.6	64.4
Western woodland softwoods	0.7	-1.3	0.0	0.9	0.2
Other western softwoods	-7.8	2.8	1.1	0.4	-3.6
All softwoods	94.4	21.5	79.7	160.6	356.2
Hardwood species groups					
Western hardwood species groups					
Cottonwood and aspen	6.3	1.2	1.3	4.3	13.1
Red alder	0.2	0.5	--	0.3	1.0
Other western hardwoods	0.4	0.5	-0.1	3.3	4.1
Western woodland hardwoods	0.9	0.4	0.1	0.3	1.7
All hardwoods	7.8	2.7	1.2	8.2	19.9
All species groups	102.2	24.2	80.9	168.8	376.2

All table cells without observations in the inventory sample are indicated by --. Table value of 0.0 indicates the volume rounds to less than 0.1 million cubic feet. Columns and rows may not add to their totals due to rounding.

Table 24—Average annual net growth of growing stock trees on timberland by species group and ownership group, Idaho, cycle 2, 2004-2009. (In million cubic feet).

Species group	Ownership group				All owners
	Forest Service	Other Federal	State and local government	Undifferentiated private	
Softwood species groups					
Western softwood species groups					
Douglas-fir	67.2	9.8	13.5	47.1	137.6
Ponderosa and Jeffrey pines	17.3	0.5	5.7	16.1	39.5
True fir	114.4	6.6	34.7	49.7	205.4
Western hemlock	15.7	0.9	2.9	10.3	29.9
Western white pine	0.1	-0.1	-0.4	2.6	2.2
Engelmann and other spruces	32.3	0.2	6.0	3.2	41.6
Western larch	10.7	0.3	3.3	5.3	19.7
Lodgepole pine	-50.1	-0.5	0.3	3.8	-46.6
Western redcedar	29.0	1.2	12.4	20.5	63.1
Other western softwoods	4.2	2.1	0.7	0.3	7.2
All softwoods	240.8	20.9	79.0	158.8	499.5
Hardwood species groups					
Western hardwood species groups					
Cottonwood and aspen	6.0	1.0	1.1	3.8	12.0
Red alder	0.2	0.5	--	0.3	1.0
Other western hardwoods	0.4	0.5	-0.1	3.3	4.1
All hardwoods	6.6	2.1	1.0	7.4	17.1
All species groups	247.4	23.0	80.1	166.3	516.6

All table cells without observations in the inventory sample are indicated by --. Table value of 0.0 indicates the volume rounds to less than 0.1 million cubic feet. Columns and rows may not add to their totals due to rounding.

USDA Forest Service Resour. Bull. RMRS-RB-14. 2012

103

Table 25—Average annual mortality of all live trees by owner class and forest land status, Idaho, cycle 2, 2004-2009. (In million cubic feet).

Owner class	Unreserved forests			Reserved forests			All forest land
	Timberland	Unproductive	Total	Productive	Unproductive	Total	
Forest Service							
National forest	483.8	10.8	494.6	259.7	3.6	263.3	757.9
Other Federal							
National Park Service	- -	- -	- -	0.2	- -	0.2	0.2
Bureau of Land Management	4.8	1.9	6.7	- -	- -	- -	6.7
Department of Defense or Energy	0.2	- -	0.2	- -	- -	- -	0.2
State and local government							
State	22.1	0.1	22.2	1.6	- -	1.6	23.8
Private							
Undifferentiated private	25.7	0.2	25.9	- -	- -	- -	25.9
All owners	536.5	13.0	549.5	261.4	3.6	265.0	814.6

All table cells without observations in the inventory sample are indicated by --. Table value of 0.0 indicates the volume rounds to less than 0.1 million cubic feet. Columns and rows may not add to their totals due to rounding.

Table 26—Average annual mortality of all live trees on forest land by forest type group and stand-size class, Idaho, cycle 2, 2004-2009. (In million cubic feet).

Forest-type group	Stand-size class					All size classes
	Large diameter	Medium diameter	Small diameter	Chaparral	Non stocked	
Pinyon / junip group	0.3	--	--	--	--	0.3
Douglas-fir g oup	150.5	7.3	9.2	--	--	167.0
Ponderosa pine group	24.9	--	2.4	--	--	27.3
Western white pin group	2.1	--	--	--	--	2.1
Fir / spruce / mountain hemlock group	197.1	15.9	20.6	--	--	233.6
Lodgepole pi e group	49.3	40.6	34.4	--	--	124.3
Hemlock / Sitka sp uce group	26.1	0.1	4.5	--	--	30.8
Western la ch group	8.3	0.5	0.7	--	--	9.5
Other western softwoods group	5.8	0.4	2.0	--	--	8.3
Elm / ash / cotto wood gr up	0.0	--	--	--	--	0.0
Aspen / birch group	0.4	1.9	9.8	--	--	12.2
Woodland hardwoods group	--	0.0	0.0	--	--	0.0
Nonstocked	--	--	--	--	199.1	199.1
All forest-type groups	465.1	66.8	83.6	--	199.1	814.6

All table cells without observations in the inventory sample are indicated by --. Table value of 0.0 indicates the volume rounds to less than 0.1 million cubic feet. Columns and rows may not add to their totals due to rounding.

USDA Forest Service Resour. Bull. RMRS-RB-14. 2012

105

Table 27—Average annual mortality of all live trees on forest land by species group and ownership group, Idaho, cycle 2, 2004-2009. (In million cubic feet).

| Species group | Ownership group | | | | | All owners |
	Forest Service	Other Federal	State and local government	Undifferentiated private	
Softwood species groups					
Western softwood species groups					
Douglas-fir	228.7	2.2	7.6	2.3	240.7
Ponderosa and Jeffrey pines	25.3	0.2	0.0	2.8	28.3
True fir	210.9	0.9	7.6	12.6	232.0
Western hemlock	1.9	--	0.0	0.0	2.0
Western white pine	6.2	0.3	2.1	0.3	8.9
Engelmann and other spruces	33.8	--	2.3	0.2	36.3
Western larch	5.6	--	0.3	0.5	6.4
Lodgepole pine	202.5	0.9	2.7	3.1	209.2
Western redcedar	6.6	--	0.1	2.5	9.2
Western woodland softwoods	0.2	1.9	--	--	2.2
Other western softwoods	32.2	0.6	0.1	--	32.9
All softwoods	753.9	7.0	22.7	24.4	808.0
Hardwood species groups					
Western hardwood species groups					
Cottonwood and aspen	3.1	0.0	0.5	1.1	4.7
Other western hardwoods	0.7	--	0.6	0.4	1.6
Western woodland hardwoods	0.2	0.0	--	--	0.2
All hardwoods	4.0	0.0	1.0	1.5	6.5
All species groups	757.9	7.1	23.8	25.9	814.6

All table cells without observations in the inventory sample are indicated by --. Table value of 0.0 indicates the volume rounds to less than 0.1 million cubic feet. Columns and rows may not add to their totals due to rounding.

Table 28—Average annual mortality of growing stock trees on timberland by species group and ownership group, Idaho, cycle 2, 2004-2009. (In million cubic feet).

Species group	Ownership group				
	Forest Service	Other Federal	State and local government	Undifferentiated private	All owners
Softwood species groups					
Western softwood species groups					
Douglas-fir	112.8	2.2	7.6	2.3	124.8
Ponderosa and Jeffrey pines	14.0	0.2	- -	2.8	17.0
True fir	150.2	0.8	7.3	12.6	170.8
Western hemlock	1.9	- -	0.0	0.0	2.0
Western white pine	6.2	0.3	2.1	0.3	8.9
Engelmann and other spruces	19.2	- -	1.0	0.2	20.4
Western larch	5.5	- -	0.3	0.5	6.3
Lodgepole pine	145.7	0.9	2.7	3.1	152.3
Western redcedar	5.1	- -	0.1	2.5	7.7
Other western softwoods	16.8	0.6	0.1	- -	17.5
All softwoods	477.3	4.9	21.1	24.4	527.6
Hardwood species groups					
Western hardwood species groups					
Cottonwood and aspen	2.2	0.0	0.4	0.8	3.5
Other western hardwoods	0.7	- -	0.6	0.4	1.6
All hardwoods	2.9	0.0	1.0	1.2	5.1
All species groups	480.2	4.9	22.0	25.6	532.7

All table cells without observations in the inventory sample are indicated by --. Table value of 0.0 indicates the volume rounds to less than 0.1 million cubic feet. Columns and rows may not add to their totals due to rounding.

Table 29a—Aboveground dry weight (regional equations method) of all live trees by owner class and forest land status, Idaho, cycle 2, 2004-2009. (In thousand dry tons).

Owner class	Unreserved forests			Reserved forests			All forest land
	Timberland	Unproductive	Total	Productive	Unproductive	Total	
Forest Service							
National Forest	552,941	8,845	561,786	115,021	586	115,608	677,394
Other Federal							
National Park Service	- -	- -	- -	1,204	121	1,325	1,325
Bureau of Land Management	20,056	3,365	23,421	- -	- -	- -	23,421
Department of Defense or Energy	2,389	225	2,615	- -	- -	- -	2,615
State and local government							
State	54,460	942	55,402	918	- -	918	56,320
Private							
Undifferentiated private	88,925	2,595	91,520	- -	- -	- -	91,520
All owners	718,772	15,972	734,744	117,144	707	117,850	852,595

All table cells without observations in the inventory sample are indicated by --. Table value of 0 indicates the aboveground tree biomass rounds to less than 1 thousand dry tons. Columns and rows may not add to their totals due to rounding.

Table 29b—Aboveground dry weight (component ratio method) of all live trees by owner class and forest land status, Idaho, cycle 2, 2004-2009. (In thousand dry tons).

Owner class	Unreserved forests			Reserved forests			All forest land
	Timberland	Unproductive	Total	Productive	Unproductive	Total	
Forest Service							
National forest	543,198	7,637	550,834	112,207	502	112,709	663,544
Other Federal							
National Park Service	--	--	--	1,067	109	1,176	1,176
Bureau of Land Management	19,975	2,658	22,633	--	--	--	22,633
Department of Defense or Energy	2,546	250	2,796	--	--	--	2,796
State and local government							
State	54,136	755	54,890	844	--	844	55,735
Private							
Undifferentiated private	86,429	2,363	88,792	--	--	--	88,792
All owners	706,283	13,663	719,946	114,118	612	114,730	834,676

All table cells without observations in the inventory sample are indicated by --. Table value of 0 indicates the aboveground tree biomass rounds to less than 1 thousand dry tons. Columns and rows may not add to their totals due to rounding.

USDA Forest Service Resour. Bull. RMRS-RB-14. 2012

109

Table 30a—Aboveground dry weight (regional equations method) of all live trees on forest land by species group and diameter class, Idaho, cycle 2, 2004-2009. (In thousand dry tons).

Species group	Diameter class (inches)															All classes
	1.0-2.9	3.0-4.9	5.0-6.9	7.0-8.9	9.0-10.9	11.0-12.9	13.0-14.9	15.0-16.9	17.0-18.9	19.0-20.9	21.0-22.9	23.0-24.9	25.0-26.9	27.0-28.9	29.0+	
Softwood species groups																
Western softwood species groups																
Douglas-fir	2,543	5,229	7,979	13,495	21,054	27,487	30,661	30,309	25,104	25,153	21,012	14,730	13,419	8,903	23,361	270,438
Ponderosa and Jeffrey pine	293	592	950	1,258	2,009	2,696	3,322	4,546	4,259	5,418	5,203	5,355	6,566	2,986	13,313	58,765
True fir	7,567	11,069	15,513	19,424	21,444	21,694	20,715	19,732	17,487	13,371	11,310	8,684	6,358	4,850	19,554	218,771
Western hemlock	708	952	1,293	2,020	2,085	1,997	2,175	1,708	1,064	569	1,484	1,205	301	366	1,668	19,595
Western white pine	175	371	299	321	278	424	475	517	614	442	447	798	312	215	211	5,900
Engelmann and other spruces	724	1,229	1,781	2,707	3,323	4,564	5,324	4,908	5,700	4,794	5,587	4,292	3,021	2,893	6,399	57,246
Western larch	85	186	698	1,435	2,324	2,763	3,087	3,065	2,019	1,619	1,862	833	955	591	1,992	23,515
Lodgepole pine	2,317	5,400	13,567	19,042	19,705	16,272	10,405	6,242	2,967	1,490	931	--	--	--	--	98,338
Western redcedar	1,052	1,529	2,304	2,302	2,599	2,622	2,280	2,842	3,519	1,733	1,959	1,998	1,466	1,881	14,359	44,448
Western woodland softwoods	35	93	193	316	432	469	407	554	475	310	134	103	131	121	239	4,013
Other western softwoods	1,131	1,931	1,839	2,791	3,152	3,275	2,939	2,577	3,390	1,867	2,749	1,266	776	884	2,300	32,868
All softwoods	16,631	28,582	46,417	65,112	78,404	84,264	81,789	77,000	66,597	56,767	52,679	39,264	33,305	23,690	83,396	833,897
Hardwood species groups																
Western hardwood species groups																
Cottonwood and aspen	433	519	905	1,834	1,905	1,949	954	604	404	347	197	139	449	126	318	11,081
Red alder	13	7	24	25	14	99	139	69	--	95	--	--	--	--	--	486
Other western hardwoods	26	44	585	551	536	445	126	85	53	--	--	--	--	--	--	2,451
Western woodland hardwoods	445	640	689	839	609	482	348	152	144	157	116	60	--	--	--	4,681
All hardwoods	917	1,210	2,204	3,249	3,064	2,975	1,567	910	601	598	312	199	449	126	318	18,698
All species groups	17,547	29,792	48,621	68,360	81,468	87,239	83,356	77,909	67,198	57,365	52,991	39,464	33,754	23,816	83,714	852,595

All table cells without observations in the inventory sample are indicated by --. Table value of 0 indicates the aboveground tree biomass rounds to less than 1 thousand dry tons. Columns and rows may not add to their totals due to rounding.

Table 30b—Aboveground dry weight (component ratio method) of all live trees on forest land by species group and diameter class, Idaho, cycle 2, 2004-2009. (In thousand dry tons).

Species group	Diameter class (inches)															All classes
	1.0-2.9	3.0-4.9	5.0-6.9	7.0-8.9	9.0-10.9	11.0-12.9	13.0-14.9	15.0-16.9	17.0-18.9	19.0-20.9	21.0-22.9	23.0-24.9	25.0-26.9	27.0-28.9	29.0+	
Softwood species groups																
Western softwood species groups																
Douglas-fir	1,225	3,261	6,923	12,798	20,807	27,904	31,604	31,265	26,170	26,283	21,873	15,281	14,052	9,246	24,293	273,005
Ponderosa and Jeffrey pines	87	260	575	1,145	1,925	2,615	3,163	4,299	4,007	5,074	4,789	5,001	5,939	2,714	11,942	53,516
True fir	3,229	7,127	13,595	17,969	20,514	21,283	20,746	19,935	17,881	13,701	11,508	8,752	6,406	4,923	19,316	206,884
Western hemlock	351	791	1,128	1,991	2,173	2,121	2,367	1,841	1,161	636	1,635	1,358	338	392	1,870	20,153
Western white pine	67	212	215	312	287	445	488	519	614	441	416	772	292	207	185	5,475
Engelmann and other spruces	259	724	1,567	2,541	3,267	4,595	5,444	5,109	5,971	5,066	5,943	4,585	3,212	3,114	6,783	58,180
Western larch	52	170	645	1,440	2,405	2,920	3,266	3,212	2,149	1,711	1,962	881	980	638	2,094	24,525
Lodgepole pine	1,520	5,507	11,127	19,326	20,414	16,606	10,430	6,475	3,048	1,533	969	--	--	--	--	96,956
Western redcedar	674	1,252	1,998	2,019	2,362	2,453	2,180	2,719	3,453	1,653	1,926	1,960	1,441	1,832	14,107	42,028
Western woodland softwoods	39	96	155	268	402	443	403	530	452	289	103	110	145	126	239	3,800
Other western softwoods	343	941	1,316	2,658	3,166	3,291	2,959	2,595	3,496	1,909	2,782	1,292	780	925	2,369	30,812
All softwoods	7,846	20,342	39,245	62,467	77,723	84,676	83,050	78,518	68,392	58,296	53,886	39,992	33,585	24,117	83,197	815,333
Hardwood species groups																
Western hardwood species groups																
Cottonwood and aspen	696	912	1,082	2,030	2,003	1,967	916	564	401	370	196	142	481	156	369	12,286
Red alder	32	11	28	28	14	94	138	69	--	68	--	--	--	--	--	483
Other western hardwoods	63	135	883	766	700	553	151	98	62	--	--	--	--	--	--	3,411
Western woodland hardwoods	834	912	277	340	230	188	147	63	54	56	41	20	--	--	--	3,163
All hardwoods	1,625	1,971	2,270	3,164	2,948	2,802	1,353	794	516	495	237	162	481	156	369	19,343
All species groups	9,471	22,312	41,515	65,630	80,671	87,478	84,403	79,313	68,908	58,791	54,124	40,154	34,067	24,273	83,566	834,676

All table cells without observations in the inventory sample are indicated by --. Table value of 0 indicates the aboveground tree biomass rounds to less than 1 thousand dry tons. Columns and rows may not add to their totals due to rounding.

USDA Forest Service Resour. Bull. RMRS-RB-14. 2012

111

Table 31—Area of accessible forest land by Forest Survey Unit, county and forest land status, Idaho, cycle 2, 2004-2009.
(In thousand acres).

Forest Survey Unit and county	Unreserved forests				Reserved forests			All forest land
	Timberland	Unproductive	Total	Productive	Unproductive	Total		
Northern								
Benewah	402.6	- -	402.6	9.8	- -	9.8		412.4
Bonner	976.2	- -	976.2	- -	- -	- -		976.2
Boundary	670.0	- -	670.0	21.5	- -	21.5		691.6
Clearwater	1,428.4	- -	1,428.4	- -	- -	- -		1,428.4
Idaho	2,403.4	21.2	2,424.5	1,955.7	21.2	1,976.9		4,401.4
Kootenai	523.8	12.8	536.6	- -	- -	- -		536.6
Latah	364.8	- -	364.8	- -	- -	- -		364.8
Lewis	67.3	- -	67.3	- -	- -	- -		67.3
Nez Perce	122.7	- -	122.7	- -	- -	- -		122.7
Shoshone	1,528.8	- -	1,528.8	- -	- -	- -		1,528.8
Total	8,488.2	34.0	8,522.2	1,987.1	21.2	2,008.3		10,530.4
Southwestern								
Ada	9.6	- -	9.6	- -	- -	- -		9.6
Adams	458.8	- -	458.8	22.3	- -	22.3		481.0
Boise	800.6	9.9	810.5	9.9	- -	9.9		820.4
Elmore	444.3	18.1	462.4	48.8	- -	48.8		511.3
Gem	46.6	- -	46.6	- -	- -	- -		46.6
Owyhee	224.4	180.6	405.0	- -	- -	- -		405.0
Valley	1,376.6	10.7	1,387.3	614.4	21.3	635.7		2,023.0
Washington	82.2	- -	82.2	- -	- -	- -		82.2
Total	3,443.0	219.3	3,662.4	695.4	21.3	716.7		4,379.1

(Table 31 continued on next page)

(Table 31 continued)

Forest Survey Unit and county	Unreserved forests			Reserved forests			All forest land
	Timberland	Unproductive	Total	Productive	Unproductive	Total	
Southeastern							
Bannock	74.9	103.2	178.0	--	--	--	178.0
Bear Lake	155.5	8.7	164.2	--	--	--	164.2
Bingham	23.3	24.9	48.2	--	--	--	48.2
Blaine	321.4	17.2	338.5	--	--	--	338.5
Bonneville	391.1	33.5	424.5	--	--	--	424.5
Butte	59.5	71.6	131.0	--	8.8	8.8	139.8
Camas	206.4	9.2	215.6	--	--	--	215.6
Caribou	342.6	72.4	415.0	--	--	--	415.0
Cassia	45.5	216.9	262.4	--	--	--	262.4
Clark	216.2	7.6	223.8	--	--	--	223.8
Custer	952.6	94.1	1,046.7	359.7	--	359.7	1,406.4
Franklin	60.0	51.6	111.6	--	--	--	111.6
Fremont	436.4	19.8	456.2	61.6	10.3	71.8	528.0
Jefferson	10.4	--	10.4	--	--	--	10.4
Lemhi	1,153.7	145.5	1,299.1	377.4	25.6	403.1	1,702.2
Madison	47.0	--	47.0	--	--	--	47.0
Oneida	32.5	54.9	87.4	--	--	--	87.4
Power	43.6	12.8	56.4	--	--	--	56.4
Teton	105.7	--	105.7	--	--	--	105.7
Twin Falls	7.4	7.4	14.7	--	--	--	14.7
Total	4,685.6	951.2	5,636.8	798.7	44.7	843.4	6,480.1
All counties	16,616.8	1,204.5	17,821.3	3,481.1	87.2	3,568.3	21,389.6

All table cells without observations in the inventory sample are indicated by --. Table value of 0.0 indicates the acres round to less than 0.1 thousand acres. Columns and rows may not add to their totals due to rounding.

Table 32—Area of accessible forest land by Forest Survey Unit, county, ownership group and forest land status, Idaho, cycle 2, 2004-2009. (In thousand acres).

Forest Survey Unit and county	Forest Service		Other Federal		State and local government		Undifferentiated private		All forest land
	Timber-land	Other forest land	Timber-land	Other forest land	Timber-land	Other forest land	Timber-land	Other forest land	
Northern									
Benewah	59.0	--	9.8	--	60.3	9.8	273.5	--	412.4
Bonner	459.4	--	19.7	--	168.8	--	328.3	--	976.2
Boundary	495.1	--	10.8	--	78.0	21.5	86.1	--	691.6
Clearwater	726.3	--	21.5	--	278.6	--	402.0	--	1,428.4
Idaho	2,087.6	1,998.1	60.9	--	34.2	--	220.7	--	4,401.4
Kootenai	230.3	--	19.5	--	19.5	--	254.6	12.8	536.6
Latah	156.2	--	--	--	52.7	--	155.8	--	364.8
Lewis	--	--	--	--	--	--	67.3	--	67.3
Nez Perce	--	--	11.1	--	44.5	--	67.1	--	122.7
Shoshone	1,079.7	--	60.6	--	76.6	--	311.9	--	1,528.8
Total	5,293.7	1,998.1	213.9	--	813.3	31.4	2,167.3	12.8	10,530.4
Southwestern									
Ada	--	--	--	--	9.4	--	0.2	--	9.6
Adams	365.3	22.3	9.9	--	39.6	--	44.0	--	481.0
Boise	633.0	19.8	9.9	--	90.7	--	66.9	--	820.4
Elmore	393.1	56.5	9.6	--	9.6	10.5	32.0	--	511.3
Gem	43.9	--	--	--	--	--	2.7	--	46.6
Owyhee	--	--	142.5	108.9	64.5	49.4	17.4	22.3	405.0
Valley	1,243.0	646.4	--	--	53.3	--	80.3	--	2,023.0
Washington	61.0	--	--	--	21.2	--	--	--	82.2
Total	2,739.2	744.9	171.9	108.9	288.3	59.9	243.6	22.3	4,379.1

(Table 32 continued on next page)

(Table 32 continued)

Forest Survey Unit and county	Forest Service		Other Federal		State and local government		Undifferentiated private		All forest land
	Timber-land	Other forest land	Timber-land	Other forest land	Timber-land	Other forest land	Timber-land	Other forest land	
Southeastern									
Bannock	26.7	42.8	29.7	--	--	9.9	18.5	50.5	178.0
Bear Lake	146.9	8.7	--	--	--	--	8.7	--	164.2
Bingham	--	--	--	--	--	5.0	23.3	20.0	48.2
Blaine	264.5	7.4	9.9	--	7.4	--	39.6	9.8	338.5
Bonneville	365.2	14.9	6.0	--	11.5	--	8.4	18.6	424.5
Butte	51.7	41.4	7.8	38.9	--	--	--	--	139.8
Camas	177.5	5.4	10.4	--	9.2	--	9.2	3.9	215.6
Caribou	276.7	31.9	20.2	20.3	33.4	--	12.3	20.2	415.0
Cassia	45.5	71.0	--	105.1	--	10.2	--	30.6	262.4
Clark	196.5	7.6	10.1	--	9.6	--	--	--	223.8
Custer	917.2	423.0	35.5	30.8	--	--	--	--	1,406.4
Franklin	60.0	28.7	--	--	--	--	--	22.9	111.6
Fremont	416.0	7.4	--	84.2	--	--	20.4	--	528.0
Jefferson	--	--	10.4	--	--	--	--	--	10.4
Lemhi	1,074.0	540.8	66.8	7.7	2.5	--	10.3	--	1,702.2
Madison	39.2	--	--	--	7.8	--	--	--	47.0
Oneida	20.0	15.0	2.5	22.5	--	--	10.0	17.5	87.4
Power	12.8	--	30.8	2.6	--	--	--	10.3	56.4
Teton	96.1	--	9.6	--	--	--	--	--	105.7
Twin Falls	7.4	7.4	--	--	--	--	--	--	14.7
Total	4,193.8	1,253.3	249.5	312.1	81.6	25.1	160.7	204.1	6,480.1
All counties	12,226.7	3,996.3	635.3	421.0	1,183.2	116.3	2,571.6	239.2	21,389.6

All table cells without observations in the inventory sample are indicated by --. Table value of 0.0 indicates the acres round to less than 0.1 thousand acres. Columns and rows may not add to their totals due to rounding.

USDA Forest Service Resour. Bull. RMRS-RB-14. 2012

115

Table 33—Area of timberland by Forest Survey Unit, county and stand-size class, Idaho, cycle 2, 2004-2009.
(In thousand acres).

Forest Survey Unit and county	Stand-size class					All size classes
	Large diameter	Medium diameter	Small diameter	Chaparral	Nonstocked	
Northern						
Benewah	295.3	17.2	90.1	- -	- -	402.6
Bonner	615.2	158.9	179.9	- -	22.2	976.2
Boundary	409.0	148.0	99.6	- -	13.5	670.0
Clearwater	887.8	134.5	338.0	- -	68.0	1,428.4
Idaho	1,761.1	212.1	306.6	- -	123.6	2,403.4
Kootenai	400.3	14.6	77.9	- -	31.0	523.8
Latah	228.2	33.4	81.9	- -	21.3	364.8
Lewis	39.4	- -	8.3	- -	19.6	67.3
Nez Perce	69.9	30.6	22.2	- -	- -	122.7
Shoshone	1,209.8	131.3	187.7	- -	- -	1,528.8
Total	5,916.1	880.6	1,392.3	- -	299.2	8,488.2
Southwestern						
Ada	9.6	- -	- -	- -	- -	9.6
Adams	361.3	9.9	70.3	- -	17.3	458.8
Boise	594.8	9.9	96.7	- -	99.2	800.6
Elmore	275.1	5.3	65.6	- -	98.3	444.3
Gem	43.9	- -	- -	- -	2.7	46.6
Owyhee	104.1	- -	27.3	- -	93.0	224.4
Valley	1,004.0	103.8	148.8	- -	120.0	1,376.6
Washington	82.2	- -	- -	- -	- -	82.2
Total	2,475.0	128.9	408.7	- -	430.5	3,443.0

(Table 33 continued on next page)

116

USDA Forest Service Resour. Bull. RMRS-RB-14. 2012

(Table 33 continued)

Forest Survey Unit and county	Large diameter	Medium diameter	Stand-size class Small diameter	Chaparral	Nonstocked	All size classes
Southeastern						
Bannock	45.1	22.5	7.3	- -	- -	74.9
Bear Lake	97.4	34.7	23.4	- -	- -	155.5
Bingham	10.0	10.0	3.3	- -	- -	23.3
Blaine	239.5	39.8	32.1	- -	9.9	321.4
Bonneville	264.3	37.8	63.1	- -	26.0	391.1
Butte	51.7	7.8	- -	- -	- -	59.5
Camas	169.2	13.8	20.8	- -	2.6	206.4
Car bou	199.5	60.0	80.2	- -	2.8	342.6
Cassia	41.3	- -	2.5	- -	1.6	45.5
Clark	161.9	19.3	25.0	- -	10.1	216.2
Custer	621.3	158.1	75.3	- -	98.0	952.6
Franklin	49.6	10.4	- -	- -	- -	60.0
Fremont	200.1	103.9	124.7	- -	7.7	436.4
Jefferson	10.4	- -	- -	- -	- -	10.4
Lemhi	683.3	222.8	159.2	- -	88.3	1,153.7
Madison	18.3	10.4	7.8	- -	10.4	47.0
Oneida	22.5	- -	10.0	- -	- -	32.5
Power	28.2	10.3	- -	- -	5.1	43.6
Teton	62.5	- -	43.3	- -	- -	105.7
Twin Falls	- -	7.4	- -	- -	- -	7.4
Total	2,975.9	769.1	678.0	- -	262.5	4,635.6
All counties	11,367.1	1,778.6	2,479.0	- -	992.2	16,616.8

All table cells without observations in the inventory sample are indicated by --. Table value of 0.0 indicates the acres round to less than 0.1 thousand acres. Columns and rows may not add to their totals due to rounding.

USDA Forest Service Resour. Bull. RMRS-RB-14. 2012

117

Table 34—Area of timberland by Forest Survey Unit, county and stocking class, Idaho, cycle 2, 2004-2009. (In thousand acres).

Forest Survey Unit and county	Stocking class of growing-stock trees					All classes
	Nonstocked	Poorly stocked	Moderately stocked	Fully stocked	Over-stocked	
Northern						
Benewah	- -	188.0	122.8	89.3	2.5	402.6
Bonner	22.4	320.9	373.8	259.1	- -	976.2
Boundary	13.5	180.3	309.5	164.1	2.7	670.0
Clearwater	68.0	392.7	665.4	288.8	13.5	1,428.4
Idaho	134.2	767.0	923.7	566.1	12.4	2,403.4
Kootenai	31.0	169.5	236.2	87.1	- -	523.8
Latah	21.3	133.9	116.1	92.1	1.5	364.8
Lewis	19.6	39.4	- -	8.3	- -	67.3
Nez Perce	- -	77.9	41.7	- -	3.1	122.7
Shoshone	- -	393.1	696.1	411.9	27.8	1,528.8
Total	310.0	2,662.8	3,485.3	1,966.8	63.4	8,488.2
Southwestern						
Ada	0.2	9.4	- -	- -	- -	9.6
Adams	17.3	164.2	203.8	68.5	4.9	458.8
Boise	99.8	431.6	214.7	52.1	2.5	800.6
Elmore	98.3	178.1	152.8	14.8	0.2	444.3
Gem	2.7	- -	43.9	- -	- -	46.6
Owyhee	93.0	111.6	14.8	5.0	- -	224.4
Valley	120.0	552.4	608.3	93.2	2.7	1,376.6
Washington	- -	21.2	53.0	8.0	- -	82.2
Total	431.3	1,468.4	1,291.4	241.6	10.3	3,443.0

(Table 34 continued on next page)

(Table 34 continued)

Forest Survey Unit and county	Stocking class of growing-stock trees					All classes
	Nonstocked	Poorly stocked	Moderately stocked	Fully stocked	Over-stocked	
Southeastern						
Bannock	- -	35.5	25.3	14.1	- -	74.9
Bear Lake	- -	52.2	58.6	44.7	- -	155.5
Bingham	- -	10.0	10.0	3.3	- -	23.3
Blaine	10.2	49.5	204.3	57.4	- -	321.4
Bonneville	26.0	173.7	125.1	66.3	- -	391.1
Butte	- -	21.0	8.8	29.7	- -	59.5
Camas	13.0	41.1	109.6	40.4	2.3	206.4
Caribou	7.3	67.3	153.6	112.2	2.2	342.6
Cassia	1.6	- -	28.6	6.4	8.9	45.5
Clark	10.1	101.6	77.5	22.1	4.8	216.2
Custer	108.0	329.6	386.5	128.3	0.3	952.6
Franklin	- -	39.1	20.9	- -	- -	60.0
Fremont	7.7	184.8	177.4	51.2	15.4	436.4
Jefferson	- -	- -	- -	10.4	- -	10.4
Lemhi	98.8	411.1	409.4	205.7	28.7	1,153.7
Madison	10.4	7.8	20.9	7.8	7.8	47.0
Oneida	- -	22.5	- -	10.0	- -	32.5
Power	5.1	18.0	2.6	18.0	- -	43.6
Teton	- -	33.6	52.9	19.2	- -	105.7
Twin Falls	- -	- -	- -	7.4	- -	7.4
Total	298.1	1,598.3	1,871.9	846.8	70.5	4,685.6
All counties	1,039.4	5,729.5	6,648.5	3,055.2	144.2	16,616.8

All table cells without observations in the inventory sample are indicated by – –. Table value of 0.0 indicates the acres round to less than 0.1 thousand acres. Columns and rows may not add to their totals due to rounding.

USDA Forest Service Resour. Bull. RMRS-RB-14. 2012

119

Table 35—Net volume of growing stock and sawtimber (International 1/4 inch rule) on timberland by Forest Survey Unit, county, and major species group, Idaho, cycle 2, 2004-2009.

Forest Survey Unit and county	Growing stock					Sawtimber				
	Major species group					Major species group				
	Pine	Other softwoods	Soft hardwoods	Hard hardwoods	All species	Pine	Other softwoods	Soft hardwoods	Hard hardwoods	All species
	(In million cubic feet)					(In million board feet)				
Northern										
Benewah	149.4	945.1	2.2	--	1,096.7	796.1	4,788.7	--	--	5,584.7
Bonner	239.5	2,014.5	123.6	42.2	2,419.8	1,205.1	9,631.0	273.4	199.3	11,308.8
Boundary	345.6	1,527.4	15.6	13.6	1,902.1	1,424.9	7,507.6	33.8	68.9	9,035.3
Clearwater	495.3	3,701.0	25.8	--	4,222.1	2,630.1	18,945.0	110.9	--	21,686.0
Idaho	1,536.9	6,256.5	25.2	--	7,818.6	7,520.9	33,692.0	61.8	--	41,274.7
Kootenai	173.4	1,257.1	14.3	8.5	1,453.3	937.1	6,663.9	32.2	47.1	7,680.3
Latah	187.9	794.9	1.3	--	984.1	952.5	4,108.3	--	--	5,060.8
Lewis	19.3	49.2	--	--	68.5	113.4	226.0	--	--	339.4
Nez Perce	56.0	88.9	--	--	144.9	287.1	414.9	--	--	702.0
Shoshone	617.4	4,759.1	0.2	0.5	5,377.2	3,042.7	24,255.1	--	--	27,297.9
Total	3,820.7	21,393.6	208.2	64.8	25,487.4	18,910.0	110,232.7	512.1	315.3	129,970.0
Southwestern										
Ada	3.8	--	--	--	3.8	20.2	--	--	--	20.2
Adams	338.3	861.0	4.6	--	1,204.0	2,103.7	4,712.9	20.7	--	6,837.3
Boise	561.9	792.0	0.1	0.8	1,354.7	3,535.3	4,219.9	--	3.5	7,758.7
Elmore	145.9	378.1	1.4	--	525.3	870.3	1,990.6	6.0	--	2,866.8
Gem	27.7	160.3	--	--	188.0	184.6	1,051.4	--	--	1,236.0
Owyhee	--	69.2	1.5	--	70.8	--	296.6	6.9	--	303.5
Valley	728.1	2,015.2	0.3	--	2,743.7	3,587.1	10,634.5	--	--	14,221.6
Washington	46.8	211.8	--	--	258.6	245.5	1,240.4	--	--	1,485.9
Total	1,852.5	4,487.7	8.0	0.8	6,348.9	10,546.7	24,146.3	33.6	3.5	34,730.1

(Table 35 continued on next page)

USDA Forest Service Resour. Bull. RMRS-RB-14. 2012

(Table 35 continued)

Forest Survey Unit and county	Growing stock					Sawtimber				
	Major species group					Major species group				
	Pine	Other softwoods	Soft hardwoods	Hard hardwoods	All species	Pine	Other softwoods	Soft hardwoods	Hard hardwoods	All species
	(In million cubic feet)					(In million board feet)				
Southeastern										
Bannock	--	95.9	30.4	--	126.3	--	531.4	60.3	--	591.7
Bear Lake	31.9	236.1	22.8	--	290.8	125.3	1,223.1	24.6	--	1,373.0
Bingham	0.3	11.8	6.0	--	18.1	--	26.9	23.7	--	50.6
Blaine	122.9	581.1	15.8	18.0	737.8	476.6	2,800.3	52.4	97.3	3,426.6
Bonneville	100.0	523.4	99.2	--	722.6	397.7	2,685.9	259.3	--	3,342.9
Butte	13.6	90.4	--	--	104.0	72.1	454.3	--	--	526.5
Camas	26.2	498.5	1.7	--	526.3	105.8	2,713.5	--	--	2,819.3
Caribou	76.9	399.3	96.2	--	572.3	298.6	1,824.4	177.3	--	2,300.3
Cassia	33.6	63.0	0.5	--	97.1	139.5	305.5	--	--	445.0
Clark	59.3	276.4	1.4	--	337.2	285.4	1,471.0	--	--	1,756.4
Custer	305.9	1,232.0	2.3	--	1,540.2	1,038.1	6,013.7	--	--	7,051.8
Franklin	16.5	85.8	5.8	--	108.2	85.6	457.5	5.4	--	548.5
Fremont	267.5	268.5	19.3	--	555.3	883.5	1,411.6	49.8	--	2,344.9
Jefferson	--	--	46.7	--	46.7	--	--	186.4	--	186.4
Lemhi	622.9	1,163.8	2.2	11.8	1,800.6	1,976.4	5,358.1	8.4	62.4	7,405.3
Madison	25.5	2.1	2.4	--	30.1	125.2	8.2	--	--	133.4
Oneida	--	26.1	2.7	--	28.8	--	116.2	2.2	--	118.3
Power	--	59.8	13.8	--	73.6	--	303.4	--	--	303.4
Teton	26.2	98.5	1.5	--	126.3	94.7	438.8	--	--	533.5
Twin Falls	--	--	18.7	--	18.7	--	--	52.0	--	52.0
Total	1,729.3	5,712.3	389.6	29.8	7,861.0	6,104.3	28,143.9	901.9	159.7	35,309.7
All counties	7,402.3	31,593.6	605.7	95.4	39,697.2	35,560.9	162,522.9	1,447.5	478.5	200,009.8

All table cells without observations in the inventory sample are indicated by --. Table value of 0.0 indicates the volume rounds to less than 0.1 million cubic or board feet. Columns and rows may not add to their totals due to rounding.

USDA Forest Service Resour. Bull. RMRS-RB-14. 2012

121

Table 36—Average annual net growth of growing stock and sawtimber (International 1/4 inch rule) on timberland by Forest Survey Unit, county, and major species group, Idaho, cycle 2, 2004-2009.

Forest Survey Unit and county	Growing stock					Sawtimber				
	Major species group (In million cubic feet)					Major species group (In million board feet)				
	Pine	Other softwoods	Soft hardwoods	Hard hardwoods	All species	Pine	Other softwoods	Soft hardwoods	Hard hardwoods	All species
Northern										
Benewah	3.2	27.5	0.0	--	30.7	29.3	163.9	--	--	193.2
Bonner	4.8	45.7	4.3	0.8	55.5	24.1	261.7	38.2	3.5	327.6
Boundary	1.5	19.9	0.3	0.2	21.9	30.5	129.3	0.7	0.9	161.3
Clearwater	-1.9	102.0	1.0	--	101.1	-17.4	559.2	3.3	--	545.1
Idaho	-17.3	94.5	0.7	--	77.8	-8.3	648.8	1.9	--	642.4
Kootenai	4.2	30.7	0.3	0.1	35.3	27.4	216.5	0.9	0.2	245.0
Latah	1.7	23.3	0.0	--	24.9	17.5	121.9	--	--	139.4
Lewis	0.9	1.4	--	--	2.3	6.6	8.4	--	--	15.0
Nez Perce	2.3	2.1	--	--	4.4	10.1	10.0	--	--	20.0
Shoshone	-0.3	105.1	0.0	0.0	104.9	21.1	701.7	--	--	722.8
Total	-0.9	452.2	6.6	1.1	458.9	140.8	2,821.4	45.0	4.6	3,011.8
Southwestern										
Ada	0.2	--	--	--	0.2	1.7	--	--	--	1.7
Adams	7.1	16.9	0.2	--	24.3	51.6	111.7	0.9	--	164.2
Boise	10.3	11.3	0.0	0.0	21.6	75.3	74.5	--	0.0	149.8
Elmore	2.7	-2.4	0.0	--	0.3	21.1	2.0	0.1	--	23.2
Gem	0.7	0.4	--	--	1.2	5.8	10.3	--	--	16.1
Owyhee	--	1.0	0.0	--	1.0	--	4.2	0.1	--	4.3
Valley	-8.0	-14.6	0.0	--	-22.6	-12.5	-18.3	--	--	-30.8
Washington	1.7	2.8	--	--	4.5	12.2	17.5	--	--	29.7
Total	14.8	15.5	0.3	0.0	30.6	155.1	201.9	1.1	0.0	358.1

(Table 36 continued on next page)

(Table 36 continued)

	Growing stock					Sawtimber				
	Major species group					Major species group				
Forest Survey Unit and county	Pine	Other softwoods	Soft hardwoods	Hard hardwoods	All species	Pine	Other softwoods	Soft hardwoods	Hard hardwoods	All species
	(In million cubic feet)					(In million board feet)				
Southeastern										
Bannock	--	1.5	0.4	--	1.9	--	9.1	1.1	--	10.2
Bear Lake	0.5	5.1	0.3	--	5.9	5.3	23.0	0.4	--	28.6
Bingham	0.0	0.7	0.1	--	0.8	--	5.0	0.4	--	5.3
Blaine	1.0	1.5	0.7	0.6	3.7	8.1	17.9	1.4	3.2	30.6
Bonneville	0.3	8.3	1.8	--	10.4	2.9	47.5	7.8	--	58.3
Butte	0.1	0.5	--	--	0.7	0.6	7.3	--	--	7.9
Camas	-0.4	0.5	0.1	--	0.1	-3.6	4.4	--	--	0.8
Caribou	1.9	9.1	2.3	--	13.4	5.5	52.6	7.7	--	65.9
Cassia	0.8	0.6	0.1	--	1.4	3.1	4.2	--	--	7.4
Clark	-2.4	3.5	0.2	--	1.3	-12.7	25.5	--	--	12.8
Custer	-45.0	-5.9	-0.1	--	-51.0	-186.0	-7.4	--	--	-193.4
Franklin	-1.9	1.9	0.0	--	0.0	-10.4	9.5	0.1	--	-0.8
Fremont	13.8	6.6	0.9	--	21.4	55.7	43.2	0.6	--	99.5
Jefferson	--	--	0.4	--	0.4	--	--	1.5	--	1.5
Lemhi	5.8	3.5	0.1	0.5	9.9	48.7	23.4	0.1	6.6	78.8
Madison	0.6	0.1	0.3	--	0.9	4.6	0.3	--	--	4.8
Oneida	--	0.8	0.1	--	0.9	--	3.7	2.2	--	5.8
Power	--	1.9	0.4	--	2.3	--	8.7	--	--	8.7
Teton	0.7	2.0	0.0	--	2.7	0.3	10.3	--	--	10.6
Twin Falls	--	--	0.3	--	0.3	--	--	4.4	--	4.4
Total	-24.2	42.1	8.2	1.0	27.2	-77.9	288.2	27.6	9.8	247.7
All counties	-10.3	509.8	15.0	2.1	516.6	218.1	3,311.4	73.7	14.4	3,617.6

All table cells without observations in the inventory sample are indicated by --. Table value of 0.0 indicates the volume rounds to less than 0.1 million cubic or board feet. Columns and rows may not add to their totals due to rounding.

Table 37—Sampling errors by Forest Survey Unit and county for area of timberland, volume, average annual net growth, average annual removals, and average annual mortality on timberland, Idaho, cycle 2, 2004-2009.

(Sampling error in percent)

Forest Survey Unit and county	Forest area	Timberland area	Growing stock				Sawtimber			
			Volume	Average annual net growth	Average annual removals	Average annual mortality	Volume	Average annual net growth	Average annual removals	Average annual mortality
Northern										
Benewah	6.12	6.58	16.90	16.94	--	51.13	18.73	16.02	--	55.47
Bonner	2.95	2.95	9.37	13.22	--	17.50	10.84	14.88	--	21.04
Boundary	4.61	5.09	10.85	23.24	--	20.90	12.76	20.13	--	23.55
Clearwater	2.49	2.49	8.14	16.95	--	31.89	9.25	18.36	--	36.36
Idaho	1.56	4.65	7.47	22.40	--	12.76	8.23	14.91	--	13.40
Kootenai	5.63	6.13	13.47	15.82	--	29.75	14.58	14.94	--	34.61
Latah	7.45	7.45	20.14	19.58	--	41.24	22.09	19.55	--	48.37
Lewis	34.07	34.07	62.00	50.36	--	100.00	65.80	49.63	--	100.00
Nez Perce	17.86	17.86	23.23	90.88	--	88.15	27.47	100.00	--	91.82
Shoshone	2.23	2.23	6.84	10.92	--	16.50	7.67	10.05	--	19.40
Total	1.05	1.68	3.52	6.54	--	8.33	3.96	5.88	--	9.69
Southwestern										
Ada	100.00	100.00	100.00	100.00	--	--	100.00	100.00	--	--
Adams	6.32	6.95	14.88	24.74	--	91.39	15.65	18.76	--	91.59
Boise	4.78	5.09	10.79	19.80	--	51.15	11.97	18.11	--	56.12
Elmore	7.96	9.05	18.02	100.00	--	60.63	19.41	100.00	--	63.49
Gem	43.58	43.58	50.36	100.00	--	70.78	51.41	100.00	--	73.60
Owyhee	12.08	19.72	36.41	97.07	--	100.00	43.92	86.58	--	100.00
Valley	2.18	5.33	8.92	74.90	--	21.66	10.08	100.00	--	24.21
Washington	26.12	26.12	31.86	35.02	--	100.00	35.83	28.88	--	94.40
Total	2.22	3.26	5.87	89.46	--	18.27	6.51	34.93	--	20.08

(Table 37 continued on next page)

124

USDA Forest Service Resour. Bull. RMRS-RB-14. 2012

(Table 37 continued)

Forest Survey Unit and county	Forest area	Timberland area	Growing stock				Sawtimber			
			Volume	Average annual net growth	Average annual removals	Average annual mortality	Volume	Average annual net growth	Average annual removals	Average annual mortality
Southeastern										
Bannock	12.67	28.04	37.05	49.40	--	82. 2	39.31	40.49	--	
Bear Lake	7.21	9.15	23.70	21.04	--	37.29	27.59	26.77	--	100 00
Bingham	40.28	62.51	75.19	90 67	--	100.0	71.28	91 47	--	-
Blaine	6.79	6.96	13.27	100.00	--	36.86	15.05	78.83	--	42 69
Bonneville	7.43	7.89	14.52	29.60	--	40.47	15.77	28.35	--	48.37
Butte	16.91	31.90	46.01	80.39	--	76.98	43. 7	78.63	--	100 00
Camas	12.44	13.50	26 33	100.00	--	60.27	28.94	100.00	--	62.95
Caribou	8. 3	9.99	15.95	18 36	--	50.66	18.09	20.99	--	--
Cassia	15.34	40.21	63 59	100 0	--	100.00	62.63	100.00	--	100 00
Clark	12.95	12.99	19.73	100.0	--	51. 8	21.18	100.00	--	54.76
Custer	3.66	6.87	11.29	23.01	--	15.92	12.63	28.10	--	17.30
Franklin	25.58	38.22	41.18	100.00	--	88.31	41.85	100.00	--	99.54
Fremont	6.38	8.69	17 26	15 23	--	53.84	20.52	16 68	--	51.51
Jefferson	99.22	99.22	99.22	99.22	--	--	99.22	99.22	--	--
Lemhi	3.29	5.99	10.25	71.43	--	25.63	11.27	45.84	--	28.86
Madison	41.84	41.84	68.44	67 34	--	83.45	78.20	71 26	--	--
Oneida	30.40	53.62	78.65	74 23	--	--	77.54	71 33	--	--
Power	38.86	42.47	62 22	54 05	--	--	71.16	58 87	--	--
Teton	25.45	25.45	42.76	36 42	--	54.59	43.73	42 48	--	63 35
Twin Falls	71.80	100.00	100 00	100 00	--	100.00	100.00	100 00	--	100 00
Total	2.06	2.92	4.92	65 17	--	11.35	5.51	35 78	--	12 73
All counties	0.93	1.37	2.64	8.00	--	6.54	2.98	6.36	--	7.47

Sampling errors that exceed 100% are reported as 100%.

Appendix E: Soil Indicator Core Tables.

Table S1a: Mean water, carbon, and nitrogen contents of forest floor and soil cores by forest type, Idaho, soil visit 1, 2000, 2001, 2002, 2004, 2007, 2008.

Table S1b: Mean water, carbon, and nitrogen contents of forest floor and soil cores by forest type, Idaho, soil visit 2, 2006, 2007, 2009.

Table S2a: Mean physical and chemical properties of soil cores by forest type, Idaho, soil visit 1, 2000, 2001, 2002, 2004, 2007, 2008.

Table S2b: Mean physical and chemical properties of soil cores by forest type, Idaho, soil visit 2, 2006, 2007, 2009.

Table S3: Mean physical and chemical properties of soil cores by forest type, Idaho, soil visit 2, 2006, 2007, 2009.

Table S4: Mean exchangeable cation concentrations in soil cores by forest type, Idaho, soil visit 2, 2006, 2007, 2009.

Table S5a: Mean extractable trace element concentrations in soil cores by forest type, Idaho, soil visit 1, 2000, 2001, 2002, 2004, 2007, 2008.

Table S5b: Mean extractable trace element concentrations in soil cores by forest type, Idaho, soil visit 2, 2006, 2007, 2009.

Table S1a—Mean water, carbon, and nitrogen contents of forest floor and soil cores by forest type, Idaho, soil visit 1, 2000, 2001, 2002, 2004, 2007, 2008.

Forest type	Soil layer	Number of plots	Water content[a]	Organic carbon	Inorganic carbon	Total nitrogen	C/N ratio	Forest floor mass[a]	Organic carbon	Total nitrogen
	cm		%	%	%	%		Mg/ha	Mg/ha	Mg/ha
Cercocarpus woodland	Forest floor	1								
	0–10	1	4.95	2.41	1.67	0.335	7.2		19.77	2.75
	10–20	1	4.65	2.01	5.02	0.237	8.5		9.52	1.124
Juniper group[b]	Forest floor	5	3.64	31.09		0.624	67.2	1.01	0.29	0.006
	0–10	5	3.7	2.08	0.21	0.162	12.8		16.74	1.303
	10–20	5	6.77	0.95	0.18	0.103	9.3		8.31	0.898
Ponderosa pine	Forest floor	17	28.81	30.56		0.891	34.6	24.5	6.62	0.207
	0–10	17	16.44	2.71	0.17	0.128	21.3		21.12	0.994
	10–20	17	11.95	1.54	0.16	0.094	16.4		13	0.794
Lodgepole pine	Forest floor	16	39.98	31.93		0.869	41.3	13.94	4.23	0.117
	0–10	16	15.99	2.82	0.18	0.124	22.8		19.07	0.836
	10–20	16	10.69	1.61	0.16	0.065	24.6		13.02	0.53
Douglas fir	Forest floor	70	22.89	31.27		0.868	38.5	18.32	5.34	0.149
	0–10	70	7.62	3.23	0.18	0.15	21.5		19.57	0.91
	10–20	70	8.6	1.93	0.18	0.095	20.4		13.21	0.647
Cottonwood/aspen	Forest floor	11	29.79	35.49		1.073	34.6	13.9	4.44	0.143
	0–10	11	18.77	5.87	0.19	0.421	14		25.08	1.798
	10–20	11	17.23	3.34	0.19	0.231	14.4		19.2	1.33
Spruce/fir group[c]	Forest floor	51	42.29	30.89		0.907	35.5	23.81	6.88	0.206
	0–10	51	18.34	4.75	0.17	0.218	21.8		26.26	1.203
	10–20	51	18.18	2.67	0.16	0.137	19.6		18.12	0.925
Western hemlock/ redcedar/larch	Forest floor	14	53.97	26.02		0.706	38.3	39.1	9.68	0.259
	0–10	14	17.7	4.27	0.21	0.211	20.2		19.5	0.964
	10–20	14	14.41	1.87	0.18	0.104	17.9		12.16	0.678
Limber pine	Forest floor	1	7.39	25.16		0.553	46.5	2.85	0.75	0.018
	0–10	1	19.35	7.23	0.12	0.331	21.8		56.85	2.604
	10–20	1	4.49	2.47	0.06	0.098	25.3		24.39	0.964

[a]Water content and forest floor mass are reported on an oven-dry weight basis (105 °C).

[b]Juniper group includes Rocky Mountain juniper, western juniper, and juniper woodland.
[c]Spruce/fir group includes Engelmann spruce, subalpine fir, mixed Engelmann spruce/subalpine fir, and grand fir.

Table S1b—Mean water, carbon, and nitrogen contents of forest floor and soil cores by forest type, Idaho, soil visit 2, 2006, 2007, 2009.

Forest type	Soil layer	Number of plots	Water content[a]	Organic carbon	Inorganic carbon	Total nitrogen	C/N ratio	Forest floor mass[a]	Organic carbon	Total nitrogen
	cm		%	%	%	%		Mg/ha	Mg/ha	Mg/ha
Cercocarpus woodland	Forest floor	1								
	0–10	1	1.05	2.67	5.18	0.287	9.3		13.06	1.403
	10–20	1								
Juniper group[b]	Forest floor	1	20.5	38.27		0.989	47	3.22	1.25	0.042
	0–10	1	7.52	2.65	0.33	0.211	12.5		18.84	1.502
	10–20	1	14.51	1.71	0.36	0.139	12.3		15.82	1.282
Ponderosa pine	Forest floor	5	21.23	32.38		0.975	35.7	30.81	9.84	0.313
	0–10	5	12.96	2.89	0.28	0.182	15.9		24.32	1.531
	10–20	5	12.85	1.52	0.23	0.111	13.7		14.75	1.08
Lodgepole pine	Forest floor	4	102.79	33.56		0.854	38.9	32.28	10.57	0.254
	0–10	4	16.39	3.47	0.33	0.112	31		22.72	0.732
	10–20	4	9.82	1.18	0.34	0.043	27.9		8.08	0.29
Douglas fir	Forest floor	23	28.56	33.15		1.044	33.5	18.8	6.41	0.194
	0–10	23	13.8	3.34	0.28	0.169	19.8		20.9	1.056
	10–20	23	9.28	1.34	0.27	0.077	17.5		8.43	0.483
Cottonwood/aspen	Forest floor	5	40.35	34.79		1.08	34.3	12.51	4.32	0.134
	0–10	5	47.17	7.76	0.27	0.413	18.8		36.79	1.959
	10–20	5	43.25	3.93	0.34	0.219	18		14.31	0.797
Spruce/fir group[c]	Forest floor	15	46.94	36.07		1.072	37.4	17.46	6.08	0.178
	0–10	15	28.47	4.45	0.29	0.224	19.9		24.69	1.241
	10–20	15	26.65	2.73	0.25	0.153	17.9		17.45	0.976
Western hemlock/ redcedar/larch	Forest floor	5	53.84	29.84		0.923	36.3	46.83	14.46	0.394
	0–10	5	23.94	4.35	0.21	0.207	21		22.05	1.051
	10–20	5	27.48	2.08	0.23	0.108	19.3		11.4	0.59
Limber pine	Forest floor	0								
	0–10	0								
	10–20	0								

[a]Water content and forest floor mass are reported on an oven-dry weight basis (105 °C).
[b]Juniper group includes Rocky Mountain juniper, western juniper, and juniper woodland.
[c]Spruce/fir group includes Engelmann spruce, subalpine fir, mixed Engelmann spruce/subalpine fir, and grand fir.

Table S2a—Mean physical and chemical properties of soil cores by forest type, Idaho, soil visit 1, 2000, 2001, 2002, 2004, 2007, 2008.

Forest type	Soil layer cm	Number of plots	SQI[a] %	Bulk density g/cm³	Coarse fragments %	pH H₂O	pH CaCl₂	Bray 1 extractable phosphorus mg/kg	Olsen extractable phosphorus mg/kg
Cercocarpus woodland	0–10	1	56	1.49	44.86	8.03	0.59	8.1	4.8
	10–20	1	52	1.41	66.53	7.94	0.53	0.1	2.6
Juniper group	0–10	5	71	1.12	27.25	6.21	0.26	17	12.7
	10–20	5	65	1.35	34.87	6.17	0.31	4.4	1
Ponderosa pine	0–10	17	69	0.97	18.81	5.94	0.15	40.4	22.7
	10–20	17	65	1.17	26.53	6.01	0.13	25.9	11.7
Lodgepole pine	0–10	16	62	0.97	28.59	5.45	0.16	37.9	19.3
	10–20	16	59	1.25	32.89	5.49	0.15	30.2	15.1
Douglas fir	0–10	70	70	0.96	34.73	6.04	0.08	56.5	31.7
	10–20	70	64	1.14	36.93	6.01	0.08	35.4	16.6
Cottonwood/aspen	0–10	11	74	0.76	35.82	6.33	0.2	112.6	46.5
	10–20	11	72	0.99	36.41	6.36	0.17	19.6	33.1
Spruce/fir group	0–10	51	67	0.8	28.25	5.28	0.09	32	15.4
	10–20	51	59	0.95	25.77	5.5	0.08	18	9.4
Western hemlock/ redcedar/larch	0–10	14	67	0.76	35.48	5.94	0.16	25.9	13.8
	10–20	14	61	1.02	30	6.09	0.15	19	12
Limber pine	0–10	1	74	1.05	25.29	5.69	0.59	55.4	25.4
	10–20	1	56	1.98	50.26	5.77	0.53	31.2	15.8

[a]SQI = Soil Quality Index

USDA Forest Service Resour. Bull. RMRS-RB-14. 2012

129

Table S2b—Mean physical and chemical properties of soil cores by forest type, Idaho, soil visit 2, 2006, 2007, 2009.

Forest type	Soil layer	Number of plots	SQI[a]	Bulk density	Coarse fragments	pH		Bray 1 extractable phosphorus	Olsen extractable phosphorus
	cm		%	g/cm³	%	H₂O	CaCl₂	mg/kg	mg/kg
Cercocarpus woodland	0–10	1	52	1.54	68.17	7.78	0.61	7.5	8.2
	10–20	1							
Juniper group	0–10	1	70	1.27	43.82	6.72	0.61	25.7	7.5
	10–20	1	70	1.24	25.21	7.02	0.47	8.6	0.9
Ponderosa pine	0–10	5	74	1.03	17.71	5.99	0.27	73	38.6
	10–20	5	71	1.18	16.86	6.23	0.21	45.3	24.5
Lodgepole pine	0–10	4	53	0.84	21.94	5.25	0.31	23.7	10.6
	10–20	4	46	1.36	46.87	5.29	0.23	17.8	6.1
Douglas fir	0–10	23	70	0.97	33	6.04	0.14	45.6	26.3
	10–20	23	63	1.21	42.74	6	0.11	34.8	19.9
Cottonwood/aspen	0–10	5	74	0.59	19.94	6.19	0.31	48.9	35.5
	10–20	5	67	0.77	48.85	6.29	0.27	11.7	40.4
Spruce/fir group	0–10	15	69	0.77	25.21	5.66	0.19	39.9	24.3
	10–20	15	67	0.96	31.46	5.81	0.15	28.3	16.1
Western hemlock/ redcedar/larch	0–10	5	68	0.85	31.32	5.74	0.27	25.1	11.5
	10–20	5	61	0.85	29.41	5.81	0.21	5.2	8
Limber pine	0–10	0							
	10–20	0							

[a]SQI = Soil Quality Index

130

USDA Forest Service Resour. Bull. RMRS-RB-14. 2012

Table S3—Mean physical and chemical properties of soil cores by forest type, Idaho, soil visit 2, 2006, 2007, 2009.

Forest type	Soil layer cm	Number of plots	1 M NH$_4$Cl Exchangeable cations					
			Na	K	Mg	Ca	Al	ECEC
			mg/kg					cmolc/kg
Cercocarpus woodland	0–10	1	22	413	168	6742	0	36.18
	10–20	1	30	93	127	5199	0	27.36
Juniper group	0–10	5	22	252	213	1907	1	12.24
	10–20	5	28	337	394	2235	3	15.56
Ponderosa pine	0–10	17	9	295	142	1486	32	9.97
	10–20	17	11	208	102	1141	13	7.7
Lodgepole pine	0–10	16	17	179	54	570	68	5.29
	10–20	16	16	145	31	450	46	3.96
Douglas fir	0–10	70	12	248	123	1569	15	10.03
	10–20	70	12	205	92	1128	20	7.61
Cottonwood/aspen	0–10	11	18	373	159	1960	6	12.74
	10–20	11	13	432	181	1839	7	12.58
Spruce/fir group	0–10	51	14	160	90	909	80	8
	10–20	51	12	119	51	488	77	5.16
Western hemlock/redcedar/larch	0–10	14	8	161	96	1509	111	10.47
	10–20	14	17	145	59	894	15	5.8
Limber pine	0–10	1	30	109	193	2512	5	14.59
	10–20	1	1	65	105	1319	3	7.64

USDA Forest Service Resour. Bull. RMRS-RB-14. 2012

131

Table S4—Mean exchangeable cation concentrations in soil cores by forest type, Idaho, soil visit 2, 2006, 2007, 2009.

Forest type	Soil layer	Number of plots	1 M NH₄Cl Exchangeable cations					
			Na	K	Mg	Ca	Al	ECEC
	cm				mg/kg			cmolc/kg
Cercocarpus woodland	0–10	1	6	455	140	6327	1	33.93
	10–20	1						
Juniper group	0–10	1	15	317	319	2547	0	16.21
	10–20	1	9	645	457	3740	5	24.16
Ponderosa pine	0–10	5	25	453	218	1911	1	13.01
	10–20	5	64	396	208	1657	2	11.48
Lodgepole pine	0–10	4	8	125	22	171	75	2.5
	10–20	4	12	98	15	79	59	1.66
Douglas fir	0–10	23	32	333	151	1896	9	12.17
	10–20	23	32	231	110	1213	13	8.37
Cottonwood/aspen	0–10	5	65	219	218	3132	0	20.03
	10–20	5	47	144	166	1874	4	12.74
Spruce/fir group	0–10	15	63	197	90	1267	46	9.19
	10–20	15	82	158	64	887	23	7.12
Western hemlock/ redcedar/larch	0–10	5	52	148	83	1071	51	8.22
	10–20	5	49	126	54	599	37	5.3
Limber pine	0–10	0						
	10–20	0						

Table S5a—Mean extractable trace element concentrations in soil cores by forest type, Idaho, soil visit 1, 2000, 2001, 2002, 2004, 2007, 2008.

Forest type	Soil layer	Number of plots	1 M NH$_4$Cl Extractable							
			Mn	Fe	Ni	Cu	Zn	Cd	Pb	S
	cm		mg/kg							
Cercocarpus woodland	0–10	1	0.03	0	0	0	0	0	0.47	7.5
	10–20	1	0	0	0	0	0	0.02	0	10.3
Juniper group	0–10	5	13.22	0.05	0	0	0.42	0.11	0.1	5.5
	10–20	5	11.32	0	0.07	0.11	0	0.01	0.02	8.1
Ponderosa pine	0–10	17	25.99	0	0.15	0	1.94	0.06	0.11	5.3
	10–20	17	19.89	0.38	0.19	0.02	0.78	0.05	0.08	10.4
Lodgepole pine	0–10	16	22.43	0.76	0	0	0.69	0.11	0.09	4.9
	10–20	16	22.43	0.57	0.02	0.03	0.26	0.08	0.25	17.8
Douglas fir	0–10	70	23.89	0.38	0.03	0	0.42	0.07	0.09	5.5
	10–20	70	15.63	0.1	0.01	0	0.05	0.05	0.15	10.1
Cottonwood/aspen	0–10	11	9.63	0.78	0.06	0	0.18	0.18	0.1	5.9
	10–20	11	9.41	0.02	0.03	0.05	0.02	0.12	0.11	6.6
Spruce/fir group	0–10	51	34.63	4.71	0.24	0.02	1.14	0.15	0.36	4.7
	10–20	51	21.67	1.07	0.02	0.03	0.45	0.07	0.21	8.6
Western hemlock/redcedar/larch	0–10	14	27.5	0.01	0.03	0	0.73	0.06	0.06	5.4
	10–20	14	12.75	0	0.02	0.01	0.24	0.05	0.15	29.5
Limber pine	0–10	1	20.85	0	0	0	0.67	0.08	0	5.2
	10–20	1	10.62	0	0	0	0.25	0	0.11	0

USDA Forest Service Resour. Bull. RMRS-RB-14. 2012

133

Table S5b—Mean extractable trace element concentrations in soil cores by forest type, Idaho, soil visit 2, 2006, 2007, 2009.

Forest type	Soil layer	Number of plots	1 M NH₄Cl Extractable							
			Mn	Fe	Ni	Cu	Zn	Cd	Pb	S
	cm		mg/kg							
Cercocarpus woodland	0–10	1	0.34	0	0		0	0.01	0	6.1
	10–20	1								
Juniper group	0–10	1	5.57	0	0		0	0.06	0.67	4.1
	10–20	1	2.02	0	0		0	0.05	0	3.7
Ponderosa pine	0–10	5	16.08	0.54	0		0.37	0.05	0.23	4
	10–20	5	9.41	0.08	0		0	0.03	0.07	1.6
Lodgepole pine	0–10	4	27.24	4.52	0.04		0.07	0.04	0.34	4.1
	10–20	4	4.19	2.97	0.01		0	0.01	0.52	4.8
Douglas fir	0–10	23	19.46	0.19	0.01		0.16	0.08	0.1	3.8
	10–20	23	8.6	0.41	0.02		0.02	0.05	0.3	2.3
Cottonwood/aspen	0–10	5	11.48	0.72	0		0	0.07	0.16	71.5
	10–20	5	4.93	0	0.01		0	0.01	0.19	53.2
Spruce/fir group	0–10	15	28.65	2.53	0		0.46	0.08	0.65	5.2
	10–20	15	14.84	1.36	0		0.29	0.05	0.44	4.2
Western hemlock/ redcedar/larch	0–10	5	22.3	2.05	0		0.08	0.05	0.33	6.5
	10–20	5	13.35	0.63	0		0	0.02	0.04	4.2
Limber pine	0–10	0								
	10–20	0								

134

USDA Forest Service Resour. Bull. RMRS-RB-14. 2012